Hidden Criticism?

Hidden Criticism?

The Methodology and Plausibility of the Search for a Counter-Imperial Subtext in Paul

Christoph Heilig

Fortress Press
Minneapolis

HIDDEN CRITICISM?
The Methodology and Plausibility of the Search for a Counter-Imperial Subtext in Paul

Originally published by Mohr Siebeck GmbH & Co. KG Tübingen © 2015

New preface copyright © 2017 Fortress Press. All rights reserved. Except for brief quotations in critical articles or reviews, no part of this book may be reproduced in any manner without prior written permission from the publisher. Email copyright@fortresspress.com or write to Permissions, Fortress Press, PO Box 1209, Minneapolis, MN 55440-1209.

Cover image: Robert Etienne: *Pompeji, die eingeäscherte Stadt* by Casa della Rissa nell'Anfiteatro / Wikimedia Commons / Public Domain
Cover design: Alisha Lofgren

Print ISBN: 978-1-5064-2812-3
eBook ISBN: 978-1-5064-3256-4

*To Theresa and Anthony —
for a magnificent year in St Andrews*

Table of Contents

Preface to the Fortress Press Edition xi
Preface to the 2015 Edition... xv
Abbreviations xvii

Chapter 1: Analogy 1

1. Introduction.. 1
   1.1 Point of Departure 1
   1.2 Goodenough's Proposal: Veiled Criticism of the Roman Empire
       in *Somn.* 2 2
   1.3 Philo's Political Theory 3

2. Analysis of Somn. *2*... 5
   2.1 Preliminary Remarks on Procedure 5
   2.2 *Somn.* 2 and the Allegory of the Soul.. 6
   2.3 Political Allegory in *Somn.* 2?... 8

3. Conclusions 17
   3.1 Summary 17
   3.2 Outlook... 19

Chapter 2: Approach 21

1. Counter-Imperial "Echoes" in the Subtext... 21

2. Evaluating Hypotheses.. 24
   2.1 On the Nature of Criteria.. 24
   2.2 The Structure of Historical Inferences 26
   2.3 Bayes's Theorem 27
   2.4 Explanatory Potential and Background Plausibility
       of a Hypothesis.. 28
   2.5 Background Knowledge... 30

2.6 Comparing Hypotheses 33
  2.7 Conclusions 34

  3. "Echoes" of the Empire 35
    3.1 Hays's Criteria for Identifying Scriptural "Echoes" 35
    3.2 Application to Imperial Ideology 36
    3.3 Methodological Evaluation 40

  4. Excursus: Inference to the Best Explanation 46

Chapter 3: Discourse Context 50

  1. Introduction 50

  2. James C. Scott's Categories 50
    2.1 The Public Transcript 50
    2.2 The Hidden Transcript 51
    2.3 The Hidden Transcript and the Public Sphere 52

  3. Application to the Pauline Letter 54
    3.1 The Pauline Letters as Hidden Transcript in Veiled Form? 54
    3.2 Pauline Letters as Hidden Transcript in Pure Form? 58
    3.3 Conclusions 65

Chapter 4: Roman Context 68

  1. The Public Transcript 68
    1.1 Criticism within the Framework of the Public Transcript? 68
    1.2 Different Objects of Criticism 70
    1.3 Conclusions: Modification of the Object of Criticism 90

  2. Roman Ideology in the Environment of Paul 92
    2.1 Introduction 92
    2.2 Imperial Cults as an Expression of Imperial Ideology 93
    2.3 Other Expressions of Imperial Ideology 104
    2.4 Conclusions 108

Chapter 5: Pauline Context 110

1. Counter-Imperial Attitude? 110
   1.1 Introduction 110
   1.2 N. T. Wright: The Empire as Oppressor of God's People 110
   1.3 John M. G. Barclay: The Empire as a Consciously Ignored
       Peripheral Phenomenon 113
   1.4 Evaluation: What is the Real Plight? 114

2. From Attitude to Expression: Modifications of the Echo-Hypothesis 125
   2.1 Paul's Personality as Obstacle for the Echo-Hypothesis 125
   2.2 Two Modification of the Classical Echo-Hypothesis 129

Chapter 6: Explanatory Context 139

1. Introducing Explanatory Potential 139

2. Establishing Parallels between Paul and the Empire 140
   2.1 Termini Technici 140
   2.2 Chance? 141
   2.3 True and False Alternatives 143

3. From Intertextuality to Criticism: Neutral Parallel or Antithesis? 146
   3.1 Non-Roman "Echoes" with and without Counter-Imperial
       "Resonance" 146
   3.2 Imperial References with and without Critical Intention:
       Neutral Parallel or Antithesis? 150

Chapter 7: Conclusion 156

   1. Summary 156
   2. Outlook 158

Bibliography 161
Index of Ancient Sources 181
Index of Modern Authors 189
Index of Subjects 194

Preface to the Fortress Press Edition

It brings me great joy to see the publication of a new edition of this book. Since reviews of the original edition have been, as I am glad to observe, generally appreciative, I do not see a need to offer any "hidden criticism" of my reviewers in this new preface. What remains for me is, thus, mainly to express my gratitude to Fortress Press for making this work more accessible. Special thanks go to Neil Elliott for his support of this project from beginning to end.

Moreover, I would also like to use this opportunity to make some comments on where and how I have further developed some aspects of the research presented here and how this might influence the reading of *Hidden Criticism?*

First, although I am still quite satisfied with the overall argument of the book, there are also some areas where I would put things a little bit differently now—or at least place them in a broader context. This applies, for example, to the assessment of the relationship between "abduction" or "inference to the best explanation" and Bayesian confirmation theory as found in chapter 2 (especially section 4). A more detailed—and probably also more nuanced—discussion of this issue can now be found in an essay I have coauthored with Theresa Heilig.[1]

Second, it should be noted that this book explicitly deals with a subset of voices who argue that Paul is "counter-imperial" in some sense.[2] It would probably be wrong to claim that this quite specific paradigm has yielded a significant amount of concrete research over the last two years. Thus, whether this paradigm will be able to establish itself as a heuristically fruitful research program, in the sense used by Imre Lakatos,[3] still remains to be seen. I do, however, continue to believe that it is indeed the most promising background for addressing the issue of Paul and the Roman Empire. An alternative approach to the one taken by N. T. Wright and Neil Elliott, which I scrutinize in this book, has recently been

---

1. "Historical Methodology," in *God and the Faithfulness of Paul: A Critical Examination of the Pauline Theology of N. T. Wright*, ed. Christoph Heilig, J. Thomas Hewitt, and Michael F. Bird (Minneapolis: Fortress Press, 2017), 115–50. The original edition was published by Mohr Siebeck (Tübingen) in 2016 in WUNT II (volume 413).

2. Rightly noted by James Miller, review of *Hidden Criticism?*, BBR 26, no. 3 (2016): 443.

3. Imre Lakatos, "Falsification and the Methodology of Scientific Research Programmes," in *The Methodology of Scientific Research Programmes*, vol. 1 of *Philosophical Papers*, ed. John Worrall and Gregory Currie (Cambridge: Cambridge University Press, 1978), 8–101.

taken by Bruce Winter.[4] As I have explained elsewhere,[5] I think that his focus on emperor worship and the social pressure associated with it is indeed an important aspect of the larger problem (see chapter 4 in this book). However, I do not think that we have a sufficiently clear idea yet about how the all-encompassing rhetoric of, for example, the direction of Scipio, quaestor of Achaia, that "everyone . . . wear crowns and to sacrifice" in light of Gaius Caesar's escape from danger (*SEG* 23.206.13–14) affected the first Christians—that is to what extent participation in cultic activities would have been "demanded" by fellow citizens and what this would have looked like in practice. Would people even have noticed if somebody did not show up at a public celebration? And is it possible that there was a wider range of options with regard to "participating" in such activities, with some more acceptable to Christians than others? While Winter's focus certainly allows for interesting insights, his emphasis might also lead to an unnecessary narrowing of the issue to cultic practice in terms of emperor worship. Thus, I would maintain that a more *text-centered* approach is still the most promising way forward and that we cannot avoid addressing the methodological objections as formulated most prominently by John Barclay.

Third, readers might notice that at some places throughout this book I allude to a forthcoming study on the imagery of the Roman triumphal procession employed by Paul in 2 Corinthians 2:14. I am pleased that this work has appeared in print in the meantime.[6] In a certain sense, this new book is the *"textzentrierte Ausführung"* of the methodological considerations of *Hidden Criticism?*—which Knut Backhaus would have liked to see included in the present book (in a review that magnificently summarizes my argument).[7] However, I also want to emphasize that *Paul's Triumph* supplements the present work rather than completing it. For I do maintain that, on the one hand, the assessment offered in the present volume has a validity of its own, which is independent of specific exegetical proposals, and that, on the other hand, a single test case is at the same time only a first step and not sufficient to demonstrate the fruitfulness of the paradigm that is analyzed and modified here. Therefore, it is important to me to note that the kind of continuity I see between these two publications lies in the fact that the present book establishes the general plausibility of a research program and offers some guidelines for how these analyses are to be carried out, while *Paul's Triumph* is an attempt to demonstrate that it is actually possible to achieve a better (i.e., fuller) understanding of certain aspects in Paul's letters against that background.

---

4. Bruce W. Winter, *Divine Honours for the Caesars: The First Christians' Responses* (Grand Rapids: Eerdmans, 2015).

5. "The First Christians' Responses to Emperor Worship," *Reviews of Biblical and Early Christian Studies*, November 2016, http://tinyurl.com/yaoxhhrx. For a shorter version, see Christoph Heilig, review of *Divine Honours for the Caesars*, by Bruce W. Winter, *JTS* 76 (2016): 754–57.

6. *Paul's Triumph: Reassessing 2 Corinthians 2:14 in Its Literary and Historical Context*, BTS 27 (Leuven: Peeters, 2017).

7. Knut Backhaus, review of *Hidden Criticism?*, *Gn* 88 (2016): 599.

It might be helpful to contrast this with a conception that appears at least in the subtext of some of the reviews, namely, that I somehow aim at constructing a new "method." As I have already tried to communicate as forcefully as possible in *Hidden Criticism?* (e.g., p. 28), this is not the case. What I am aiming at is not yet another set of criteria that can then be simply "applied" to specific texts.[8] Rather, the book is mainly about the background plausibility of the hypothesis of a counter-imperial subtext. It thus offers a way to structure current discourse on the matter of Paul and Empire and to evaluate the significance of the general arguments brought forward by both sides. Thus, I gladly admit that *Hidden Criticism?* does "not introduce any new historical data that effectively tips the scales"[9]—it rather wants to demonstrate how the known data is to be evaluated in a methodologically sound way, how the scales work, and where the needle is currently pointed when all the relevant data has been placed upon them. In so doing, the book also offers a structure for making it easier to localize disagreement within the scholarly guild.[10] More comments on this function of confirmation theory as a tool for analyzing scholarly discourse can be found in the essay on "Historical Methodology" mentioned above.[11]

Thus, to sum up, *Hidden Criticism?* is primarily an assessment of the background plausibility of the hypothesis of a counter-imperial subtext in Paul's letters, and I continue to believe that, as such, it makes a limited but necessary contribution to scholarship. Given that the judgment that I arrive at concerning this general plausibility is more positive than, for example, the one by John Barclay, *Hidden Criticism?* also offers—in chapters 6 and 7—some considerations of how exegesis could move forward within this framework. It is in this latter context that *Paul's Triumph* now plays a role in illustrating and refining what this contribution might look like in practice. Also, for those who think that my employment of confirmation theory in *Hidden Criticism?* is "unnecessary for sound historical reasoning and confusing to the reader,"[12] the new book might serve as a reminder that sometimes the explication of inferential structures, which

---

8. Thus, I am not at all surprised that Dorothea H. Bertschmann, in her review of *Hidden Criticism?*, *JSNT* 38 (2016): 64, cannot find such criteria in my book.

9. John K. Goodrich, review of *Hidden Criticism? RSR* 42 (2016): 213.

10. The criticism by Bertschmann, review of *Hidden Criticism?*, 64—who doubts that it is clear that there was a real conflict in Paul's worldview between his "messianic beliefs" and "an earthly ruler"—demonstrates to me that in this task *Hidden Criticism?* has been successful. (Though I would also say that I do not think this question remains "untested" in the present book. Cf. pp. 103–4 and 150–55.) See also Benedikt Mankel, review of *Hidden Criticism?*, *Glauben und Denken heute* 9, no. 1 (2016): 35, who approaches the issue from the perspective of a mathematician and appreciates the opportunity for localizing exegetical disagreement within the framework as presented by *Hidden Criticism?*

11. In Heilig and Heilig, "Historical Methodology," 145–48, there is also a discussion of Wright's response to Barclay's criticism, material that was published too late in the process of *Hidden Criticism?* for me to incorporate it fully.

12. So Miller, review of *Hidden Criticism?*, 443, who nevertheless speaks of a "timely, necessary, and substantive contribution" to the debate about Paul and Empire.

are, to be sure, followed by many intuitively (see *Hidden Criticism?*, p. 28), is very useful indeed, for it can unmask incomplete arguments, which mainly convince on the basis of their rhetorical presentation even though they ignore significant portions of the relevant evidence.[13]

Zurich, April 1, 2017

---

13. More specifically, I hope to have demonstrated in *Paul's Triumph* that many of the proposals put forward for the interpretation of 2 Cor 2:14 focus exclusively on either background plausibility *or* explanatory potential of the respective hypotheses—while making much more far-reaching (i.e., unsupported) claims concerning the status of these suggested interpretations.

Preface to the 2015 Edition

As creators of texts, we constantly produce associated subtexts. This is even true for "factual" scholarly literature. Often what is important with regard to our communicative aims is not simply what we obviously state, but also what is only implied or hinted at. Reasons for such behaviour are manifold, ranging from restrictive social conventions to pure delight in playing with the ambiguous. Strategies for crafting such subtexts do not have to be sophisticated; even surprising omissions can be telling in some instances. Identifying subtexts, however, can be all the more difficult. After all, we cannot automatically use the lack of clear statements as evidence for the existence of more subtle ones.

This book is no exception in being part of a network of texts. There is the scholarly literature that is engaged explicitly, but in those parts that are of good quality, there are also countless implicit "echoes" of the incredible support of others. First and foremost, I would like to use the public transcript of this preface to state that I owe infinite gratitude to my wife Theresa Heilig, who has supported my work in so many ways that her contribution to this project cannot be overestimated. But there are many more who have become part of the process of writing this monolith and to whom I am grateful. The roots of this project go back to my undergraduate studies at the FTH Giessen. I am especially thankful for the encouragement of Dr. Philipp Bartholomä to pursue postgraduate studies and for the dialogue with Dr. Joel R. White, who supervised my thesis on Paul and Empire. When I came to St Andrews, I found research conditions that were simply exceptional, and this book would not have been possible without the opportunities afforded me there. I am especially thankful for the manifold support of Prof. Kristin De Troyer, Dr. Mark W. Elliott, Dr. Scott J. Hafemann, and Prof. N. T. Wright. During the international SBL meeting of St Andrews, I had the opportunity to present my views on "Methodological Considerations for the Search of Counter-Imperial 'Echoes' in the Pauline Literature" in the section "Sacred Texts in Their Socio-Political Contexts" (in conjunction with the third St Andrews Graduate Conference for Biblical and Early Christian Studies). In the wake of this presentation, I was invited to do a postgraduate workshop "On Hays and Bayes: A Workshop on Intertextuality, Criteria and Probability Theory" at St Mary's College (St Andrews), 25th July 2013, which was initiated by Ernest Clark Jr. I benefitted greatly from the feedback at both events. The iSBL-paper was later published in *Reactions to Empire: Proceedings of Sacred Texts in Their Socio-Political Contexts* (ed. John Anthony Dunne and Dan Batovici; WUNT II, 372; Tübingen: Mohr Siebeck, 2014), 73–92. It offers a very short summary of the argument presented in this book.

I am immensely thankful to Prof. John M. G. Barclay for providing me with constructive feedback on this essay and I hope that I was able to do justice to his critique in this book. I would also like to thank Prof. James R. Davila and Prof. Maren R. Niehoff for reading Chapter 1 on Philo and Prof. Barbara Burrell for reading Chapter 4 on Paul's Roman context. Also, I am grateful to Prof. Vasily Rudich for discussin various aspects of censorship in antiquity with me. Special thanks go to Anthony Fisher, who read the whole manuscript and offered immensely helpful feedback. Dr. Wayne Coppins also deserves great thanks for reading through the whole manuscript in a very short time. I would also like to thank Prof. Jörg Frey for his early interest in this work, helpful feedback, and the acceptance into this series. I am also grateful for the very pleasant experience of cooperating with the Mohr Siebeck team, including Dr. Henning Ziebritzki, Simon Schüz, Matthias Spitzner, and Kendra Mäschke.

Abbreviations

For abbreviations, Patrick H. Alexander, John F. Kutsko, James D. Ernest, Shirley Decker-Lucke, and David L. Petersen, *The SBL Handbook of Style: For Ancient Near Eastern, Biblical, and Early Christian Studies* (Peabody: Hendrickson, 1999) was consulted. Abbreviations that were not listed there were taken from Siegfried Schwertner, *Internationales Abkürzungsverzeichnis für Theologie und Grenzgebiete* (2nd ed.; Berlin: de Gruyter, 1992) and Simon Hornblower, Antony Spawforth, and Esther Eidinow, eds. *The Oxford Classical Dictionary* (4th ed; Oxford: Oxford University Press, 2012). Other abbreviations are listed below.

ABIG	Arbeiten zur Bibel und ihrer Geschichte
AJEC	Ancient Judaism and Early Christianity
AMUGS	Antike Münzen und Geschnittene Steine
BCAW	Blackwell Companions to the Ancient World
BCP	Blackwell Companions to Philosophy
BiTS	Biblical Tools and Studies
BMSEC	Baylor-Mohn Siebeck Studies in Early
CBR	*Currents in Biblical Research*
CCCl	Cambridge Companion to the Classics
CCSNS	Cincinnati Classical Studies. New Series
ClCT	Classics and Contemporary Thought
COQG	Christian Origins and the Question of God. London: SPCK; Minneapolis: Fortress: 1992–
CulA	*Cultural Anthropology*
ÉtPlat	*Études Platoniciennes*
FJTC	Flavius Josephus: Translation and Commentary
GGNT	Siebenthal, Heinrich von. *Griechische Grammatik zum Neuen Testament: Neubearbeitung und Erweiterung der Grammatik Hoffmann/von Siebenthal.* Gießen: Brunnen, 2011.
HelSC	Hellenistic Society and Culture
DNTB	Evans, Craig A., and Stanley E. Porter, eds. *Dictionary of New Testament Background: A Compendium of Contemporary Biblical Scholarship.* Downers Grove: InterVarsity, 2000.
EDSS	Schiffman, Lawrence H., and James C. VanderKam, eds. *Encyclopedia of the Dead Sea Scrolls.* 2 vols. Oxford: Oxford University Press, 2000.
FRHIST	Cornell, Tim J., ed. *The Fragments of the Roman Historians.* 3 vols. Oxford: Oxford University Press, 2013.
JSJSup	Journal for the Study of Judaism: Supplement Series

KlSL	Klassische Sprachen und Literaturen
MNTS	McMaster Divinity College Press New Testament Studies Series
NTMon	New Testament Monographs
OACL	Oxford Approaches to Classical Literature
ODLT	*Oxford Dictionary of Literary Terms.* Edited by Chris Baldick. 3rd ed. Oxford: Oxford University Press, 2008.
PACS	Philo of Alexandria Commentary Series
PAST	Pauline Studies
SAG	Studien zur Alten Geschichte
SBLWGRW	Society of Biblical Literature Writings from the Greco-Roman World
SHS	Scripture and Hermeneutics Series
SPhAl	Studies in Philo of Alexandria
SUNYJ	SUNY Series in Judaica
VWGTh	Veröffentlichungen der Wissenschaftlichen Gesellschaft für Theologie
ZeitSt	Zeithistoriche Studien

Chapter 1

Analogy

1. Introduction

1.1 Point of Departure

In the midst of the first century, there lived a Jew of remarkable personality. He was educated and well acquainted with the culture of Graeco-Roman society, but he was also deeply rooted in the ancient heritage of the Hebrew Scriptures. He was a pious Jew, a mystic – but at the same time a pragmatist, a leader. He spoke in the synagogue and once, as an old man, even before a Roman emperor of narcissistic reputation. He was a remarkable Jew and the heritage of his writings remains to the present day and has puzzled interpreters for two millennia. We could even add the further hint that his name begins with "P." The person I am talking about is – Philo of Alexandria. The parallels to Paul are intriguing and hence it is not surprising that some of the questions that are relevant to Philonic scholarship are also controversial topics among scholars of the Pauline literature. The relation of these two men to the realm of "politics" is one of them. Since this book addresses the hotly debated question of whether there is a political subtext in Paul's letters, I think it might be helpful to start our investigation in calmer waters in order to get accustomed to the kind of questions we need to ask and the kind of results we may expect before we tackle our main question directly. As my apology for this more uncommon route into the subject, the reader may accept that the proposal concerning Philo under consideration here is often cited in current Pauline scholarship on a "hidden" criticism of the Roman Empire but is often presupposed[1] or rejected[2] without much discussion. Although I do not think

---

[1] Cf. Nicholas T. Wright, *Paul: In Fresh Perspective* (Minneapolis: Fortress, 2005), 61 and more recently (in response to Barclay [see next footnote]) Nicholas T. Wright, *Paul and the Faithfulness of God* (COQG 4; London: SPCK, 2013), 316, fn. 135. See also Neil Elliott, "Romans 13:1–7 in the Context of Imperial Propaganda," in *Paul and Empire: Religion and Power in Roman Imperial Society* (ed. Richard A. Horsley; Harrisburg: Trinity Press International, 1997), 199–201 and Stefan Schreiber, "Caesar oder Gott (Mk 12,17)? Zur Theoriebildung im Umgang mit politischen Texten des Neuen Testaments," *BZ* 48 (2004): 77–78. James R. Harrison, *Paul and the Imperial Authorities at Thessalonica and Rome* (WUNT 273; Tübingen: Mohr Siebeck, 2011), 28–31 discusses at least some of the criticisms raised against Goodenough's suggestion. The most detailed recent adop-

that this topic is anything like a test case for determining the plausibility of similar phenomena *in Paul,* I do think that it offers a very useful point of departure in that it sensitises the exegete to better differentiate between the literary praxis of a first-century Jew and twenty-first-century scholarly imagination or lack thereof.[3]

1.2 Goodenough's Proposal: Veiled Criticism of the Roman Empire in Somn. *2*

In his *The Politics of Philo Judaeus,* Erwin R. Goodenough suggested that there are three different types of political writings in Philo's work: Firstly, those that openly discuss Jewish relations with the Roman authorities (*In Flaccum* and *Legatio*) and, secondly, those that do so in a much more inconspicuous form and are much more critical in content.[4] The first is written for Gentiles (warning them not to behave like Flaccus/Caligula towards the Jews), the second for Jews. There is also a third class written for Gentiles

---

tion of Goodenough's thesis of different rhetorical strategies for different audiences can be found in Jean-Georges Kahn, "La Valeur et la Légitimité des Activités politiques d'après Philon d'Alexandrie," *Méditerranées* 16 (1998): 117–127.

[2] John M. G. Barclay, "Why the Roman Empire was Insignificant to Paul," in *Pauline Churches and Diaspora Jews* (ed. John M. G. Barclay; WUNT 275; Tübingen: Mohr Siebeck, 2011), 381, fn. 62. Stefan Krauter, *Studien zu Röm 13,1–7: Paulus und der politische Diskurs der neronischen Zeit* (WUNT 243; Tübingen: Mohr Siebeck, 2009), 107–108 summarises the state of research as evaluating Goodenough's thesis as "unbeweisbare Spekulation": "einige wenige 'messianische' Stellen würden hier isoliert von ihrem Kontext, der eine spiriualisierende [sic] Deutung nahelege, als kodierte politische Aussagen verstanden und so zum Einfallstor für eine methodisch unkontrollierte Eintragung eines postulierten allgemeinjüdischen politischen Messianismus." Katell Berthelot, "Philo's Perception of the Roman Empire," *JSJ* 42 (2011): 177, who is not writing from the perspective of NT studies, remarks that "some of Goodenough's 'reading between the lines' in the *Allegorical Commentary* – particularly his identification of Joseph with Roman rulers – may be far-fetched."

[3] Friederike Oertelt, *Herrscherideal und Herrschaftskritik bei Philo von Alexandria: Eine Untersuchung am Beispiel seiner Josephsdarstellung in De Josepho und De somniis I* (SPhAl 8; Leiden: Brill, 2015), 3 offers still another rationale for such an analysis from the perspective of NT studies: "Da die Briefe des Paulus zeigen, dass er mit den jüdischen Traditionen seiner Zeit vertraut war, ist ein Verständnis der jüdisch-hellenistischen Literatur aus dieser Zeit für eine neutestamentliche Exegese relevant, die davon ausgeht, dass die paulinische Theologie auch den politischen Kontext reflektiert." However, I think it would need more elaboration to demonstrate that Philo's ruler ideals are significant for understanding Paul's own view on politics. Hence, the real significance of Philo's political discourse seems to lie in the fact that it offers a potential, historically close example of a counter-imperial subtext as a literary device.

[4] Erwin R. Goodenough, *The Politics of Philo Judaeus: Practice and Theory* (New Haven: Yale University Press, 1938), 7. Cf. Goodenough, *Politics,* 1–20 for the first class ("politics direct") and Goodenough, *Politics,* 21–41 for the second ("politics in code").

interested in Judaism.⁵ For Goodenough, the different addressees explain the different characterisation of the biblical figure of Joseph in *De Iosepho* – which belongs to the third category (as part of the *Exposition of the Law*) – and in *De Somniis* 2 – which belongs to the second (as part of the *Allegorical Commentary*):⁶ While the first is written "with a single purpose, namely to insinuate to its gentile readers the political philosophy which Jews wished gentiles to believe was theirs"⁷ and subsequently portrays Joseph as an ideal politician respecting ancient (Jewish) traditions, the second exhibits "bitterest hatred of the Romans"⁸ by describing Joseph – who is interpreted as standing for the prefect – with disdain. In Goodenough's view *Somn.* 2.81–92 gives insight into Philo's reasons for such a veiled criticism and offers us access to his thought,⁹ namely, that it is caution which hinders Philo from writing more openly about his hatred in his works written for Gentiles. Only in his texts written for a Jewish audience, can he dare to make some ambivalent – and thus still justifiable – statements. At the same time – read with the knowledge of this method of caution in the back of one's mind – this text also shows that Philo "loved the Romans no more than the skipper of a tiny boat loves a hurricane."¹⁰ In what follows we will analyse *Somn.* 2 with regard to such a subtext critical of the Roman Empire.¹¹

1.3 Philo's Political Theory

Before analysing the texts themselves, we will first sketch Philo's broader views on political theory, which will offer a helpful context for our following evaluation of Goodenough's claims regarding *Somn.* 2. The most obvious point of departure in assessing Philo's ideas about politics are his treatises *In*

---

⁵ Cf. Goodenough, *Politics*, 42–63 ("politics by innuendo").
⁶ The distinction between the more straightforward *Exposition of the Law* interpretation and the *Allegorical Commentary* is established in scholarship. Cf. Robert A. Kraft, "Philo and the Sabbath Crisis: Alexandrian Jewish Politics and the Dating of Philo's Works," in *The Future of Early Christianity: Essays in Honour of Helmut Koester* (ed. Birger A. Pearson; Minneapolis: Fortress, 1991), 136, fn. 9. The third category of exegetical works is the *Questions and Answers on Genesis and Exodus* (cf. Kenneth Schenck, *A Brief Guide to Philo* [Louisville: Westminster John Knox, 2005], 15–16). Samuel Sandmel, *Philo of Alexandria: An Introduction* (New York: Oxford University Press, 1979), 79 thinks this work was only preparatory for the *Allegorical Commentary*. For lists of the works belonging to each of the two main categories, cf. Schenck, *Guide*, 16–19.
⁷ Goodenough, *Politics*, 62.
⁸ Goodenough, *Politics*, 42.
⁹ Goodenough, *Politics*, 5–7.
¹⁰ Goodenough, *Politics*, 7.
¹¹ Translations are usually from the Loeb volume (Colson) if not indicated otherwise. For a recent overview of the literature and the manuscript evidence, cf. Earle Hilgert, "A Survey of Previous Scholarship on Philo's *De Somniis* 1–2," in *SBL Seminar Papers, 1987* (SBLSP 26; Atlanta: Scholars Press, 1987), 394–402.

Flaccum and *Legatio ad Gaium*.[12] They not only show that Philo, despite often having the reputation of being a mere philosopher or mystic, was a politically interested (and active) Jew from Alexandria,[13] but also that he could be very critical of Roman officials who did not defend the traditional privileges of the Jews. In the same breath, Philo is capable of speaking of Augustus very highly (cf. *Legat.* 143–158; he is even described as the πρῶτος καὶ μέγιστος καὶ κοινὸς εὐεργέτης in *Legat.* 149). Although there are rhetorical reasons for this praise (to make Caligula look even worse) and although it is possible that part of it is flattering,[14] it hints at the respect Philo had for the Roman Empire: "His emphasis on peace, law and harmony ... in describing the Roman order was in accord with the conditions he considered most desirable in a state."[15] However, the Roman state was not good in itself, but only inasmuch as the divine Logos (λόγος ὁ θεῖος) is manifested in it currently before moving on (cf. *Deus.* 173–176). Implied in this flux is the act of God and the only end of this circle could be the reign of God, superseding all human kingdoms.[16] How much Philo understood this future hope in terms of Jewish nationalism is a matter of some debate,[17] but it seems probable that Philo's expectation included a concrete restoration of Jewish superiority.[18] It

---

[12] There are commentaries on these books: Herbert Box, *Philonis Alexandrini: In Flaccum* (London: Oxford University Press, 1939), Willem van der Horst, *Philo's Flaccus: The First Pogrom: Introduction, Translation and Commentary* (PACS 2; Leiden: Brill, 2003), and E. Mary Smallwood, *Philonis Alexandrini: Legatio ad Gaium* (Leiden: Brill, 1970).

[13] On Philo as a "politically active person," see now Torrey Seland, "Philo as a Citizen: *Homo Politicus*," in *Reading Philo: A Handbook to Philo of Alexandria* (ed. Torrey Seland; Grand Rapids: Eerdmans, 2014), 47–74.

[14] Goodenough, *Politics*, 1–20 suggests that *Flacc.* and *Legat.* were written for the successors of their main characters in order to warn them that disrespectful behaviour towards the Jews would result in God's judgement. This certainly explains the different roles Caligula plays in both texts. Others have suggested that they were written for Jewish readers. See Maren R. Niehoff, *Philo on Jewish Identity and Culture* (TSAJ 86; Mohr Siebeck: Tübingen, 2011), 39: "Both the *Legatio* and *In Flaccum* aimed at defending Philo's pro-Roman politics. He wished to convince his Jewish readers back home that the more radical positions, which had been adopted by many Jews during his stay in Rome, were unwise and doomed to failure."

[15] Ray Barraclough, "Philo's Politics, Roman Rule and Hellenistic Judaism." *ANRW* 21.1:452. For a very balanced account of the ambivalent picture of Roman rule emerging from a close reading of *Flacc.* see Joshua Yoder, "Sympathy for the Devil? Philo on Flaccus and Rome," *SPhA* 24 (2012): 167–182.

[16] Cf. Goodenough, *Politics*, 76–79.

[17] Cf. Barraclough, "Politics," *ANRW* 21.1:476–486 for a de-historicised hope on the level of the soul in contrast to Goodenough's proposal.

[18] Cf. Berthelot, "Perception," 186: "Although eschatology, messianism, and the restoration of Israel both on the spiritual and the political level are not major themes in Philo's works, there is hardly any doubt that he believed in a brighter future for the Jews and expected all earthly powers to be ultimately subject to the will of God." Also, cf. the bal-

is thus not in principle implausible to look – as Goodenough did[19] – for statements critical of the Roman Empire in Philo's writings. Also the idea of a "coded" criticism does not seem too fanciful in light of the real danger associated with writings that could be interpreted as subversive.[20]

2. Analysis of *Somn.* 2

2.1 Preliminary Remarks on Procedure

One work that has received some attention with regard to Philo's view on the politician is *Ios*. In this biography[21] Philo shows great familiarity with Hellenistic ideas about kingship, which he traces back to his own Jewish tradition.[22] The politics of *Somn.* 2 has been a focus of research for some time, but the discussion usually takes place in the context of explaining the discrepancies between the respective evaluations of the figure of Joseph in *Ios.* and in *Somn.* 2.[23] While Joseph seems to be an entirely commendable person in

---

anced assessment by John J. Collins, *Between Athens and Jerusalem: Jewish Identity in the Hellenistic Diaspora* (New York: Crossroad, 1983), 111–117. Philo's eschatology is said to differ from the eschatology of writers of apocalyptic (and related) literature "not so much in the actual concepts as in the degree of urgency" (Collins, *Athens*, 116). On messianism in Egypt in general, see the overview by James C. Paget, "Egypt," in *Redemption and Resistance: The Messianic Hopes of Jews and Christians in Antiquity* (ed. Markus Bockmuehl and James C. Paget; London: T&T Clark, 2007), 181–191.

[19] For a more recent example of such an interpretation, see the postcolonial analysis by Torrey Seland, "'Colony' and 'metropolis' in Philo: Examples of Mimicry and Hybridity in Philo's Writing Back from the Empire?," *Études Platoniciennes* 7 (2010): 13–36.

[20] Here our discussion of Philo already points us to an important factor we also will have to consider with regard to Paul: Was criticism possible in public or was it dangerous? We will discuss this question later (Chapter 4, Section 1) in detail. So for the moment this assertion has to suffice.

[21] Cf. Maren R Niehoff, *The Figure of Joseph in Post-Biblical Jewish Literature* (AGJU 16; Leiden: Brill, 1992), 54–60.

[22] Goodenough, *Politics*, 62. For the question of how much this work was written with a focus on the *Roman* politician, cf. Goodenough, *Politics*, 42–63 and Barraclough, "Politics," *ANRW* 21.1:491–506. Although the prefect might well be in view, Goodenough's proposal seems to be too monolithic, since *Ios.* 72–73 clearly envisages a range of political roles.

[23] Joseph also features in other writings of Philo – often negatively. Cf. Goodenough, *Politics*, 33, fn. 50 and Kraft, "Philo," 136–138. The patriarchs are represented quite consistently in Philo's works (Deborah Sills, "Strange Bedfellows: Politics and Narrative in Philo," in *The Seductiveness of Jewish Myth: Challenge or Response?* [ed. S. Daniel Breslauer; SUNYJ; Albany: State University of New York Press, 1997], 171). Cf. also Oertelt, *Herrscherideal*, 6–8, who builds on the work of Martina Böhm, *Rezeption und Funktion der Vätererzählungen bei Philo von Alexandria: Zum Zusammenhang von Kontext, Hermeneutik und Exegese im frühen Judentum* (BZNW 128; Berlin: de Gruyter, 2005).

Ios.,[24] many details are interpreted much more negatively in *Somn.* 2. Many different solutions have been proposed, Goodenough's suggestion of different audiences being only one of them.[25] But since the *thesis of a subtext* critical of the Roman Empire in *Somn.* 2 does not depend on the assumption of different audiences for *Somn.* 2 and *Ios.*, we will concentrate on evaluating the claim of Roman references in *Somn.* 2 (and comment on its literary place in the Philonic corpus only shortly in the conclusion).[26]

2.2 Somn. 2 and the Allegory of the Soul

Somn. 2 is the third book in a series devoted to an interpretation of dreams. While the first, lost treatise discusses dreams that are directly sent by God,[27] the second (*Somn.* 1) addresses dreams that belong to the inspired mind that can foresee the future (*Somn.* 1.2). The third (*Somn.* 2) focusses on dreams that have nothing to do with God's intervention but are due to the mind's motion in sleep (*Somn.* 2.1). Those are the kind of dreams Philo identifies in the case of Joseph, Pharaoh, and his chief baker and butler (*Somn.* 2.5). The three categories differ with regard to their clarity: While the first two are straightforward (*Somn.* 2.2–3), the third category demands care in interpretation (*Somn.* 2.4).

As Hay pointed out, there is a further difference (which seems to be based on the degree of God's involvement in my view) between the dreams of *Somn.* 1 and 2: "[T]he former reveal an admirable spiritual mindset, whereas

---

[24] For the tension within *Ios.* itself, cf. Françoise Frazier, "Les visages de Joseph dans le *De Josepho,*" *SPhA* 14 (2002): 1–30.

[25] They include: Uncritical use of different sources (suggested by Wilhelm Bousset; cf. Jouette M. Bassler, "Philo on Joseph: The Basic Coherence of *De Iosepho* and *De Somniis* II," *JSJ* 16 [1985]: 240), different geographical settings (Joseph does well in an Egyptian context [*Ios.*] but not in the context of the Holy Land [*Somn.* 2]; Jaques Cazeaux, "'Nul n'est prophète en son pays': Contribution à l'étude de Joseph d'après Philon," in *The School of Moses: Studies in Philo and Hellenistic Religion in Memory of Horst R. Moehring* [BJS 304 = SPhM 1; ed. John P. Kenney; Atlanta: Scholars Press, 1995], 41–81), different periods in Jewish-Roman relations (for proponents and opponents of this view, cf. Bassler, "Philo," 241), and Philo's different age (Sandmel, *Philo*, 64: *Ios.* "comes from Philo's old age, and reflects fatigue and a lack of zest."). For a survey of research on this issue, see now Oertelt, *Herrscherideal*, 11–31.

[26] By itself, the fact that Goodenough may have been too optimistic in his reconstruction of the audience does not imply that one needs to confine oneself to more general questions of Philo's "Herrscherideal." Here, I differ from the approach of Oertelt, *Herrscherideal*, 32–33. Accordingly, her detailed study is very helpful for locating Philo in the wider framework of discourse on rulership at that time, but it does not evaluate the specific theses put forth by Goodenough in equal depth.

[27] That there was a treatise preceding *Somn.* 1 is clear from *Somn.* 1.1. Eusebius talks about five books on dreams (*Hist. eccl.* 2.18.4).

the latter reveal only folly and wickedness."[28] Thus, the literary flow already evokes the expectation of a discussion not only of isolated dreams but also of human character. This first impression is strengthened by the analysis of the place of *Somn.* 2 in its larger literary context. The opening description of Joseph is clearly interwoven with the discussion of Jacob in *Somn.* 2. In *Somn.* 1.124–126, the friends of reason are described as being "real genuine men" characterised by self-control (*Somn.* 1.124) in contrast to those ruled by passions (*Somn.* 1.122) and vainglory (*Somn.* 1.126).[29] The book ends accordingly, summoning the Jacob-like soul to battle against passion and vainglory (*Somn.* 1.155). Joseph, on the other hand, is said (*Somn.* 2.15) to embody "the rational strain of self-control, which is of the masculine family, fashioned after his father Jacob," but also (*Somn.* 2.16) "the irrational strain of sense-perception, assimilated to what he derives from his mother."[30] This negative trait is accompanied (*Somn.* 2.16) by "the breed of bodily pleasure, impressed on him by association with chief butlers and chief bakers and chief cooks" and "the element of vainglory." Bassler thus rightly concludes: "[I]n *Somn.* ii Philo presents in allegorical form the two elements Jacob is summoned to battle."[31] This basic structure can be traced through the rest of the book since Joseph's two dreams embody vainglory and the dreams of the baker and butler are understood as expressions of gluttony (cf. *Somn.* 2.155 for this explicit division), which is linked to passion by Philo (cf. *Somn.* 2.203). Bassler thus concludes that the "dominant message is the one found so frequently in his writings, that is, the antagonistic relationship between rationality and irrationality within the soul, with Joseph presented as a paradigm of irrationality."[32] It is thus comprehensible that Barraclough writes: "The contrary picture of Joseph sketched in 'De Somniis' can be explained as Philo's use of allegorical interpretation to suit a different purpose. In 'De Somniis' the emphasis is on the superiority of the soul over the body."[33]

---

[28] David M. Hay, "Politics and Exegesis in Philo's Treatise on Dreams," in *SBL Seminar Papers, 1987* (SBLSP 26; Atlanta: Scholars Press, 1987), 431.

[29] Cf. Bassler, "Philo," 249.

[30] On this passage, cf. Oertelt, *Herrscherideal,* 154–156.

[31] Bassler, "Philo," 250.

[32] Bassler, "Philo," 250. Cf. also Bassler, "Philo," 251: The level of allegory in *Somn.* 2 is "that of the individual soul."

[33] Barraclough, "Politics," *ANRW* 21.1:487. However, Barraclough is quite confusing on this point. Later (Barraclough, "Politics," *ANRW* 21.1:501–502) he writes that the difference in the portrayal of Joseph between *Ios.* and *Somn.* 2 is likely due to the negative experience with Flaccus. Cf. Erich S. Gruen, *Heritage and Hellenism: The Reinvention of Jewish Tradition* (HelSC 30; Berkeley: University of California Press, 1998), 85: "Barraclough ... devotes most of his discussion to arguing with Goodenough, only to accept his basic premise that Philo had two different political objectives in mind when composing the two works."

2.3 Political Allegory in Somn. 2?

2.3.1 Preliminary Remarks

It is certainly right that, of all the different types of allegories we find in *Somn.* 1 and 2, the most prevalent one is the "allegory of the soul."[34] And undoubtedly, one of Goodenough's shortcomings is that he did not take this basic concern into consideration enough and that he interpreted remarks on the soul only as subordinate descriptions of the soul of the (Roman) politician.[35] Nevertheless, one needs to be careful not to restrict Philo's discourse to only one level at the outset. There may be different types of allegory side by side or even one within another. We will begin by looking for the first type – clear political allegory – and, on that basis, ask whether it is reasonable to see a political subtext in other allegories of the soul also.[36]

The search for such political references is not as illegitimate as one might suppose on the grounds of Bassler's treatment. Although the contrast with Jacob – applied to the level of the soul – certainly is an important connection between *Somn.* 1 and *Somn.* 2, Bassler ignores the fact that already in *Somn.* 1, the figure is introduced in an explicitly political context. In *Somn.* 1.219–223, Jacob's dream of multi-coloured sheep triggers a comment about Joseph's coat (*Somn.* 1.220; cf. Gen 37:3), which is interpreted as implying that he is "the man whose desires are set on human statecraft (τῆς ἀνθρωπίνης πολιτείας)" (*Somn.* 1.219).[37] The robe of statecraft (τῆς πολιτείας) is variegated because it is "a most meagre admixture of truth" with "many large portions of false, probable, plausible, conjectural matter," which form the origin of all kinds of Egyptian occult evil (*Somn.* 1.220).[38] The robe is described as stained with blood (cf. Gen 37:31) because the political life is characterised by conflict (*Somn.* 1.221). Contrary to what one would infer from the admiration some people give to a man who is involved in the affairs of the city (τὰ πόλεως πράγματα), there are many problems in his life and he has to fear his downfall due to either a revolt by the people or a more power-

---

[34] Other types include epistemological, cosmological, metaphysical, ethical, and political allegory. Cf. for the classification Hay, "Politics, "432.

[35] Cf. Goodenough, *Politics,* 22: "This is the sort of man, the *politicus,* the meaning of whose dream Philo goes on to expound."

[36] For a similar procedure, see Hay, "Politics," 432–437.

[37] Bassler, "Philo," 250 refers to the section in a footnote but only writes: "The allegorization of Joseph as a mixture was already introduced in *I,* 219–223, where the negative aspects were emphasized more." She does not mention that it is Joseph *the politician* who is discussed in this light.

[38] These evils are associated with the "sophists of Egypt," on whom cf. Bruce W. Winter, *Philo and Paul among the Sophists* (SNTSMS 96; Cambridge: Cambridge University Press, 1997), 59–79.

ful rival (*Somn.* 1. 222). As the following sentences in *Somn.* 1.224–225 show, Philo was fully aware that he himself belonged to this group.[39]

2.3.2 Political Allegory

2.3.2.1 Joseph's Second Dream[40]

The most obvious political remarks in *Somn.* 2 occur in Philo's discussion of Joseph's heavenly dream (Gen 37:9). After a cosmological allegory,[41] he begins a new thought (λέγομεν δὲ ἡμεῖς; the English translations signal this through the insertion of horizontal blank spaces or line breaks), mentioning men who are – among other things – characterised as lovers of vainglory, and who exalt themselves "not only above men but above the world of nature" (*Somn.* 2.115). He mentions three examples: The Persian King Xerxes, who tried to shoot arrows at the sun (*Somn.* 2.117–120), German tribes, who were threatening the sea with weapons (*Somn.* 2.121–122), and "one of the ruling class" (ἄνδρα τινὰ ... τῶν ἡγεμονικῶν), who had charge and authority over Egypt (προστασίαν καὶ ἐπιμέλειαν; *Somn.* 2.123). The two specific examples given before suggest that this also refers to a concrete person. This impression is strengthened by Philo's explicit comment that he had only recently come to know this person (χθὲς δ᾽ οὐ πρῴην ... οἶδα).[42] The "lively and impassioned" flow of words[43] with which Philo describes this person's attempt to force and later to persuade the Jews to give up their keeping of the Sabbath also speaks in favour of this view. The person in view is probably the prefect of Egypt.[44] Which prefect he was has been the subject of some debate. If he was Flaccus, this would imply that Philo would have written very much as a very old man.[45] The same objection applies to the suggestion that the person in view is a Jewish insider, namely Tiberius Julius Alexander, the nephew of

---

[39] It need not bother us here whether the change of clothes implies a retreat from political engagement (Goodenough, *Politics,* 32) or "that he should ... simply beware of political temptation" (cf. Hay, "Politics," 433).

[40] Depending on the text one assumes for *Somn.* 2.136, it is even judged not to be a real dream at all. This is the case if one assumes ἀλλ᾽ οὐκ ἐνύπνιον εἶδες (Yonge, Colson). If the conjecture ἆρ᾽ οὐκ is presupposed, the resulting question means something like (Heinemann/Adler; cf., e.g., *Opif.* 129): "Es war doch wohl nur ein Traum, den du sahst?"

[41] Cf. Hay, "Politics," 434–435.

[42] Cf. LSJ, 1543 and 1991.

[43] Cf. Kraft, "Philo," 134.

[44] Cf., e.g., Goodenough, *Politics,* 29. For arguments against this position, cf. Daniel R. Schwartz, "Philonic Anonyms of the Roman and Nazi Periods: Two Suggestions," *SPhA* 1 (1989): 66–67.

[45] Philo describes himself as old during the reign of Caligula: In *Legat.* 1 he calls himself an old man (γέρων). Cf. also *Legat.* 182 (ἡλικία). Hence he was probably at least 57 years old at this time (*Opif.* 105).

Philo.[46] For our present purpose, the identity of the person is not very important, but we can conclude the following things: 1) At least in this instance, Philo interprets dream and dreamer explicitly in the political terms of his own day.[47] 2) The criticism is directed against a specific individual not against the Roman Empire as a whole.[48]

After concluding this interpretation in *Somn.* 2.133, "the Political Allegory submerges and the rest of the treatise focuses primarily on the Allegory of the Soul."[49] Even Goodenough admits that "[t]his discussion is general" and he thinks that only the connection with the preceding section and the continual use of words like "vainglory" and "arrogance" and their counterparts "would suggest that Philo is still speaking of the Romans."[50] But as we have seen at the beginning of this section, it is mistaken to see the Roman Empire as the huge meta-structure *always* looming in the background. Rather, it is reasonable to see in *Somn.* 2.115–133 a very clear application of Philo's general thought regarding human nature to political affairs.

2.3.2.2 Joseph's First Dream

The other clearly political allegory occurs earlier in the discussion of Joseph's first dream on the sheaves (Gen 37:7), which begins in *Somn.* 2.78.[51] Joseph is first identified very generally as "all the votaries of vainglory" who "set themselves up above everything." But this is immediately specified as "above cities and laws and ancestral customs and the affairs of the several citizens." *Somn.* 2.79 makes this even more explicit by describing the development from leadership to dictatorship over the people as a next step. Again, the object of criticism does not seem to be Roman rule as a whole, but every misuse of power. What Philo fears is the violation of Jewish rights and customs, which he defends in his political treatises (see above). Read in light of

---

[46] This view was developed by Daniel R. Schwartz, "Anonyms," 63–73 and Kraft, "Philo," independently. On the implications for the dating of the works of Philo and his age, cf. Kraft, "Philo," 140. For a critique of this view, see Gruen, *Heritage*, 85–86, fn. 69.

[47] It is puzzling to me why Bassler, "Philo," 250 describes this passage as referring to Joseph as "a soul ... impiously seeking honors due to God alone." Excluding such clear political references, it is not astonishing that she cannot find a dimension beyond a discussion of the human soul in *Somn.* 2.

[48] Cf. Barraclough, "Politics," *ANRW* 21.1:523: "[I]t was his actions, not his Roman authority, which manifested his vainglory."

[49] Hay, "Politics," 435.

[50] Goodenough, *Politics*, 30.

[51] Again, Bassler, "Philo," 250 refers to this section only briefly and only to show that "at least for the episode under consideration the masculine rational principle has been suppressed and the effeminate principle prevails." This certainly is correct, but it is also important that this is not part of an abstract discussion of the soul, but referring to the soul of a politician going the wrong way.

2. Analysis of Somn. 2

the later section, which we have just discussed, it could even be that Philo is thinking of the same conflict. After all, the person there thought "that if he could destroy the ancestral rule of the Sabbath it would lead the way to irregularity in all other matters, and general backsliding" (*Somn* 2.123). Be that as it may, Philo does not concentrate on the persons in power but on the subordinate people, represented by the other sheaves that made obeisance (*Somn*. 2.80). It is pure caution (εὐλάβεια) that demands such behaviour (*Somn*. 2.80–82). There is every reason to suppose that Philo is still talking about engagement with officials since subsequently, in *Somn*. 2.83, he defines inappropriate behaviour towards "kings and tyrants" (βασιλεῦσι καὶ τυράννοις). Only foolish people would oppose them by word and deed since they are under their "yoke" and the "harness" extends to their whole environment. They are thus under complete control (*Somn*. 2.83) and their death is only logical (*Somn*. 2.84). Philo has no respect at all for this kind of falsely understood "free speech" and, in a vivid description, compares it to sailing in wrong weather conditions (*Somn*. 2.85–86):

> Who if he sees a storm at its height, a fierce counter-wind, a hurricane swooping down and a tempest tossed sea, sets sail and puts out to sea when he should remain in harbour? What pilot or skipper was ever so utterly intoxicated as to wish to sail with all these terrors launched upon him, only to find the ship water-logged by the down-rushing sea and swallowed up, crew and all.

In contrast, safe dealings with these mighty men are compared to "a safe voyage" at the right time (*Somn*. 2.86). Philo then changes the metaphor and expresses the same thought with regard to wild beasts: It would be foolish to attack them instead of calming them down (*Somn*. 2.87–88). That these are an illustration for "men more fierce and malicious than boars, scorpions or asps" is made explicit in *Somn*. 2.89. In accordance with the behaviour towards these beasts, it is appropriate to soothe and tame (τιθασείαις καὶ μειλίγμασι) them. In Philo's view this is exactly what the wise Abraham did with the sons of Cheth (Gen 23:3) when he did obeisance to them (προσκυνήσει)[52] in order to get the double cave.[53] *Somn*. 2.91 then makes a connection with the situation of Philo and his implied readers: He asks "What now?"(τί δέ;) And continues: "Are not we also, when we are spending time in the market-place, accustomed to make way for the rulers, and also to make room for the pack animals?" (my translation; οὐχὶ καὶ ἡμεῖς, ὅταν ἐν ἀγορᾷ διατρίβωμεν,

---

[52] Philo interprets the name to mean "admiring" (cf. Yonge; Colson translates literally as "removing," but the metaphorical meaning makes much more sense in the context. Cf. LSJ, 595).

[53] On the meaning of the double cave as referring to the contemplation of the created world as well as its maker, cf. *Somn*. 2.26.

εἰώθαμεν ἐξίστασθαι⁵⁴ μὲν τοῖς ἄρχουσιν, ἐξίστασθαι δὲ καὶ τοῖς ὑποζυγίοις;) The implication is clear: Throughout the whole section, Philo has argued for the importance of caution in order to avoid danger. Behind all the metaphors for these risky favours lay the worry about powerful rulers, who were able to take away ancient rights and who thus needed to be soothed instead of provoked.⁵⁵ Philo immediately hastens to add that there is, of course, a difference in motivation between both kinds of making room:⁵⁶ It is honour (τιμή) in the case of the rulers (ἄρχων) and fear (φόβος) in the case of the pack animals. But in light of the flow of the whole argument, this assertion is most probably ironic.⁵⁷

Otherwise, the structure of the argument becomes completely obscure: Beginning with caution for fear of leaders, Philo would end with the opposite conclusion. Talking about rulers all the time – through different metaphors – this carefully structured discourse would culminate in making room for the pack animals ... One could of course argue that the beginning refers to "Gentile power groups" in general and after discussing them, Philo wants to add some (honest) remarks concerning the specific case of the Romans.⁵⁸ But in arguing that *Somn.* 2.83–92 refers to the Alexandrian mob, Barraclough does not take into consideration enough that the preceding *Somn.* 2.78–79 refers explicitly to *rulers*. One could modify his position and argue that there is a distinction between rulers in general and contemporary rulers, including Romans. But the present-day situation is not just peripheral to the argument, but the climax of all the illustrations. After all, the Egyptian situation is carefully put into focus by mentioning Egyptian beasts (*Somn.* 2.88), the link to men is not a digression but the human side of the metaphor is carefully linked to all

---

⁵⁴ In *Somn.* 2.89, the active voice is used ("admiring") and here the middle voice ("making room"). Against Yonge: "Do we not also ... wonder ... ?"

⁵⁵ Goodenough, *Politics*, 7: "Philo has compared harsh rulers to savage and deadly animals throughout." Harrison, *Paul*, 31 tries to save Goodenough's argument against criticism by pointing to the motif of beasts for tyrants. But even without such a background the equation is clear from the flow of the argument.

⁵⁶ In Colson's translation it is difficult to see that this question is a sentence standing on its own: "Again, do not we too, when we are spending time in the market-place, make a practice of standing out of the path of our rulers and also of beasts of carriage, though our motive in the two cases is entirely different?" (*Somn.* 2.91).

⁵⁷ Hence I agree with Neil Elliott, "The 'Patience of the Jews': Strategies of Resistance and Accommodation to Imperial Cultures," in *Pauline Conversations in Context: Essays in Honor of Calvin J. Roetzel* (ed. Janice C. Anderson, Philip Sellew, and Claudia Setzer; JSNTSup 221; London: Sheffield Academic, 2002), 39–40: "Of course these qualifications come a moment too late. The distinction between rulers and brute animals is explicit – but is undermined by everything else Philo has said about the brutality of rulers. His insistence that 'honor' is shown to rulers is belied by his preceding comment that fear, not honor, compels the outward deference of the subordinate."

⁵⁸ Cf. Barraclough, "Politics," *ANRW* 21.1:536.

the beasts mentioned before (*Somn.* 2.89), and the application to the Alexandrian situation is consciously introduced by asking "What now?" (*Somn.* 2.91).[59] The example of Abraham is intriguing, too: His behaviour is explicitly called not an act of honouring but an act of fear (δείδω instead of τιμάω). Goodenough therefore seems to be correct in asserting that "it is part of the very caution he is counselling that he should distinguish between the two ... If the passage were called into question, he could insist that the first part was perfectly general and had no reference to the Romans, while he had properly indicated that one gives way to Romans out of honour. But his Jewish readers would have understood quite well that the reason Philo gave way to each was the same, because he knew that if he did not he would be crushed."[60] Philo ends his discussion in *Somn.* 2.93, concluding "somewhat cryptically":[61] "And if ever occasions permit it is good to subdue the violence of enemies by attack, but if they do not permit, the safe course is to keep quiet, and if we wish to gain any help from them the fitting course is to soften and tame them." Philo thus does not seem to be rejecting the use of violence (βία) to end suppression in principle – as long as it can be done without endangering oneself.[62] If this is not the case, Philo can be very diplomatic – and this should cause us to read praise for Roman rule in other works carefully.[63] He is okay with flattery[64] because he knows that God still remains the judge over

---

[59] Oertelt, *Herrscherideal,* 240 does not seem to have taken this fact into account.
[60] Goodenough, *Politics,* 7.
[61] Hay, "Politics," 434.
[62] Barraclough, "Politics," *ANRW* 21.1:536–637, who argues against such a view, points to *Abr.* 228 to show that Philo would not approve of such behaviour. But he overlooks that *Abr.* 229 makes clear that this kind of rebellion was untimely because it ended in a disaster. Furthermore, it is not clear how this element of violent resistance could be integrated into Barraclough's *own* interpretation of *Somn.* 2.83–92: He summarises *Somn.* 2.90–92 without any reference to this aspect (Barraclough, "Politics," *ANRW* 21.1:536): "If the Jews wished to gain greater rights, they were to avoid conflict and impress their Alexandrian neighbours by their reasonable and subservient lives, thus softening and taming their fierce opposition." Does this imply that Philo would have approved of violent resistance *to the Alexandrians* if the situation would have been more promising? Then Barraclough faces his own objections against resistance towards rulers.
[63] Collins, *Athens,* 114 sees this implication but remarks with *Legat.* and *Flacc.* in view: "Admittedly the quotation from *De Somniis* 2.91–92 may make any positive statements suspect as an attempt to 'soften and tame' the Romans, but the fact that these praises are found in works which are so outspoken in criticism of Roman rulers tells against such a view." But while we already noted that Philo has seen positive aspects in Roman rule, the more important implication – not noticed by Collins – is that this passage might explain what is *not* there: The absence of evidence for a generally critical attitude towards the Roman Empire cannot simply be taken as evidence for the absence of such a view.
[64] Bassler, "Philo," 250 suggests that Abraham's submissive behaviour is the negative foil before which the resistance of the brothers looks even better. But this does not do justice to 1) the fact that Philo seems to approve of both kinds of behaviour – depending on

his enemies. Thus, it is not surprising that βία – although not carried out by the Jews themselves – plays a role in the end of one of the enemies of the Jews, namely in the execution of Flaccus (*Flacc.* 188).

Although Goodenough is probably right about the ironical character of *Somn.* 2.91, he nevertheless seems to go too far in his conclusions when he writes that Philo "loved the Romans no more than the skipper of a tiny boat loves a hurricane."[65] There is no reason to assume that Philo is talking about "the Romans" in general here. In fact, he gives quite a detailed description of the people in view at the beginning of the section in *Somn.* 2.78–79. He is talking about the votaries of vainglory (θιασῶται τῆς κενῆς δόξης),[66] who behave disrespectfully toward other people. This includes opposition to "ancestral customs" (ἐθῶν πατρίων) – the very thing that Flaccus (*Flacc.* 53: ἐθῶν τε πατρίων) and the unnamed individual who was in Philo's recent memory (*Somn.* 2.123) were accused of. We have already seen in *Ios.* that vainglory is a serious threat to the soul of any politician. But it is not a necessary trait nor is it necessarily a Roman phenomenon. Romans happened to have (the highest) power over Philo's environment, so they happened to produce individuals who were in danger of becoming vainglorious, and worse, who yielded to the temptation. Again, we have the impression that, for Philo, the primary problem was a problem of the human soul – which could find expression in the acts of powerful individuals. This impression is strengthened by the comments starting in *Somn.* 2.93, which elucidate the notion of resistance in *Somn.* 2.92: The resistance of the brothers is approved, who resisted when Joseph was "not yet" strong.[67] But now Joseph is explicitly interpreted as representing the craving for glory that exists in *"every man's soul"* (*Somn.* 2.98). Philo thus includes himself (*Somn.* 2.101–104) among those who have already acted like "Joseph" and who have to put themselves under the judgement of the "brothers."[68] Accordingly, a change of mind for

---

the concrete situation – and 2) that a shift in reference (unjust rulers → vainglorious inclination of the soul) occurs with *Somn.* 2.93, as is evident from *Somn.* 2.98.

[65] Goodenough, "Politics," 7.

[66] On this phrase, cf. Oertelt, *Herrscherideal*, 235–239.

[67] Arnaldo Momigliano, review of Erwin R. Goodenough, *An Introduction to Philo Judaeus, JRS* 34 (1944): 164 thinks the sense of the passage is that one "must resist the tyrant before he becomes too strong." But the sequence seems to be triggered by the biblical story itself, and Philo's emphasis is on the lack of danger without dating it. See in contrast *Somn.* 2.86, where the person should even "wait" for a better time. Additionally, it is doubtful that political resistance is still Philo's concern here.

[68] Hay, "Politics," 437 agrees with Goodenough, *Politics,* 27–28 that this refers to political follies. More recently, Oertelt, *Herrscherideal,* 167 has also assumed a "politische Aussage" for this text. Although it is possible, of course, that such a dimension is included, there is nothing in the text that makes such a reference probable. Other than in *Somn.* 1.122–124 the *immediate* context does not support an explicitly political dimension. Maren R. Niehoff, "New Garments for Biblical Joseph," in *Biblical Interpretation: History, Con-*

"Joseph" is possible (*Somn.* 2.105–109). The real object of Philo's dislike is not the politician in himself but the vainglorious character. Therefore, Philo would not deny the possibility of rulers who do not fall prey to the danger of vainglory (cf. Augustus in *Legat.*) or stop being vainglorious and thus detestable. These observations confirm Hay's conclusion: "It seems evident that Philo has deliberately set side by side Political Allegory and Allegory of the Soul."[69] At the same time, this also suggests that it is reasonable to look for concrete, political references in Philo's allegories of the soul.[70]

2.3.3 Political Subtext in Allegories of the Soul?

On the grounds of our investigation so far, it seems reasonable to look for less overt political references in Philo's allegories of the soul in *Somn.* 2.[71] Since Joseph has already been identified with the politician in *Somn.* 1, it is reasonable to suggest that, when the figure is introduced in *Somn.* 2.5–16, this also has implications for the picture of the politician Philo is sketching in his work on dreams.[72] But although Philo would probably not have rejected the application of these thoughts to political figures (since he did it later in the book explicitly himself), it is impossible to say whether he had in mind such a concrete referent here. In what follows we will focus on one instance in *Somn.* 2,[73] in which a political subtext seems very likely to me.

---

text, and Reality (ed. Christine Helmer and Taylor G. Petrey; SBLSymS 26; Atlanta: Society of Biblical Literature, 2005), 46 argues that the passionate tone of this section demonstrates that Philo had in view the Jewish adaptation to Egyptian culture. If true, this would demonstrate Philo's ability to include concrete referents in abstract discussions and increase the probability that there are similar references to political realities embedded in allegories of the soul.

[69] Hay, "Politics," 434.

[70] Even the very next sentence (*Somn.* 2.99) about the association of Joseph with the soul could be a good candidate for such an assessment. Cf. Oertelt, *Herrscherideal,* 168.

[71] Cf. Hay, "Politics," 363, who warns against looking for too subtle a criticism but remarks: "It seems altogether possible ... to detect Political Allegory beneath or mixed with Allegory of the Soul in several other passages of *De Somniis.* ... [I]t is a fact that political terms and images occur within passages that concentrate on allegory of the Soul. In these passages we may then detect some political 'overtones,' particularly if the message conveyed seems consonant with the more overt Political Allegory we have already examined and with Philo's political thought as expressed in other writings."

[72] Cf. Hay, "Politics," 436: "[W]e may be inclined to view any description of his nature, even without obvious political terminology, as conveying a political message ... ." He then refers to *Somn.* 2.5–16 as an example.

[73] In *Somn.* 1 there is also a strong case: In the midst of the discussion of the Jacob-like soul, Philo suddenly writes about persons who erect inscriptions for themselves in *Somn.* 1.244. Even Barraclough, "Politics," *ANRW* 21.1:541 thinks a connection to monuments like Augustus's *Res gest. divi Aug.* could be intended. Cf. also Hay, "Politics," 436 (incorrectly referencing *Somn.* 1.243).

Somn. 2.42–64 seems to be a promising candidate. Here, Philo's primary concern is the worthlessness of all kinds of luxury. In the course of this argument, he describes the career of Joseph. Although Goodenough might have overplayed the lexical evidence by claiming that the title ἐπίτροπος is a terminus technicus for the prefect,[74] there is a clear conceptual similarity. Joseph's new position is described as "procurator or protector of all Egypt, to stand second only to the sovereign in the signs of honour shewn to him" (*Somn.* 2.43) and immediately interpreted negatively as "a position set down as more insignificant and absurd in wisdom's judgement than the infliction of indignity and defeat." There is no reason to suppose that the whole discussion centres on Roman individuals since Philo describes the different luxurious wishes – for example, exotic foods – in the first person plural,[75] even though the luxurious lifestyle of some politicians could conceivably have been one of his concerns. Accordingly, in *Somn.* 2.62 this background comes to the surface of the discourse again when he describes people who "pose over their head golden wreaths … without any shame in mid-market at the hour when it is full."[76] They assert that they are "lords and rulers of many others,"[77] but they are rather "slaves of vainglory."

The conclusion of the section in *Somn.* 2.64 is also interesting. The "life of falsity and vanity" is a parasite to the true and simple life and has to be removed just like superfluous growths on trees are removed by the farmer. Philo concludes that "no husbandman has hitherto been found to excise the mischievous overgrowth, root and all." For Goodenough, "Philo has gone out of his way to make his reference clear" in the concluding section from 61–64:[78] "The arrogant ones he is describing are those people who call themselves rulers of many peoples and whom all his audience will have seen daily vaunting themselves in the marketplace. Philo's hatred of them glows at white heat." The husbandman is said to be a clear reference to the Messiah[79] and Philo "was not only awaiting the Husbandman, but would swing an axe

---

[74] Cf. Goodenough, *Politics,* 22–23 with Barraclough, "Politics," *ANRW* 21.1:499–500. Cf. also Louis H. Feldman, *Scholarship on Philo and Josephus, 1937–1962* (New York: Yeshiva University, 1963), 5. For a recent discussion of Joseph's titles, see Oertelt, *Herrscherideal,* 266–272.

[75] Cf., for example, *Somn.* 2.48 in contrast with 49.

[76] Even Barraclough, "Politics," *ANRW* 21.1:492 "undeniably" sees an allusion to "Roman practice and claims" here.

[77] Literally: "asserting not only to be free but also …" (φάσκοντες οὐκ ἐλεύθεροι μόνον ἀλλὰ καὶ πολλῶν ἄλλων ἡγεμόνες εἶναι).

[78] Goodenough, *Politics,* 24.

[79] Goodenough, *Politics,* 25 refers to the language of Q's portrayal of John the Baptist's Messianic announcement in Matt 3:10; Luke 3:9 and of John 15.

with him when he came."⁸⁰ However, this interpretation seems to be problematic and Goodenough misrepresents the evidence here.

Somn. 2.63–64 does not only refer to the vainglorious behaviour of officials (*Somn.* 2.62). Rather, it seems to conclude the whole section, which includes the aspect expressed in *Somn.* 2.62 as one of several aspects of unnecessary luxury, which can also be found in Joseph's career (cf. *Somn.* 2.44 on the parallel on clothing in Joseph's life). In Goodenough's translation this is veiled by excluding one question from *Somn.* 2.63, namely: "The day will pass before I have given the sum of the corruption of human life, and indeed why need we dwell at length upon them?" This seems to refer to *all* the various behaviours (τὰς διαφθορὰς τοῦ ἀνθρωπείου βίου) he has described before. The next question ("For who has not heard, who has not seen them?") is thus referring not just to the politicians but to all people who live overly luxurious lives as is further supported by the reference to Joseph's name as an "addition," which refers back to the beginning of the discussion in *Somn.* 2.47.⁸¹ The closing statement, therefore, seems to refer to the removal of human arrogance as a whole, and the participles are better translated as referring back to βίος instead of being understood as introducing a new person. Philo is writing about a parasitic kind of "life" not about "the false man full of arrogance grow[ing] out as a sucker" (Goodenough).⁸² That the husbandman is a messianic figure and not simply "a reformer who would put an end to corruption" thus seems doubtful.⁸³

3. Conclusions

3.1 Summary

Our analysis has shown that *Somn.* 2 includes political allegory and also probably a political subtext at least in parts of its allegories of the soul.⁸⁴ Nevertheless, Goodenough seems to have overemphasised this aspect at some points so that the following qualifications are in order.

First, there is no reason to assume that Joseph has to be associated with concrete political figures *every time* he is mentioned, especially since he is

---

⁸⁰ Goodenough, *Politics,* 25.
⁸¹ On the interpretation of Joseph's name, see Oertelt, *Herrscherideal,* 136–138.
⁸² Goodenough, *Politics,* 24.
⁸³ Collins, *Athens,* 115. On the lack of messianic expectations in Philo, cf. Sandmel, *Philo,* 109–110. Oertelt, *Herrscherideal,* 144 follows Goodenough to the degree that she affirms "dass der von Philo erwartete Landwirt die Hoffnung auf einen messianischen König durchschimmern lässt."
⁸⁴ Thus, Krauter, *Studien,* 107 is wrong to say that the "Kontext" demands a spiritualised interpretation. This treats Philo's allegorical interpretations too one-dimensionally.

explicitly equated with each individual's soul. Certainly, this figure easily evoked political implications due to its career in the biblical story, and where Philo's more general concerns for human nature had striking resemblance in concrete political circumstances of his day, he thus was able to make the connection in the text.[85]

Second, the references which we have identified are not related to Roman power as a whole, but rather seem to focus on actual or potential misbehaviour of people with a Joseph-like soul in political positions.[86] That, in his view, such Roman misbehaviour was not simply coincidental but symptomatic of the superior status of the Jewish race can be inferred from his other writings (see above, Section 1.3), but this is not the subject matter of *Somn.* 2. Thus, the inference of a general hatred by Goodenough does not seem to be based on the text itself.

Third, this also has implications for Goodenough's framework for explaining the differences regarding the figure of Joseph in *Ios.* and *Somn.* 2. While in the former Philo uses the biblical character to show how politicians should behave by offering a paradigm of the good politician,[87] in the latter he stands for the human soul in general and some of the deviations from the ideal explained in *Ios.* are mentioned.[88] Goodenough is probably correct that overt

---

[85] Similarly Hay, "Politics," 437: "Rather than having an elaborate deliberate plan to locate political comments and interpretations at carefully chosen points near or not so near the surface of his commentary, Philo seems simply to have approached the writing of *De Somniis* with strong convictions about politics and the political significance of the dreams in the Joseph story."

[86] Thus, vainglory could also take on non-political forms or political forms other than Roman ones (referring, e.g., to Philo himself as in *Somn.* 1.224). The critical remarks against *Egyptian* political action, which Hay, "Politics," 437 identifies in *Somn.* 2.182–184 and 219, would nicely fit such an evaluation. Cf. also Barraclough, "Politics," *ANRW* 21.1:525 on *Somn.* 2.283–302 as a critique of the Alexandrian mob as an expression of ochlocracy. Oertelt, *Herrscherideal,* 111 also recognises the tendency in Philo "dass er in der Herrschaft aller eine Gefahr für die Gesellschaft sieht."

[87] For an intriguing reading of *Flacc.* against the background of *Ios.* as a paradigm for the politician, cf. Sills, "Bedfellows," 186–187, who wants to follow Bassler, "Philo," in looking for "a deeper exegetical grammar" (Bassler, "Philo," 181). But from my perspective, there is one important difference: While Bassler concentrates on the *figure* of Joseph, Sills is looking for the *concept* of the politician. This move helps her to avoid some of the reductionist readings we found in Bassler's work.

[88] It is also important to note in this connection that *Ios.* already hints at these potential dangers. Cf. Bassler, "Philo," 251. Oertelt, *Herrscherideal,* 259 reaches similar conclusions with regard to the different depictions of Joseph although she sees a more thoroughgoing political discourse in *Somn.* 2: "[D]ie unterschiedliche Bewertung Josephs [entsteht] aus den unterschiedlichen Perspektiven, die beide Schriften einnehmen ... . Geht es Philo in *somn.* ii um die Ursachen tyrannischer Herrschaft, aus der er Verhaltensweisen für die Beherrschten ableitet, stellt er in *Jos.* den idealen Staatsmann dar, der die Beherrschten

criticism of imperial ideology or living powerful officials (unlike Flaccus and Caligula, who were dead at the time of the critique!) would have been a dangerous thing for a man in Philo's position, and his exegesis of the veiling in *Somn.* 2.91 seems plausible. However, avoiding danger should not be overemphasised as Philo's motivation for using allegorical discourse to make critical remarks about contemporary political affairs,[89] and absence of such criticism in *Ios.* seems to be adequately explained by authorial intention. Philo had different purposes in writing and the ambivalent figure of Joseph could be used in different ways to serve these ends.[90]

3.2 Outlook

How can these conclusions help sharpen the focus in our assessment of the Empire in *Paul*? Our observation of a variety of different ways of dealing with Roman power in Philo should make us cautious about monolithic descriptions of Paul's relation to the Empire and at the same time open to subtle literary phenomena.[91] I even think that the different categories we found in Philo might be a helpful way of classifying Pauline handling of imperial claims.[92] As the book of Acts vividly demonstrates, Paul also had his issue with individual Roman officials who, from his perspective, did not perform their duties appropriately (cf., e.g., Acts 16:20–39). Although not a prominent theme in his letters, we will later (Chapter 5, Section 2.1) examine traces of direct criticism of this kind. When searching for irony with regard to imperial authority, we should probably start where, on the surface of the text, Paul is making direct statements concerning this entity, which basically amounts to Rom 13:1–7 (one could add some statements about social behaviour like 1

---

nicht für seine eigenen Begierden missbraucht, sondern ihnen an seinem Wissen Anteil gibt und sie lehrt."

[89] Philo is not writing primarily about politics and looking for a safe way to communicate his criticism; rather, he is writing allegorically about Joseph as the vainglorious soul and comes up with some political associations. Perhaps his political references would have been clearer if he had nothing to fear – but the choice of writing about politics in terms of "Joseph" is due to the genre itself. Cf. also Oertelt, *Herrscherideal*, 308, fn. 7.

[90] Gruen, *Heritage,* 87: "All of this suggests that for Hellenistic Jews Joseph was more persona than personage, an acknowledged literary artifice available and versatile. No monolithic figure determined the discourse. The ambiguities of Joseph's personality and achievements made him readily malleable to serve a variety of purposes."

[91] This openness is further demanded by the subtlety and complexity of "resistance" in Greek literature during the Roman period. See Tim Whitmarsh, "Resistance is Futile? Greek Literary Tactics in the Face of Rome," in *Les Grecs héritiers des Romains* (ed. Paul Schubert; EnAC 59; Geneva: Hardt Foundation, 2013), 57–78.

[92] Cf. the similar first three points in Scot McKnight and Joseph B. Modica, "Introduction," in *Jesus Is Lord, Caesar Is Not: Evaluating Empire in New Testament Studies* (ed. Scot McKnight and Joseph B. Modica; Downers Grove: IVP Academia, 2013), 17–18.

Thess 4:10–12; if we want to include the pastorals, also Titus 3:1). This kind of engagement with Roman ideology has indeed been suggested with regard to the topos of using the sword "not in εἰκῇ" (Rom 13:4). Usually read as a concession to state power at first sight, this statement becomes cutting irony in light of the governmental emphasis on the non-use of violence.[93] What we are going to consider in this book is the third category, which stands between these two extremes, namely between open criticism in a text explicitly referring to the political realm on the one hand and intentional irony on the other, which reverses the sense of a text that is also clearly speaking about this sphere. While in Philo the soul was the vehicle for concomitantly communicating a critical assessment of political circumstances and ideas, in Paul it is his christological discourse, which is often assumed to be open for double entendre, i.e., for a subtext that complements what he says on the surface of the text. We now turn to the question of how to handle this problem methodologically.

---

[93] Suggested by Neil Elliott, "Romans." For a critical assessment, see Krauter, *Studien*, esp. 28–32. He concludes his exegesis (Krauter, *Studien*, 239): "Versuche, bestimmten Wendungen im Text einen herrschaftskritischen, die Ansprüche von Herrschern einschränkenden oder gar gegen sie polemisierenden Hintersinn zu entnehmen, lassen sich nicht plausibel begründen."

Chapter 2

Approach

1. Counter-Imperial "Echoes" in the Subtext

In the last two decades, an increasing number of scholars have argued for a much more critical evaluation of the Roman Empire in the Pauline letters than has often been assumed.[1] The fundamental criticism that is raised against

---

[1] Some forerunners include, for example, G. Adolf Deissmann, *Licht vom Osten: Das Neue Testament und die neuentdeckten Texte der hellenistisch-römischen Welt* (4th ed.; Tübingen: Mohr, 1923), Klaus Wengst, *Pax Romana: Anspruch und Wirklichkeit: Erfahrungen und Wahrnehmungen des Friedens bei Jesus und im Urchristentum* (München: Kaiser, 1986), and Dieter Georgi, "Gott auf den Kopf stellen: Überlegungen zu Tendenz und Kontext des Theokratiegedankens in paulinischer Praxis und Theologie," in *Theokratie* (ed. Jacob Taubes; vol. 3 of *Religionstheorie und Politische Theologie;* ed. Jacob Taubes; München: Ferdinand Schöningh/Wilhelm Funk, 1987), 148–205. The last contribution has gained some influence due to its partial inclusion in the important anthology of Richard A. Horsley, ed., *Paul and Empire: Religion and Power in Roman Imperial Society* (Harrisburg: Trinity Press International, 1997). Nevertheless, caution is necessary when attributing an uncritical position to earlier (exegetical and systematic-theological) scholarship. One only has to compare some of the nuanced contributions from post-war Germany, sensitised to tyranny. Compare, for example, Oscar Cullmann, *Der Staat im Neuen Testament* (2nd ed.; Tübingen: Mohr Siebeck, 1961), with the rather pompous statements of some current interpreters of Paul, who deny that former generations had a nuanced position on this topic. For the current discussion, there are three foundational anthologies by Horsley: Horsley, *Paul,* Richard A. Horsley, ed., *Paul and Politics: Ekklesia, Israel, Imperium, Interpretation: Essays in Honor of Krister Stendahl* (Harrisburg: Trinity Press International, 2000), and Richard A. Horsley, ed., *Paul and the Roman Imperial Order* (Harrisburg: Trinity Press International, 2004). Warren Carter, "Paul and the Roman Empire: Recent Perspectives," in *Paul Unbound: Other Perspectives on the Apostle* (ed. Mark D. Given; Peabody: Hendrickson, 2009), 7–18 offers a very good summary. For a less incisive but more detailed summary of scholarship on anti-imperialism in the Pauline letters, see Judith A. Diehl, "Empire and Epistles: Anti-Roman Rhetoric in the New Testament Epistles," *CBR* 10 (2012): 217–252. For a continental perspective, which declares itself to be an outsider perspective on a largely American phenomenon, see Wiard Popkes, "Zum Thema 'Anti-imperiale Deutung neutestamentlicher Schriften,'" *ThLZ* 127 (2002): 850–862. The most detailed German survey of relevant scholarship can be found in Christian Strecker, "Taktiken der Aneignung: Politische Implikationen der paulinischen Botschaft im Kontext der römischen imperialen Wirklichkeit," in *Das Neue Testament und politische Theorie: Interdisziplinäre Beiträge zur Zukunft des Politischen* (ed. Eckart Reinmuth; ReligionsKul-

such an interpretation of Paul is, naturally, the apparently *positive* evaluation of state power in Rom 13:1–7 in combination with the *lack of clear criticism* in the rest of the *Corpus Paulinum*.² Since, on the *surface of the text*, such a critical attitude is not apparent, the search for critical allusions in the *subtext* – "[a]ny meaning or set of meanings which is implied rather than explicitly stated in a literary work"³ – has become increasingly important.⁴ In this framework, the idea of a politically passive Paul as implied by Rom 13 has to be read either in dialogue with the less accessible critical remarks or the passage is interpreted as itself displaying criticism if analysed with scrutiny. The object of all this criticism is defined in a variety of ways by different proponents of this view. There is probably most agreement on the position that the ideology underlying the imperial cult is challenged by Paul's reference to Christ as the true κύριος. Sometimes, the references to Roman ideology are broadened to the whole imperial system and its society.⁵

---

turen 9; Stuttgart: Kohlhammer, 2011), 114–148. That this topic is almost exclusively an anglophone phenomenon can also be seen in the fact that the detailed discussion of Pauline scholarship in Friedrich W. Horn, ed., *Paulus Handbuch* (Tübingen: Mohr Siebeck, 2013), has only two short paragraphs on the "Imperium Romanum."

² Cf. Joel R. White, "Anti-Imperial Subtexts in Paul: An Attempt at Building a Firmer Foundation," *Bib* 90 (2009): 305–307 on the problem of a positive evaluation of the Roman Empire in Rom 13:1–7 and the lack of overt negative criticism. For a typical summary combining these two observations, see Volker Gäckle, "Historische Analyse II: Die griechisch-römische Umwelt," in *Das Studium des Neuen Testaments* (ed. Heinz-Werner Neudorfer and Eckhard J. Schnabel; 2nd ed.; Wuppertal: R. Brockhaus, 2006), 151: "Zunächst stellte der Kaiserkult auch für die christliche Gemeinde keine unüberwindliche Herausforderung dar (vgl. nur Röm 13,1–7). Eine Spannung zwischen Christuskult und Kaiserkult ist im Neuen Testament abgesehen von der Johannesapokalypse nirgendwo spürbar." See also the overview by Jost Eckert, "Das Imperium Romanum im Neuen Testament: Ein Beitrag zum Thema 'Kirche und Gesellschaft,'" *TthZ* 96 (1987): 259–264, in which the apostle Paul is seen as demanding "ohne Einschränkung … Unterordnung unter die staatliche Obrigkeit" and where Luke's preparation of the "Konstantinische[n] Wende" is only a consequent development of this position.

³ Chris Baldick, "Subtext," *ODLT* n. p. (online version).

⁴ White, "Subtexts," 308: "In view of the absence of direct evidence, proponents of an anti-imperial Paul have turned their attention to examining the subtexts of Paul's writing." See also Strecker, "Taktiken," 130–131. It is intriguing to compare the selection of passages in recent arguments for a "counter-imperial" attitude of Paul with the selection by Rodney L. Parrott, "Paul's Political Thought: Rom 13:1–7 in the Light of Hellenistic Political Thought" (Ph.D. diss., The Claremont Graduate School, 1980), 217–228.

⁵ Or beyond – John D. Crossan and Jonathan L. Reed, *In Search of Paul: How Jesus' Apostle Opposed Rome's Empire with God's Kingdom: A New Vision of Paul's Words and World* (San Francisco: HarperSanFrancisco, 2004), x write: "What is *newest* about this book is our insistence that Paul opposed Rome with Christ against Caesar, not because that empire was particularly unjust or oppressive, but because he questioned *the normalcy of civilization* itself, since civilization has always been imperial, that is, unjust and oppressive." For a different classification of the position of Crossan/Reed as some kind of mid-

I cannot even begin discussing the many different exegetical suggestions developed within this paradigm (let alone post-colonial applications).[6] Also, I am not sure whether this would be especially helpful since more opinions on the same texts do not per se advance the discussion, so long as there is no consensus on how to evaluate them.[7] Hence, what is needed in the first place, from my perspective, is a methodological discussion which picks up some important suggestions and develops them into a reliable framework. Until now, such a methodological analysis is lacking.[8] The need for such an assessment is also demonstrated by Harrill's telling remark: "If Paul wrote coded and ambiguous speech in order to avoid detection, how can modern readers detect his 'real' message in Romans 13? After all, it's supposedly *hidden*!"[9] On the one hand, this rhetorical question is absurd: How could anyone try to decode messages of the Nazis in the Second World War? After all, they were coded! On the other hand, the comment points to an important aspect: Such a task certainly demands a sound methodological foundation, which has to be developed carefully. The questions that need to be answered – to name the most obvious ones – are: How could such a critical subtext be identified in a methodologically sound way? How could such an enquiry fulfil the requirements of historical-critical scholarship? How could one guarantee that ideological positions of the interpreter are not foisted on Paul's letters by a subjective procedure, only to be read out of the text again? What are the rules that should govern such analyses and how can their results be re-

---

dle-ground, see Strecker, "Taktiken," 119. For an overview regarding the spectrum of opinions on the object of the alleged criticism, see Barclay, "Empire," 366–367.

[6] A very recent assessment of the NT writings is provided by Scot McKnight, and Joseph B. Modica, eds., *Jesus Is Lord, Caesar Is Not: Evaluating Empire in New Testament Studies* (Downers Grove: IVP Academic, 2013). With focus on the gospels, see now Gilbert Van Belle and Joseph Verheyden, eds., *Christ and the Emperor: The Gospel Evidence* (BiTS 20; Leuven: Peeters, 2014).

[7] Paradigm-changes happen quickly these days. Many already think that we are living in a post-NPP world, that we have learned a lot from these scholars, but now we are supposed to move beyond their one-sidedness. Michael F. Bird, ed., *Four Views on the Apostle Paul* (Counterpoints: Bible & Theology; Grand Rapids: Zondervan, 2012), for example, does not even include a contribution from the point of view of the NPP anymore. However, sometimes endeavours of this kind make the impression of an artificial synthesis which aims to produce some balanced consensus after a short time of nasty disagreement. The aim of the volume of McKnight and Modica seems to me to fall into this category. I do not think it is appropriate to already look for a synthesis (cf. McKnight and Modica, "Conclusion," 212). Sure, there are a lot of exegetical suggestions in the literature, but I do not yet see either the detailed exegetical evaluation of these proposals, in most cases at least, nor even the necessary methodological groundwork.

[8] If one takes a look at the short description of "methods" by McKnight and Modica, "Introduction," 17–19, one gets quite a good impression of what is lacking.

[9] J. Albert Harrill, *Paul the Apostle: His Life and Legacy in Their Roman Context* (Cambridge: Cambridge University Press, 2012), 93; emphasis original.

evaluated by other scholars? Answers to these questions have often been presupposed rather than demonstrated convincingly as Joel R. White complains.[10] It is the aim of this book to provide its readers with such an evaluation. An assessment like this is, of course, not an end in itself, and in saying that a methodological assessment is lacking, I do not wish to imply that concrete case studies abound. Rather, the contrary is the case, and detailed exegetical analyses should be encouraged.[11] Nevertheless, they should be done on the basis of a general evaluation of the plausibility of the paradigm of a counter-imperial subtext in Paul. Although space limits require restriction to this preparatory step in this book, it is obviously true that, for the discussion as a whole to advance, we should do the former without neglecting the latter.

The attentive reader will have noticed the allusion to Matt 23:23 in the last sentence. Indeed, it seems natural to use research on other forms of intertextuality in order to shed light on Paul's letters in their Roman context. Accordingly, N. T. Wright[12] and Neil Elliott[13] suggest the use of Richard B. Hays's criteria[14] for identifying "echoes" of the Hebrew Bible in the NT as a methodological help for the search of a counter-imperial subtext in Paul. In this chapter, I will shortly summarise their specific suggestion for understanding the critical subtext *as "echoes."* In the rest of the book, we will take these considerations as a point of departure for our own analysis of the plausibility of the assumption that there is hidden criticism of the Roman Empire in Paul. Even if this is only a minor step towards getting a full and, at the same time, precise picture of Paul's engagement with the imperial ideology of his day, it is a necessary one nevertheless.

2. Evaluating Hypotheses

2.1 On the Nature of Criteria

When discussing Wright's and Elliott's approach, we encountered concrete "criteria," which are suggested as means to identify echoes that are critical of

---

[10] Cf. White, "Subtexts," 308–311 on "The Difficulty in Identifying Anti-Imperial Subtexts in Paul."

[11] The analyses of Krauter, *Studien* on Rom 13:1–7 and Joseph D. Fantin, *The Lord of the Entire World: Lord Jesus, a Challenge to Lord Caesar?* (NTMon 31; Sheffield: Sheffield Phoenix, 2011) on lordship terminology in Paul are the most notable detailed studies so far.

[12] Nicholas T. Wright, *Paul: In Fresh Perspective* (Minneapolis: Fortress, 2005), 61.

[13] Neil Elliott, *The Arrogance of Nations: Reading Romans in the Shadow of Empire* (Minneapolis: Fortress, 2008), 22.

[14] Richard B. Hays, *Echoes of Scripture in the Letters of Paul* (New Haven: Yale University Press: 1989).

the Roman Empire. Before we discuss their specific value, we first have to consider the function of criteria in historical research in general. Developing and using criteria to answer questions is a common practice in scientific research in general and in the field of New Testament research in particular: "Does text X have feature A, B, and C? If so, it follows that it (probably) also has feature D." To give one example, the judgement on the historicity of statements or deeds attributed to Jesus in the Gospels is dependent on the fulfilment of certain criteria.[15] The same is true for "mirror-reading" Paul's letters in order to determine what can be learnt from them about his opponents.[16] And tests, such as the ones suggested by Hays, are also used to identify echoes of the Hebrew Bible in the letters of Paul. All these phenomena[17] are in some sense intertextual,[18] and the analysis of specific criteria aims to check whether a postulated connection is historically plausible (Jesus → Gospels; Scripture/Opponents → Paul's letters). In principle then, one may also want to formulate criteria for the relationship at the centre of Wright's and Elliott's investigation (imperial propaganda → letters of Paul).

However, before borrowing criteria from one field and applying them to another,[19] we first need to clarify what "criteria" really are. First of all, it is important to note that usually a much weaker concept of 'criterion' is used in biblical studies compared to philosophical discourse, in which criteria for the predicate P being the case for a thing x are "nichts anderes als die jeweils notwendigen und zusammengenommen hinreichenden Bedingungen dafür, dass P auf x zutrifft."[20] By contrast, in the areas of application just mentioned, the term "criteria" is used more with the meaning of 'symptom' or 'mark' and implies a tendency rather than a necessary consequence. This realism does justice to the fact that historical events usually cannot be broken

---

[15] It should be noted that the classical use of criteria in the *Leben-Jesu-Forschung* has become increasingly less popular. See, e.g., Chris Keith and Anthony Le Donne, eds., *Criteria, and the Demise of Authenticity* (London: T&T Clark, 2012).

[16] See, e.g., the classical treatment by John M. G. Barclay, "Mirror-Reading a Polemical Letter: Galatians as a Test Case," *JSNT* 10 (1987): 73–93. Cf. p. 84: "What is needed is a carefully controlled method of working which uses logical criteria and proceeds with suitable caution." He then proposes seven criteria.

[17] A similar focus on the value of criteria can be found in (mostly popular) books on textual criticism.

[18] The term "intertextuality" is used in this book not in the wider technical poststructuralist sense of Julia Kristeva, "Bakhtine, le mot, le dialogue et le roman," *Critique* 33 (1967): 438–465, but in the more specific sense of actual dependency between texts, the usage that is most frequent in New Testament studies.

[19] This is also a popular procedure in New Testament studies. See, e.g., the adoption of Barclay, "Mirror-Reading" for ethical issues in Nijay Gupta, "Mirror-Reading Moral Issues in Paul," *JSNT* 34 (2011): 361–381.

[20] Heinrich Schmidt and Martin Gessmann, eds., *Philosophisches Wörterbuch* (23rd ed.; Stuttgart: Kröner, 2009), 411.

down to a few verifiable basic points. However, this automatically implies that, in the final analysis, the use of criteria is not a phenomenon of logic but of pragmatism. The examination of certain criteria allows one to classify objects without having to comprehend them in their entirety, which is an immense practical advantage. But what makes such a predication true in the end is not the fulfilment of the criteria itself but their agreement with the *logical inference* for which the criteria are only the shortcut.

Criteria can thus be legitimised in two ways. First, by showing a multiplicity of cases in which they lead to the right – independently established – result or, secondly (and far better), by explicating how these criteria relate to the complete inference.[21] If criteria are applied to another field, it is prudent to see whether they fit their new inferential context.[22] We thus want to take a look at the implicit foundation of the whole argument in the next section in order to see whether Hays's criteria are a useful representation of the inference they were originally developed for. Only then will we ask the question whether it is fitting to transfer them to another context. In order to be in the position to evaluate how helpful Hays's criteria are, we will have to determine first how historical inferences are properly structured. Only on that basis, a kind of "meta-criterion," will it be possible to see whether criteria offer a helpful route in assessing the plausibility of a hypothesis.

2.2 The Structure of Historical Inferences

In historical research, we evaluate the plausibility of hypotheses that aim to explain the occurrence of a specific event. The explanations we develop for this purpose have to be considered in light of the historical evidence that is available to us. Data functions as evidence that supports or contradicts a hypothesis in two different ways, corresponding to two different questions that need to be answered with regard to a hypothesis:
 1. How well does the event fit into the explanation given for its occurrence?
 2. How plausible are the basic parameters presupposed by the hypothesis?

---

[21] Hence, it is odd that Harrison, *Paul,* 37 says: "Several of Hays' methodological criteria, as reconfigured by Wright, coincide with my own, though my criteria have been formulated independently of Wright and Hays. They flow methodologically from my engagement of the ancient literary, documentary, numismatic, iconographic and archaeological evidence with the texts of Paul." To say that criteria are methodologically derived from the object of investigation is as incorrect as a cook who claims that his recipes are derived from his products alone (and not from principles of composition with regard to taste, texture, and colour).

[22] Cf. Christoph Heilig, "Anonymes oder Spezifisches Design? Vergleich zweier methodischer Ansätze für Forschung im Rahmen der teleologischen Perspektive," in *Die Ursprungsfrage: Beiträge zum Status teleologischer Antwortversuche* (ed. Christoph Heilig and Jens Kany; Edition Forschung 1; Münster: Lit, 2011), 102–109.

Every good historical enquiry will always pay attention to both factors. If only the first aspect is considered, we are in danger of getting scenarios which would inevitably lead to the observed event – but are completely absurd in themselves. If only the second aspect is heeded in our analysis, we might end up with processes which very probably took place in the past – but which also probably are not associated in any way with the phenomenon we had observed and wanted to explain.

Two very important comments are in order here. First, these principles for evaluating historical hypotheses are ineluctable and *not* a matter that could be debated in order to justify an approach that does not consider these elements in the same way. As soon as we say that a hypothesis is "plausible" we enter a specific *Sprachspiel* in which the rules of probability theory have to be respected. In the rest of this section, I will demonstrate that these two parameters for evaluating hypotheses are directly deducible from basic mathematical principles. Second, although this basic structure of historical arguments is so immensely important and its disregard inevitably leads to wrong, or at least insufficiently reasoned, conclusions, it is *not* a sufficient condition for valid inferences. Historical data does not come with tags attached to it, informing us about (a) how – or whether at all – it relates to one of the two categories we have mentioned and (b) how much plausibility it contributes to the overall picture. The historian will never be replaced by the mathematician.[23]

In accordance with these observations, I will spend the rest of this chapter explicating these two points. First, I will demonstrate, on the basis of Bayes's theorem, that the two questions I have claimed to be decisive for the evaluation of hypotheses are deducible from basic principles of probability theory. Second, I will discuss how this basic structure of an historical inference could be fleshed out for our specific issue of a potential counter-imperial subtext in Paul.

2.3 Bayes's Theorem

At this point, in order to justify the two-part plausibility of hypotheses, we can make use of Bayes's theorem.[24] It offers the basic structure of an infer-

---

[23] This becomes painfully clear when one considers that one of the few adaptations of Bayes's theorem in biblical studies, namely Richard Carrier, *On the Historicity of Jesus: Why We Might Have Reason for Doubt* (Sheffield: Sheffield Phoenix, 2014), aims to demonstrate that Jesus was not a historical figure.

[24] For a very detailed discussion of the aspects which can only be treated very briefly here, cf. Colin Howson and Peter Urbach, *Scientific Reasoning: The Bayesian Approach* (Chicago: Open Court, 1993). For the original essay by Thomas Bayes, see the appendix in Richard Swinburne, ed., *Bayes's Theorem* (PBA 113; Oxford: Oxford University Press,

ence by stating which elements amount to the overall plausibility of a hypothesis. The theorem can be derived easily from the axioms of probability theory.[25] It is very simple in its structure, and its use for historical research is obvious since it determines the plausibility of a hypothesis in light of specific data.[26] Accordingly, following this theorem in historical judgements is *not* another new "method," or yet another tool adapted from another academic field. It simply means to *make the logical substructure more explicit that underlies all solid historical conclusions*.[27] It reads:

$$p(H|E)=p(E|H) \cdot p(H)/p(E)$$

p(H|E) is the probability we want to determine, the probability of a hypothesis H in light of (that is the function of "|") the occurrence of the event E. Since we are talking about past events, it is best to think of this value as corresponding to the confidence in the truth of H. How much would you be willing to bet on the truth of H?

2.4 Explanatory Potential and Background Plausibility of a Hypothesis

The first element that is necessary in order to determine this value is the probability of the event E if the hypothesis H is presupposed (this is called "likelihood" or, less misleadingly, "predictive power" of H).[28] It is the *explanatory potential* of the hypothesis that is investigated at this point. Does the occurrence of E fit nicely into what one would expect on the basis of H or is it surprising? This corresponds to the first question mentioned in the last section.

2002), 117–149. The relation to the "inference to the best explanation" will be discussed in an excursus below (Chapter 2, Section 4).

[25] Richard Swinburne, "Introduction," in *Bayes's Theorem* (ed. Richard Swinburne; PBA 113; Oxford: Oxford University Press, 2002), 5–10.

[26] For Bayes's theorem in historical research, cf. Aviezer Tucker, *Our Knowledge of the Past: A Philosophy of Historiography* (Cambridge: Cambridge University Press, 2008), 92–140. Cf. also the introductions of Mark Day, *The Philosophy of History: An Introduction* (London: Continuum, 2008), 31–49 and Mark Day and Gregory Radick, "Historiographic Evidence and Confirmation," in *A Companion to the Philosophy of History and Historiography* (ed. Aviezer Tucker; BCP; Oxford: Blackwell, 2009), 87–97. Unfortunately, the theorem itself contains errors in both works. The chapter by Philip Dawid, "Bayes's Theorem and Weighing Evidence by Juries," in *Bayes's Theorem* (ed. Richard Swinburne; PBA 113; Oxford: Oxford University Press, 2002) discusses the evaluation of evidence in court and has many intriguing impulses for dealing with data in the historical sciences.

[27] Poignantly stated by Dawid, "Theorem," 88 (italics mine): "Bayesian statistics is just *the logic of rational inference* in the presence of uncertainty. It is a valuable intellectual resource, bringing clarity to the formulation and analysis of many perplexing problems."

[28] Cf. Swinburne, "Introduction," 10.

The other values are called "priors" since they describe probabilities *before* taking into account the occurrence of the event E itself and without presupposing the hypothesis. Hence, the probabilities p(H) and p(E) are not conditional upon (there is no "|") the evidence in the former and the hypothesis in the latter case. In other words: How probable is the hypothesis H (irrespective of E) and how probable is the occurrence of E at all?[29] To use less technical terms, we will refer to the former aspect as the *background plausibility* of a hypothesis, meaning the plausibility of a hypothesis without having taken into account the effect of the evidence in question. It is mandatory for any inference to ask the question of not only how well a certain theory would explain the evidence but *also* whether there is any independent reason for assuming that this theory could be true. Where inferences rest on only one of these factors, they are incomplete. Nowadays it seems customary to assume scriptural echoes in the Pauline letters solely on the grounds that it would "make sense" out of an otherwise rather strange wording. Although this is an important observation, scholars sometimes seem to forget completely to take into account the prior p(H). If we assume, for example, that only in a quarter of all the Pauline phrases do we find an intertextual link to the Hebrew Scriptures, this makes the statistical background plausibility $p(H_{intertextual\ link})=0.25$. If we come to a specific verse, we should thus be careful to assume intertextuality just because it would fit the evidence better. The question is *how much better* it would explain the phrase. Is the explanatory/predictive advantage high enough in order to balance out the disadvantage of the lower background plausibility? Of course, it may well be that $p(H_{intertextual\ link})$ is much higher, but this too would have to be demonstrated first.[30]

We can thus conclude – and this is the most important aspect of this whole chapter – that for every inference one has to consider both the predictive power *and* the background plausibility of a hypothesis together. Let me illustrate this by taking a closer look at the argument by White.[31] His sketch of the apocalyptic background of Paul's worldview[32] conforms to Wright's description[33] to a very high degree. Nevertheless, White does not agree with Wright with regard to the question of whether counter-imperial "echoes" can be

---

[29] Accordingly, p(H|E) is called the "posterior"-probability because here the probability is dependent on the occurrence of E.

[30] I am grateful to the participants of the postgraduate workshop "On Hays and Bayes: A Workshop on Intertextuality, Criteria and Probability Theory" at St Mary's College (St Andrews), 25th July 2013, which I was invited to give. The discussion was helpful for the question of how to extend my thoughts on Hays's criteria for echoes to an application of Bayes's theorem to intertextual links to the Hebrew Scriptures.

[31] White, "Subtexts."

[32] White, "Subtexts," 315–333.

[33] See Chapter 5, Section 1.4.1.

found in passages like 1 Thess 4:13–17, 1 Thess 5:3, and Phil 3:20.[34] What is the reason for this surprising difference? At least one important aspect of the answer is a methodologically problematic step taken by White. In the first part of his paper, White rejects the echo-hypothesis by focussing on the explanatory potential of this approach and alternative approaches for Paul's christological statements.[35] He argues, for example, that ἀπάντησις and παρουσία are not "prominent in Roman imperial literature, whereas both terms often occur in decidedly non-Imperial, even banal contexts, in the NT."[36] In other words: The explanatory potential of hypotheses that do not assume an imperial reference is higher. Such an assessment in itself is valuable indeed, but it only takes one half-way toward a complete inference. The problem is that White draws a conclusion from the "argument from vocabulary"[37] *before* having looked at the background plausibility. Interestingly, he then establishes precisely this factor by immediately working out Paul's apocalyptic framework of thought in the second part of his article. If one reads his paper "from back to front," one can only wonder why he does not *combine* his insights into the background plausibility of subversive elements in Paul's worldview and writings with the explanatory potential of this hypothesis. It is commendable that he is looking for a "firmer foundation"[38] for counter-imperial readings of Paul in the second part of his paper, but should not these insights also influence his exegetical decisions in the first part? Therefore, although he discusses the second important element of Bayes's theorem, his inference is incomplete since he does not include it in his decision process but rather adds it as an appendix.

2.5 Background Knowledge

In the last section I have assumed that it is possible to determine p(H) on statistical grounds. However, this is not always possible, especially if the question is not whether a specific hypothesis, which has been established for many cases, is true in another, but whether it is true at all in any case. To determine p(H) in such situations is one of the great challenges of inferences according to Bayes's theorem. If our inferences were based only on the event E, this would be problematic indeed since the probability p(H) would have no testable reference point. How could one tell which hypothesis has the higher

---

[34] White, "Subtexts," 315.
[35] White, "Subtexts," 308–315.
[36] White, "Subtexts," 312.
[37] White, "Subtexts," 309–311.
[38] The title of his paper.

probability at the outset, before the new evidence is taken into account?[39] Fortunately, we do not look at E in isolation but against the background of our other knowledge. That this knowledge is part of Bayes's theorem can be seen by reformulating it to show that the prior of H depends on our previous knowledge P:[40]

$$p(H|E\&P)=p(E|H\&P) \cdot p(H|P)/p(E|P)$$

Much of this knowledge will, of course, be irrelevant for determining our probabilities. It is the knowledge that concerns the basic parameters presupposed by the hypothesis H that is crucial. A hypothesis can have a very high explanatory power p(E|H) (if true, the event which occurred would make perfect sense), but if our prior knowledge P contradicts the presuppositions of H, the value for p(H|P) will be very low and hence the resulting overall probability of the hypothesis may turn out to be low as well.[41] That is precisely the problem with conspiracy theories, which appeal to many because they are persuasive due to the fact that humans intuitively do not tend to think in a Bayesian mode and make huge mistakes in evaluating probabilities.

It is important to note that the background plausibility and the explanatory potential of H depend on *the same* prior knowledge P. The attempt to use different sets (or stages) of prior knowledge automatically results in an incoherent argument. Actually, this would be a more precise way of analysing White's procedure since he does not draw his conclusion about counter-imperial echoes on the basis of the explanatory potential of the hypothesis alone but includes considerations (e.g., with regard to Rom 13:1–7) about the general plausibility of the assumption of a counter-imperial stance of Paul. Hence, the problem is not the neglect of the background plausibility in general but different sets of background knowledge as a foundation for determining this factor. White discusses the explanatory potential of H for the occurrence of E *without presupposing an apocalyptic mindset for Paul* p(E|H&P$_1$) side by side with the background plausibility which includes this insight (p(H|P$_2$)). To be fair, it would be wrong to attribute to White a position that holds to a dichotomy of christological statements *or* an apocalyptic back-

---

[39] On this problem, see exemplarily Elliott Sober, "Bayesianism: Its Scope and Limits," in *Bayes's Theorem* (ed. Richard Swinburne; PBA 113; Oxford: Oxford University Press, 2002), 22–38, especially 22–24.

[40] The assignment of events to the categories P and E is, of course, artificial and derived from the problem under consideration: What counts as established knowledge, and what is debated? Cf. Swinburne, "Introduction," 10.

[41] On conspiracy theories, cf. Peter Lipton, *Inference to the Best Explanation* (2nd ed.; London: Routledge, 2004), 60: "If only it were true, it would provide a very good explanation." For astonishing illustrations of the inclination of humans to think in non-Bayesian ways, cf. Lipton, *Inference,* 108–109.

ground,[42] and it is justifiable to test the explanatory potential for "christological events" like E$_{κύριος}$ without reference to Paul's apocalyptic worldview first. But then, after having established that the "event" of many passages influenced by Danielic ideas points in the direction of an apocalyptic mindset,[43] it would have been mandatory to *revisit* the earlier exegetical questions in order to get an "updated" explanatory potential. If White would have read the christological titles[44] like κύριος in the context of Paul's Jewish apocalypticism (P$_2$), he might have found them fitting very well within the framework of subversive statements against imperial hubris. After all, the one the apostle is proclaiming is none other than the ruler of the new kingdom that will supersede all earthly kingdoms![45] We should thus be very careful not to include different sets of background information when we evaluate the two main aspects of Bayes's theorem.

While one might wish that White would have better integrated the background knowledge into his inference, on the other end of the spectrum, lurks the danger of making *too much* use of this factor. One has to keep in mind that our background knowledge is, most of the time, not self-evident but itself the result of historical inferences. Hence, the division between what counts as background knowledge and what is in need of justification, i.e., the hypothesis, will differ among scholars. That is why it is important to be consistent in one's own classification of the data. If data is used as background knowledge which can only be justified on the basis of the inference it itself supports, this is equivalent to circular reasoning. Schnelle, for example, comments on 1 Pet 2:13 in such a way. He thinks it is "eine Anspielung auf den Kaiserkult ... Der Kaiser erscheint als menschliches Geschöpf, und er wird damit dem κύριος Ἰησοῦς Χριστός untergeordnet."[46] However, with regard to the quite similar section Rom 13:1–7 (cf. with 1 Pet 2:13–17), Schnelle does not come to similar conclusions.[47] Now, in itself the section in 1 Peter is quite innocent. Galinsky even writes that the passage is characterised by "its unequivocal insistence on submission to the worldly ruler."[48] Obviously, it is correct that placing texts in different historical settings as part of our presupposed back-

---

[42] Cf. White, "Subtexts," 316.

[43] This is an inference in its own right by which the hypothesis of an apocalyptic mindset is established and can then be regarded as part of the background knowledge.

[44] Cf. White, "Subtexts," 309–310.

[45] See White, "Subtexts," 326–327!

[46] Udo Schnelle, *Einleitung in das Neue Testament* (8th ed.; UTB 1830; Göttingen: Vandenhoeck & Ruprecht, 2013), 483.

[47] To be fair, Udo Schnelle, *Paulus: Leben und Denken* (GLB; Berlin: de Gruyter, 2003), 394–395 at least speaks of "zunehmende Spannungen."

[48] Karl Galinsky, "The Cult of the Roman Emperor: Uniter or Divider?" in *Rome and Religion: A Cross-Disciplinary Dialogue on the Imperial Cult* (ed. Jeffrey Brodd and Jonathan L. Reed; SBLWGRW 5. Atlanta: Scholars Press, 2011), 15.

ground knowledge can lead to differing results with regard to their interpretation. However, Schnelle makes the circular move of arguing for a compositional date during the reign of Domitian on the basis (among others, to be fair) of this "Anspielung" to the imperial cult although this allusion can probably only be detected on the basis of the dating itself.

2.6 Comparing Hypotheses

The last aspect we have to explicate is p(E). Normally, there are several hypotheses which are suggested as an explanation for the occurrence of E. This comparative aspect is also part of the theorem although this is not apparent at first sight and it looks as if only *one* explanation is analysed. However, p(E) – the overall probability of the occurrence of E – also includes the probability of E under the presupposition of all hypotheses alternative to H (here summarised by the negation ~H) so that p(E) can be reformulated as p(E|H)·p(H)+ p(E|~H)·p(~H).[49] If two specific hypotheses H_1 and H_2 are to be compared, the theorem can be reformulated in a way in which the knowledge of the overall probability of E, p(E), is no longer necessary:[50]

$$p(H_1|E)/p(H_2|E)=p(E|H_1)\cdot p(H_1)/(p(E|H_2)\cdot p(H_2))$$

This means that a hypothesis H_1 is to be preferred over against another hypothesis H_2 if the probability – which is based on background plausibility and explanatory potential – is higher in the first case. Thus it is true that $p(H_1|E)>p(H_2|E)$ if and only if $p(E|H_1)\cdot p(H_1)>p(E|H_2)\cdot p(H_2)$.[51]

All this might seem highly theoretical at first sight, but it has very practical implications and can serve as a methodological guideline in how to use Bayes's theorem in comparative assessments of different hypotheses. Let me illustrate the importance of this by one example relevant to the topic of the Roman context of Paul's ministry. In his discussion of Rom 5:2, Dunn argues, with regard to Paul's use of the word προσαγωγή as a designation for the new "access" that was made possible by the Messiah, that a cultic background is likely for a Jew, yet he notes that "in the societies of the time (not least in Rome itself) the court imagery of access through the royal chamberlain into the king's presence would just as readily be evoked."[52] With refer-

---

[49] Or p(E|H&P)·p(H|P)+p(E|~H&P)·p(~H|P). The theorem thus reads (cf. Swinburne, "Introduction," 10):
p(H|E&P)=p((E|H&P)·p(H|P))/(p(E|H&P)·p(H|P)+p(E|~H&P)·p(~H|P)).

[50] Day, *Philosophy*, 33. Cf. the erroneous presentation in Day and Radick, "Evidence," 89–90, where the element of the prior-probability is missing.

[51] Cf. Sober, "Bayesianism," 21.

[52] James D. G. Dunn, *Romans 1–8* (WBC 38A; Dallas: Word Books, 1988), 248. He also notes that Heb 4:16 and the emperor cult demonstrate that both spheres could be merged.

ence to the intention behind Rom 5:2, Dunn apparently thinks that the two explanations are on a par. But then he remarks, taking into account the term χάρις: "Since a reference to royal 'favor' is also a quite natural part of its broader Greek usage ... its use here strengthens the court imagery of προσαγωγή ... to enter the king's presence being possible only if the king extends his royal favor to the suppliant."[53] Now, it might well be that the use of the word "grace" *fits well* into the context of the audience. But is this an argument ("strengthens") for the royal interpretation of προσαγωγή? A consistent use of Bayes's theorem helps to assess the value of the new evidence correctly. Initially, προσαγωγή itself is the evidence (E_1) on the basis of which a possible reference to a court scene is evaluated. The determined probability thus is: p(court reference in Rom 5:2|προσαγωγή). If – before considering E_2 (χάρις) – the hypotheses H_1 (court background) and H_2 (cultic background) have the same probability, this means that $p(H_1|E_1)=p(H_2|E_1)$. If – after considering E_2 – it should be true that $p(H_1|E_2)>p(H_2|E_2)$, then it must also be true that $p(E_2|H_1)>p(E_2|H_2)$, i.e., that E_2 fits in *better* with H_1. Therefore, χάρις can only be regarded as *evidence* for the truth of the hypothesis of a court reference of προσαγωγή if it can be shown that this term fits into this background *better* than into the framework of cultic imagery. I do not want to argue here that this task is impossible, but Bayes's theorem helps to recognise where Dunn's argument would need elaboration.

2.7 Conclusions

So far, we have seen that Bayes's theorem can help introduce transsubjectively accountable structures to discussions that are typically characterised by intuition (which might be reliable some times but cannot be the basis for scientific inquiry). This is even more important since human intuition has a tendency to ignore foundational aspects of probability theory and to opt for the less plausible option.[54]

I also want to point out that the intuitive objection that, for certain hypotheses, we do not have enough information in order to use Bayes's theorem appropriately is not a real counterargument. Firstly, it is clear that often we will not be able to give precise absolute numbers. However, this is not a problem, as long as we can compare different hypotheses *relatively* to each other. Secondly, this objection reveals more about the exegete in question than about the theorem. If the data does not allow us to reach a well-founded Bayesian conclusion, this situation only reflects our *limited historical knowledge* and the result Bayes's theorem offers is still the best we can pos-

---

[53] Dunn, *Romans*, 248.

[54] For truly astonishing examples, see Lipton, *Inference*, 108–109 with references to Daniel Kahneman, Paul Slovic, and Amos Tversky, eds., *Judgement under Uncertainty: Heuristics and Biases* (Cambridge: Cambridge University Press, 1982).

sibly attain. Bayes's theorem offers us an upper limit for what we can conclude. If we are not satisfied with this result, or if it is too vague from our perspective, this should cause us to be humble in our historical judgements, rather than seeking out other forms of argumentation which allow for a "better" result. There is no result that is better than the best, and Bayes's theorem is a valuable guideline in reaching it. In light of this, it is not surprising that Bayes's theorem is increasingly being applied to a multitude of practical areas in which evidence has to be weighed.[55] We would be well-advised to follow this example.

3. "Echoes" of the Empire

3.1 Hays's Criteria for Identifying Scriptural "Echoes"

Richard B. Hays's *Echoes of Scripture in the Letters of Paul* is one of the most influential books in Pauline scholarship in the second half of the 20th century.[56] He discusses the use of the Scriptures of Israel in the letters of Paul. In contrast to many other scholars, he does not merely focus on clearly recognisable quotes that Paul is said to have used as proof-texts.[57] Instead, he concentrates on short phrases reminiscent of the (Greek translation of) the Hebrew Bible (hence the metaphor of "echoes") and shows that often the whole story of the scriptural passage resonates.[58] An "echo" in Hays's terminology is more subtle than an allusion or even a quote.[59] In fact, it can be so subtle that it might not even have been intended as an intertextual link by the author himself.[60] (Just like biblical formulations in modern authors.)[61] In order to identify such echoes, Hays suggests seven criteria,[62] which in his eyes function more like guidelines rather than a procedure strictly to be followed that produces results in a mechanistic fashion:[63]

---

[55] For an easily understandable elucidation of the integration of new evidence from a forensic perspective within the paradigm of Bayes's theorem, see Dawid, "Theorem," 78.

[56] Cf. Nicholas T. Wright, "Paul in Current Anglophone Scholarship," *ExpTim* 128 (2012): 371, who calls it "groundbreaking." For a discussion of Hays's theses, cf. the anthology of Craig A. Evans and James A. Sanders, eds., *Paul and the Scriptures of Israel* (JSNTSup 83; Sheffield: Sheffield Academic, 1993).

[57] Cf. Wright, "Scholarship," 371.

[58] Cf., for example, Hays, *Echoes,* 21–24 on Phil 1:19.

[59] Hays, *Echoes,* 29. This distinction is quite vague and not very important for our investigation since the authors discussed here (Elliott and Wright) do not adopt it.

[60] Cf. the hermeneutical discussion Hays, *Echoes,* 25–29.

[61] Hays, *Echoes,* 29.

[62] Hays, *Echoes,* 29–32.

[63] Hays, *Echoes,* 29: "Precision in such judgment calls is unattainable, because exegesis is a modest imaginative craft, not an exact science; still, it is possible to specify certain

1. Availability: Was the supposed source of the echo available to the author/the original reader? The Hebrew Scriptures are assumed to be known to Paul on the grounds of many explicit quotes. On the other hand, this shows that Paul expects his readers to be familiar with this material.[64]
2. Volume: The "volume" is mainly determined by the degree of explicit repetition of words or syntactic patterns. But there are other factors, such as the question of how important the source text was in the Jewish canon and how much the echo is emphasised.[65]
3. Recurrence: How often does Paul quote the same scriptural passage or allude to it?[66]
4. Thematic Coherence: This criterion analyses how well the supposed echo fits into the flow of Paul's argument or with other quotes in his letters.[67]
5. Historical Plausibility: Is it historically plausible that Paul would have intended the effect of the echo and that his readers could have understood it?[68]
6. History of Interpretation: Has the echo been identified before? Since discoveries could be new and meanings lost for a long time, a negative test result is not a criterion for exclusion.[69]
7. Satisfaction: This criterion asks questions like: Does the new reading make sense? Does it shed light on the discourse? Does it offer a good explanation for the supposed intertextual link?[70]

3.2 Application to Imperial Ideology

3.2.1 Wright

In his book on Pauline theology *Paul: In Fresh Perspective,* Wright devotes an entire chapter to the relationship between Paul and the Roman Empire.[71] He has developed his reading of Paul in his Roman context in much more detail in his recent *Paul and the Faithfulness of God,* but since he laid the

---

rules of thumb that might help the craftsman decide whether to treat a particular phrase as an echo and whether to credit my proposed reading of it."

[64] Hays, *Echoes,* 29–30.
[65] Hays, *Echoes,* 30.
[66] Hays, *Echoes,* 30.
[67] Hays, *Echoes,* 30.
[68] Hays, *Echoes,* 30–31. The motivation for this criterion is to avoid anachronisms (Hays, *Echoes,* 30–31). From my perspective, Hays is contradicting his own hermeneutical ambivalence towards authorial intention (cf. with Hays, *Echoes,* 25–29 and 33).
[69] Hays, *Echoes,* 31.
[70] Hays, *Echoes,* 31–32.
[71] Wright, *Perspective,* 59–79: "Gospel and Empire."

methodological foundations in this earlier work, we will concentrate on that book.[72]

At the outset, he refers to cases of hidden communication, namely the literature discussed by Graham Robb,[73] which alludes to homosexual motifs by means of key words, colours, and pictures "at a time when such things could not be published openly."[74] Wright also discusses the case of a playwright who criticised the current regime during the time of the Chinese cultural revolution by means of plays which he placed in a setting long passed (apparently he was not very successful – he was detected and persecuted).[75] As for the first century, he refers to some hidden criticism under Nero and the coded criticism identified by Goodenough in some of Philo's writings (cf. Chapter 1).[76] In the field of New Testament studies, Wright refers to the work of Hays regarding the identification of allusions and echoes.[77] He wants to use this tool in order to identify "echoes of Caesar."[78]

In his analysis of Pauline texts, Wright does not work through the individual criteria in order to show that they are met in specific texts. Rather, he presupposes them as the background to his discussion instead of referring to them explicitly. First of all, Wright outlines the Roman context with its ideology[79] and shows how, in the Jewish tradition, there existed the idea of God using the reign of Gentiles in order to prevent anarchy on the one hand, alongside the conviction that the covenant God would intervene and judge the Gentiles for oppressing his people on the other.[80] These two aspects, combined with the experience of the resurrection of Jesus, are said to have generated the conviction that Jesus was Lord, and Caesar was not.[81] At the same time (and in analogy with Jewish tradition), Wright argues that this claim was compatible with a positive evaluation of Gentile power as evident in Rom 13

---

[72] Wright, *Faithfulness* does not often refer to Roman "echoes" explicitly, and where he does, he does not say much about the concrete fulfilment of criteria. Cf. Wright, *Faithfulness*, 1047, 1284, 1292, 1293 (fn. 65), 1294, 1295, 1301, 1313, 1317 (!).

[73] Graham Robb, *Strangers: Homosexual Love in the Nineteenth Century* (New York: W. W. Norton & Company, 2003).

[74] Wright, *Perspective,* 60.

[75] Wright, *Perspective,* 60–61.

[76] Edward Champlin, *Nero* (Cambridge: Belknap, 2003) and Goodenough, *Politics.*

[77] Wright, *Perspective,* 61.

[78] Wright, *Perspective,* 61. It is quite significant that he focuses on the person of Caesar. For Wright, Paul is opposed not to the Roman Empire as a whole but "only" to certain claims of the ideology of the ruler and the associated propaganda (cf. Barclay, "Empire," 370–371).

[79] Wright, *Perspective,* 62–65.

[80] Wright, *Perspective,* 65–69.

[81] Wright, *Perspective,* 69.

and Acts.⁸² Accordingly, he thinks that this integration of an apparently pro-imperial passage is compatible with the criterion of "Thematic Coherence."⁸³ Apart from this short comment, Wright does not refer to any of the individual criteria⁸⁴ but sums up generally:

> It would be possible ... to explore the relevant material by means of key words and ideas: *Kyrios, Sōter, parousia, euangelion, dikaiosynē,* and so on. At each point we would find that the material (to return to Richard Hays's categories) was available, loud in volume, frequent in recurrence and thematic coherence, historically plausible, and, though routinely not noticed within much of the history of interpretation, enormously productive of that 'aha' which is one of the results of good historical exegesis.⁸⁵

Instead of following this path, Wright proceeds to show how Paul picks up and confronts imperial themes.⁸⁶

3.2.2 Elliott

In the introductory remarks of his analysis of the letter to the Romans, Elliott emphasises that Hays's criteria can be applied to mythical and ideological themes, which were ubiquitous in the Roman capital, as well as to scriptural texts.⁸⁷ He comments on some of the criteria: With regard to "Availability," Elliott thinks that the fulfilment of this criterion can be assumed, since themes of imperial propaganda were widely known in the cities of the Roman Empire through pictures, processions, and panegyric. He adds that this presupposition can be made even firmer than the one of the familiarity of the non-Jewish addressees of Paul with the Septuagint.⁸⁸ On the criterion of

---

⁸² Cf. Wright, *Perspective*, 70 and on Rom 13:1–7 in more detail Wright, *Perspective*, 78–79.

⁸³ Wright, *Perspective*, 61.

⁸⁴ One could argue that Wright's discussion at the beginning of the chapter at least implicitly engages with the criterion of "Historical Plausibility." There, Wright emphasises that the strict distinction between theology and society, or religion and politics, which is part of our own worldview, is inappropriate to describe the situation in the first century. This distinction would not have made sense either in a Jewish or in a Graeco-Roman context (Wright, *Perspective*, 60). For Israel, YHWH was not only creator but also ruler of the world. Caesar, on the other hand, "was a living example of the uniting of the divine and human spheres" (Wright, *Perspective*, 60). The charge of anachronism thus has to be raised against those exegetes who try to understand Paul's worldview while presupposing such a dichotomy (Wright, *Perspective*, 61).

⁸⁵ Wright, *Perspective*, 70–71.

⁸⁶ Wright, *Perspective*, 71–78.

⁸⁷ Elliott, *Arrogance*, 22. For a shorter and, with regard to our question, more poignant extract of this work, see Neil Elliott, "'Blasphemed among the Nations': Pursuing an Anti-Imperial 'Intertextuality' in Romans," in *As it is Written: Studying Paul's Use of Scripture* (ed. Stanley E. Porter and Christopher D. Stanley; SBLSymS 50; Atlanta: Scholars Press, 2008), 219.

⁸⁸ Elliott, "Nations," 219.

"Volume," Elliott acknowledges that, with the exception of 1 Thess 5:3, Paul does not refer explicitly to slogans of imperial propaganda or even Roman writings. Nevertheless, he invokes Hays's remark that the volume is also determined by the prominence of the source text of the echo: "Themes that loom large in Romans – justice, mercy, piety, and virtue – were *overwhelmingly* 'distinctive and prominent' in Roman imperial ideology as well."[89] Commenting on the criterion of "Historical Plausibility," Elliott refers to Champlin's assertion of a "remarkable sensitivity" among the Roman population with regard to irony, ambiguity, and other forms of indirect communication.[90] Concerning the "History of Interpretation," Elliott points out that it is not very important for Hays. He also emphasises that there is currently a greater awareness in scholarship for political themes and allusions in the writings of Paul.[91] Altogether, Elliott thinks that these observations allow for the preliminary conclusion that it is appropriate to read the letter to the Romans with the same sensitivity for political connotations that the audience in the Roman theatre would have had.[92]

3.2.3 Summary

As we have seen, N. T. Wright and Neil Elliott use Hays's criteria in a quite similar way. Both use them in order to justify their search for a veiled criticism of the Roman Empire in Paul. Both do not apply the criteria to specific texts but rather presuppose them as justification for their approach.[93] Both seem to understand the echoes to be intentional (departing from Hays, who remains agnostic about this with regard to scriptural echoes). And very importantly, both stress that it is the combination of (a) oppression and (b) the avoidance of persecution that justify the search for "echoes" of the Empire in

---

[89] Elliott, "Nations," 220.
[90] Elliott, "Nations," 219–220. Cf. Champlin, *Nero,* 94–96.
[91] Elliott, "Nations," 220.
[92] Elliott, "Nations," 220. He adds that, "since Paul's letter would have been read in a much less surveilled social site, we may suppose that the sort of expectations that Champlin describes for the theater might have been heightened there." I am not sure what Elliott means here. What one could expect on this basis is that less control would lead to greater expectation – of *clearer and less subtle* criticism. One would not expect it, however, to lead to greater attention leading, in turn, to the detection of *less suspicious* allusions. If Elliott is implying that the context of the church, based on less control, leads to a greater sensitivity, this would be an inconsistent argument.
[93] Interestingly, this is quite similar to Hays's own approach. See Hays, *Echoes,* 29: "I do not use these criteria explicitly in my readings of the texts, but they implicitly undergird the exegetical judgments that I have made." But see, e.g., Hays, *Echoes,* 32 and now Richard B. Hays, *The Conversion of the Imagination. Paul as Interpreter of Israel's Scripture* (Grand Rapids: Eerdmans, 2005), esp. 29–49.

Paul.[94] For us to be able to decide whether such literary phenomena can be found in Paul's letters, we first need to determine whether the methodological procedure proposed by Hays is a useful tool for this aim. We now turn to this evaluation on the basis of our discussion of the structure of historical inferences (Section 2 of this chapter).

3.3 Methodological Evaluation

3.3.1 Hays's Criteria in the Context of Bayes's Theorem

We can conclude on the basis of Bayes's theorem that criteria which are supposed to establish a hypothesis have to ensure that background plausibility and explanatory potential are both considered *and* that both of these fields are covered completely. Hence, the question we need to ask next is whether Hays's criteria really are a faithful representation of these two essential elements of Bayes's theorem. First, let us turn to the background plausibility. The "Thematic Coherence" of an alleged echo with the immediate literary context can influence this plausibility. Given the flow of the argument, would we expect the proposition that emerges if we assume an echo for a specific verse? If so, then we have reason to expect the echo even before ("prior to") looking at the concrete wording of the phrase in question. (Introductory forumulae obviously are the strongest contextual indicators.) Similarly, if the phrase in question is anticipated by the flow of the passage without recourse to a scriptural link, this lowers the value of the background plausibility. "Thematic Coherence" with regard to other quotes in Paul[95] is significant for the background plausibility too. The potential explanation "echo in verse X" gains plausibility if it can be shown that Paul did similar things in the wider corpus of his letters. This aspect of criterion 4 is very similar to criterion 3, "Recurrence." Even if the assumption of an echo explains the verse very well, one still needs to ask whether it is even plausible that such a process could ever have happened. This is more probable if it is known that Paul has acted in exactly the same way in other places, and less probable if his behaviour is discontinuous. The criterion of "Availability" (criterion 1) has the same effect on the probability of the hypothesis being true. The potential explanation that Paul, in Gal 3:28, does not have Gen 1:27^{LXX} (or Jewish traditions derived from it) in mind but a phrase from a modern feminist might have a large explanatory potential. However, its background plausibility is 0 since one of its

---

[94] Cf. Elliott, "Nations," 216–217 on the oppression of hidden transcripts in the Roman Empire in the first century, and pp. 218–219, more specifically, on the situation in the capital. See also the parallels, which too are characterised by these two aspects, adduced by Wright, *Perspective*, 60–61. For a historically recent example of critical subtext in the framework of political oppression, see the very interesting observations of Sylvia Klötzer, *Satire und Macht: Film, Zeitung, Kabarett in der DDR* (ZeitSt 30; Köln: Böhlau, 2006).

[95] Hays, *Echoes*, 30.

necessary presuppositions, namely the postulated sequence, is impossible. The criterion of "Historical Plausibility" (criterion 5) belongs closely to the one just discussed. However, it does not concern the availability of the *Vorlage* but its *effect* (in the worldview of Paul/his readers), which is assumed to be intentional. The assumption of a certain echo may give a fascinating sense to a difficult passage (explanatory potential), but if the meaning that is attained by this interpretation only makes sense from a perspective later in time, Bayes's theorem exposes its low plausibility. The criterion of the "History of Interpretation" (criterion 6) is connected to the logical structure of the inference only insofar as it is understood as a subcategory of the criterion of "Historical Plausibility" or the criterion of "Availability" and is limited to a certain circle of recipients. By this I mean that if very early interpreters of the Pauline letters (or later readers who were very well informed about the original context) heard the same echo, this would add plausibility to the case that the *Vorlage* might also have been familiar to those involved in the original communication process ("Availability") and that they could have heard the same echo ("Historical Plausibility").[96]

After having sifted through the criteria with regard to the background plausibility, let us now turn to the explanatory potential. Ultimately, what Hays calls "Satisfaction" (criterion 7) corresponds exactly to this component. Provided the explanation of an OT-background (or: criticism against the Empire) were correct, would this make the concrete textual form comprehensible? Even more precisely (taking into account p(E|P) also): Would the echo-explanation explain the text at hand *better* than alternative explanations (chance, other textual traditions; in case of counter-imperial echoes: LXX, pagan cults ...)? Part of this comparison of the explanatory potential corresponds to the question of "Volume" (criterion 2). It indicates whether there is, in the text at hand, a strong correlation with the assumed *Vorlage* (quality) or an especially large piece of it (quantity) if the explanation of an echo were true.

If we sum up these observations on Hays's criteria in relation to the basic structure of Bayes's theorem, the following correlation emerges:

1. Background Plausibility: p(H)
    1. "Availability" of the *Vorlage* for the author (including parts of "History of Interpretation")

---

[96] Seyoon Kim, *Christ and Caesar: The Gospel and the Roman Empire in the Writings of Paul and Luke* (Grand Rapids: Eerdmans, 2008), 60–64 constructs a counter-argument based on the lack of such early reception. However, it is confusing, to say the least, how he can assert (Kim, *Christ,* 33) that even the original recipients (!) of the Pauline letters did not hear any message critical of the Empire.

2. "Historical Plausibility" of the achieved effect in the framework of the worldview of author and recipient (including parts of "History of Interpretation")
   3. "Thematic Coherence" with the immediate literary context
   4. "Thematic Coherence" with other allusions by Paul and "Recurrence" of the motif
2. Explanatory Potential = "Satisfaction": p(E|H)
   (Including "Volume" of the potential echo)

So what can we conclude on this basis? First, the set of criteria invites the uncritical interpreter to *overemphasise* certain factors since, in part, Hays's criteria are only sub-factors of other criteria, and they should not be used as separate touchstones since this would yield an unrealistic result. For example, one could get the impression that it is correct to treat "Satisfaction" and "Volume" as two different arguments – although "Satisfaction" cannot be determined without analysing its subordinate aspects. Second, there is the danger of *underemphasising* the aspect of "Satisfaction." Most exegetes probably are not aware of the fact that this factor makes up half (!) of the overall plausibility of an echo because it is only one of seven tests in Hays's list. Third, another danger in using Hays's criteria is that parts of the relevant data could be *overlooked* since the criteria are spread out rather chaotically across the two large factors in Bayes's theorem and defined rather vaguely. To give just one example: How do we know that we have really covered all the relevant ground to determine the crucial factor of the background plausibility? How do we know the criteria Hays suggested do not leave important gaps in the evaluation of the data? Related to this, fourth, is the problem that the *consequences* of failing and fulfilling a test are unclear. The criteria function cumulatively, and what is missing in one area in terms of plausibility can be counterbalanced by another. Without a control mechanism, this becomes quite an arbitrary way of weighing evidence.

In light of all of this, it does not seem advisable to use Hays's criteria as a methodologically sound way to identify echoes.[97] To be sure, it is *possible* to come to well-founded conclusions on their basis (conclusions that agree with

---

[97] This implies that the criticism of Barclay, "Empire," 380 against the adoption of Hays's methodology does not get to the root of the problem. It is the catalogue of criteria itself which is questionable not the application to Roman ideology. Wright, *Faithfulness*, 1317 thinks that he offers "at least a partial answer to Barclay's comment about my use of Hays's criteria for detecting allusions and echo" by referring to Revelation which also does not name Rome explicitly. However, I am not so sure whether Wright really "uses" Hays's criteria to detect individual echoes of Caesar (and not simply to justify his approach as a whole). I also think that such a response is not even necessary since Barclay's comments do not address the core issues, at least not in the form he presents them. We will incorporate his remarks on why he thinks the two contexts of Scripture and Roman ideology are not comparable in our later discussion at the points where they matter most.

3. "Echoes" of the Empire 43

an inference in terms of Bayes), but in these cases it is not the set of criteria *itself* which guarantees the success, but their *wise use*, which *attributes the correct significance to each of them*.[98] The danger of such a methodological procedure is that intuitive decisions, which are made *in advance,* are sanctioned afterwards by "tests" which have the appearance of scientific method.

3.3.2 A New Suggestion: Nested Necessary Conditions

What we need is an approach which covers all of the areas relevant for a complete inference in a *systematic* manner. We thus have to translate the two factors of Bayes's theorem into testable questions which cover all the relevant data. In many areas in which Bayes's theorem is applied the prior probability is simply calculated on the basis of statistics. If an illness occurs in 1 person among 1000, the prior-probability of a randomly chosen person being sick is p(sick|statistical knowledge)=0.001.[99] Similarly, one could argue that our knowledge of first-century Judaism might yield a rough idea of how good the background plausibility is that Paul would criticise the Roman Empire by means of a subtext. If this was the usual thing to do for a Jew of his time, one might argue that the prior-probability is quite high. This is why, for many scholars, the existence of *analogies* – or the lack thereof – is so important (e.g., coded criticism in Philo's *Somn.* 2). However, statistical prior-probabilities always have the problem of scope: which data is to be used? Are we looking for the ratio of politically subversive writers in all of history under suppressive regimes to all writers ever? Or only for the equivalent ratio among Jews during the first century? Or maybe, even more specifically, among similarly minded Jewish Christians? Should we not even narrow this down to apostles planting churches among Gentiles in Asia Minor and Greece? After all, the wider we cast our net for analogies, the more differences we will find between the two areas of comparison (Paul and a selection of people). Maybe one of these differences is decisive for why the large

---

[98] It should be clear that my critique of Hays's methodological approach does not imply that I am claiming that his results with regard to echoes of Scripture – and the the manifold adaptations by other scholars – are wrong per se. Much of what has been written on this subject from this perspective may be correct and immensely valuable. (My only contention would be that we cannot know whether this is the case on the basis of Hays's criteria alone.)

[99] If a randomly chosen group of 1000 people is tested by a test which does not have any false negatives and "only" 1% false positives, this does *not* mean that a positive test implies a 99% chance of being sick, but only ca. 9%! This is because 1 (the likelihood; there are no false negatives – if one is sick one will definitely be tested positively) is multiplied by 0.001 (the prior probability of the "hypothesis" of being sick) and divided by ca. 0.11 (the probability of the event of a positive test occurring; on average [!] 1 person will be tested positively because he or she is sick and 1% of the remaining 999 people will also be tested positively although they are not sick).

group did not criticise the Roman Empire on the subtextual level (and maybe Paul did after all)? On the other hand, if we narrow our focus, we lose statistical significance at the same time. If only two writers are left, let us say Paul and Josephus, and we assume that the latter supported the Roman regime, the resulting prior for Paul is not very meaningful. However, this whole problem rests on an overestimation of the value of parallels in contexts like the historical sciences where we are dealing with the intentions of individuals. If this preoccupation is avoided, the dilemma becomes irrelevant. The investigation of a wider group of individuals, an assessment of "the Jewish mindset" for example, may indeed help in deducing the ideas of an individual. Where possible, however (i.e., where we know enough about the person in question), it is much better to evaluate the aims and action of an individual himself. The prior-probability of Paul trusting in the God of Israel is quite high, given that he was a Jew, but it is even higher – and much more precise – if we can count some of his letters as background knowledge.

But how exactly can we evaluate the background plausibility of the hypothesis that Paul criticised the Roman Empire in the subtext? As we have already noted, we need to look at the plausibility of the parameters presupposed by H in order to determine p(H|P). This means that in order for the hypothesis to be true, certain *assumptions* need to be made, which are *necessary conditions* for (this version of) the hypothesis. If we combine the notion of necessary conditions with Bayes's theorem, we see that the failure to fulfil one of these implies that p(H|P)=0 and accordingly p(H|E & P)=0. In other words, we are asking the question: Is there any presupposition that is necessarily implied by the assumption of a counter-imperial subtext that can be falsified? If a condition is met, this is no proof (i.e., p(H|P)=1) but rather opens up the question concerning the status of another, consequential, necessary condition. This approach of *nested* necessary conditions avoids the problem of the unclear consequences mentioned above (Section 3.3.1). It is always evident which function each individual operation has. If the hypothesis falls through, it has to be rejected – or modified so that the condition no longer poses an obstacle to it. This method also has great advantages in terms of scholarly discourse. In this framework, pointless discussion about the integration of details into the parameters of a hypothesis that does not even meet its most foundational conditions is avoided. Additionally, in the case of disagreement, it allows for very precise communication about where exactly the point of divergence lies and which areas (namely the following steps) are affected by it. Other disagreements may be due to the opinion that important necessary conditions are missing. Again, this procedure allows for specific

localisation of such dispute.[100] Building on these considerations, I suggest the following steps of procedure:
1. *Discourse Context:* The subtext-hypothesis presupposes that Paul would have placed hypothetical criticism of the Empire in the subtext of his letters. In order to maintain this assumption, it needs to be clarified first in what way these letters were affected by the *rules of public discourse* at all. This is a necessary condition for the assumption that criticism would have been restricted to the subtext for security reasons.
2. *Historical/Roman Context:*
    1. Further, one needs to answer the question of how these rules were framed in the *explicit context of the Roman Empire:* Would they have sanctioned criticism of the Empire? If not, the classical echo-hypothesis would lose its justification for why the criticism was supposedly hidden.
    2. Even if, on the basis of these considerations, we could conclude that criticism of the Empire would have been sanctioned on the surface level of the text but not on the subtextual level, this still leaves open the question whether such a critical attitude can be assumed for Paul. Without a negative evaluation of the Empire on Paul's part, there is no reason to expect the discovery of pejorative comments – either on the surface level of the text or on the subtextual level. In order to attest such a critical attitude, we first have to clarify whether Paul could have had an *exposure to imperial ideology,* and if so, to what extent.
3. *Pauline Context:*
    1. We have progressively narrowed our focus, already examining Paul in his historical context in the last step. Now we have to go even further and focus on Paul himself: Even if he was exposed to imperial propaganda, is there any reason to assume that he would have judged it negatively? This is a question about Paul's *worldview* and the possible integration of a critical attitude within it.
    2. Again, even if such sentiments could be attributed to him, the question would remain how plausible it is, in light of his *personality,* that he would have limited his criticism to the subtext in order to avoid danger.

After a careful examination of these areas, we will be able to judge whether the hypothesis of a counter-imperial subtext in Paul seems generally plausible or not. Of course, this is only a preparatory step for evaluating the intention behind concrete Pauline wordings. After all, what cannot be evaluated apart

---

[100] Cf., e.g., Stefan Schreiber, "Paulus als Kritiker Roms? Politische Herrschaftsdiskurse in den Paulusbriefen," *TGl* 101 (2011): 345, who correctly mentions the restrictive public transcript in the Roman Empire (2.1) and a critical attitude (3.1) as relevant parameters of the discussion. His position would be even stronger if he did not skip some of the other necessary conditions mentioned here.

from taking into account specific words and verses is the *explanatory potential* of the hypothesis of a counter-imperial subtext. Even if all these necessary conditions helped establish an overall plausibility for the echo-hypothesis, this would only present a precondition for a successful inference because everything still depends on whether this hypothesis, with its plausible parameters, can make sense of the concrete textual phenomena. In Chapter 6, we will consider some of the important aspects that have to be kept in mind when analysing explanatory potentials of hypotheses.

4. Excursus: Inference to the Best Explanation

We are now in a position to turn to the individual steps just mentioned. However, the history of research in the field of the philosophy of science necessitates at least a short comment on the relationship between Bayes's theorem and the so called "inference to the best explanation" since the latter sometimes is adduced as a superior framework for historical research. Unfortunately, this is one of the most debated issues in the field. But since, from my perspective, it is also one of the most unnecessary debates, this will make the task of giving a short justification of our Bayesian approach easier. Readers who are not troubled by an apparent conflict between the IBE and Bayes's theorem can simply jump to the next chapter.

Since historical events belong to the past, they cannot themselves be observed. What we have are only their results, on which we base our reconstruction of hypothetical causes. In so doing, we form models for how historical sequences of events could have taken place. Normally, one can imagine different scenarios, which results in the coexistence of several models or explanations. This means that an "explanation" provides information about the potential *causal history* of a phenomenon.[101] In order to decide which model represents the *actual* events, the best potential explanation needs to be determined, so an "inference to the best explanation" (short: IBE) is necessary.[102]

It is difficult to state exactly what a "good" explanation is. At first sight it seems natural that the explanation in question is the one which is the *most probable* since the aim of the investigation is to find a reconstruction which can be hoped to represent historical reality faithfully. But things are more

---

[101] Cf. Lipton, *Inference,* 21–29 for a discussion of alternative models and pp. 30–54 for a justification of the causal interpretation of the concept of "explanation."

[102] The most detailed presentation can be found in Lipton, *Inference*. For a nice, short introduction online, see Richard Johns, "Inference to the Best Explanation," [accessed on 14 August 2012]. Online: http://faculty.arts.ubc.ca/rjohns/ibe.pdf. Since he is interested in inferences to the *likeliest* explanation (see below), his short treatment is more helpful for our purposes than many technical discussion of IBE along the lines of Lipton.

4. Excursus: Inference to the Best Explanation

complicated especially since the publication of the influential work by Peter Lipton, who differentiates between the "likeliest explanation" and the "loveliest explanation."[103] The second category describes the explanation which yields the most insight, thus being "lovely." Most of the time, likeliest and loveliest explanations are identical, but this does not have to be the case. Conspiracy theories normally are very improbable although they connect a multitude of seemingly unrelated facts and make sense out of them: "If only it were true, it would provide a very good explanation."[104] Which of these two categories should be used for the inference to the *best* explanation? Lipton knows that intuitively we tend towards the first option, but opts for the latter:

> There is a natural temptation to plump for likeliness. After all, Inference to the Best Explanation is supposed to describe strong inductive arguments, and a strong inductive argument is one where the premises make the conclusion likely. But in fact this connection is too close and, as a consequence, choosing likeliness would push Inference to the Best Explanation towards triviality. We want a model of inductive inference to describe what principles we use to judge one inference more likely than another, so to say that we infer the likeliest explanation is not helpful. To put the point another way, we want our account of inference to give the *symptoms* of likeliness, the features an argument has that lead us to say that the premises make the conclusion likely.[105]

What Lipton is saying is that defining the "best" explanation in terms of likelihood would not yield any progress for the *praxis* of inferring. The only thing we would have achieved would be a change of the attribute "best" into its synonym "likeliest" but without describing how the "likeliest" (formerly "best") explanation can be identified. We would still need some characteristics in order to differentiate between the multitude of potential explanations – "loveliness."

But is this focus on "loveliness" really an improvement over against the search for the most probable explanation? What *is* "loveliness"? This question inevitably leads to categories which are only vaguely defined (and difficult to define in principle) like "simplicity" or "coherence" (coherence, that is, with other established theories).[106] The difficulty of quantifying abstract probabilities is only replaced by relocating the problem in the realm of defining and justifying their "symptoms."

Not only is it difficult to make the concept of "loveliness" useful, it is also *unnecessary* since Bayes's theorem *does* offer a way to determine the likeliest explanation directly, by means of representing the basic structure of such an inference. Unfortunately and unnecessarily, the relationship between Bayes's theorem and the IBE is very controversial and ranges from suggestions of

---

[103] Cf. Lipton, *Inference*, 59–62.
[104] Lipton, *Inference*, 60.
[105] Lipton, *Inference*, 60.
[106] See, e.g., Lipton, *Inference*, 122.

identity to the assertion of complete contradiction.[107] From my perspective, the basic problem of this debate is that it focuses on the question of whether there are *explanatory considerations* in the different values of Bayes's theorem.[108] As helpful as these discussions may be in determining these values, they are just as irrelevant to the question of whether IBE and Bayes's theorem are compatible. With regard to this question, only *one* single factor in the theorem is of importance: The only spot where the explanatory facet has to appear in order to make the Bayesian inference an inference *to the best explanation*, is the posterior probability P (H|E). If the hypothesis H *is* an explanation, Bayes's theorem represents an inference to the most probable and thereby best explanation. Day thinks that the decision to equate "best" with "likeliest" would make it difficult "to claim that anything but decoration is added to a straightforward Bayesianism."[109] I would prefer to say (less pejoratively) that the expression "inference *to* the best explanation" describes the purpose of the inference and Bayes's theorem provides its meta-structure, which explains why the inference works.[110]

As Lipton himself admits, there is absolutely no conflict between Bayes's theorem and an inference to the likeliest explanation.[111] The problem he then tries to resolve[112] only appears because he insists on understanding the IBE in terms of loveliness. There is nothing in principle objectionable to investigating "loveliness" as a symptom of "likeliness" since this mode of inference (often also called "abduction")[113] is a useful pragmatic cutoff procedure and is employed by us on a daily basis, often successfully.[114] But one should not forget that this kind of inference will also frequently fail since it rests on only one part of the overall probability, namely the likelihood.[115] It turns into a

---

[107] For the range of different opinions, see Lipton, *Inference*, 103–107. Cf. also Igor Douven, "Abduction (The Stanford Encyclopedia of Philosophy; Spring 2011 Edition; ed. Edward N. Zalta)," n.p. [accessed on 25 September 2013]. Online: http://plato.stanford.edu/archives/spr2011/entries/abduction/.

[108] See especially the contributions of Salmon and Lipton in Giora Hon and Sam S. Rakover, eds., *Explanation: Theoretical Approaches and Applications* (Dordrecht: Kluwer, 2001). Cf. also the account of Lipton, *Inference*, 114 on the role of explanatory aspects for P (E|H), p. 115 for P (H), and p. 116 for P (E).

[109] Day, *Philosophy*, 42.

[110] For a detailed example of an IBE along the lines of Bayes's theorem, see Heilig, "Vergleich."

[111] Lipton, *Inference*, 107.

[112] Lipton, *Inference*, 103–120.

[113] Douven, "Abduction."

[114] See Douven, "Abduction" for some examples.

[115] If "likelihoods" (in the sense of Bayes's theorem) are analysed in isolation, it is possible that new evidence supports absurd hypotheses more than more sound options. Cf. Sober, "Bayesianism," 25: "If you draw the six of spades from a deck of cards, the hypothesis that this was due to the intervention of an evil demon bent on having you draw that

4. Excursus: Inference to the Best Explanation

fallacy if an inference to the loveliest explanation is not held accountable to the results of an inference to the likeliest explanation.[116] Since the inference to the loveliest explanation is a subordinate procedure of the inference to the likeliest explanation, the former cannot undo the result of the latter. And because this higher-ranking inference is perfectly compatible with Bayes's theorem, there is no way in which IBE could pose any problem for our analysis.

---

very card has a likelihood of unity, but few of us would regard this hypothesis as very plausible." As Colin Howson, "Bayesianism in Statistics," in *Bayes's Theorem* (ed. Richard Swinburne; PBA 113; Oxford: Oxford University Press, 2002), 53 states: "Assessments of support depend on relevant prior information." It is certainly possible to look at likelihoods themselves, but "likelihood ratios by themselves do not tell you anything."

[116] Cf. the example of Dawid, "Theorem," 76. Sometimes one encounters a strange methodological mixture in which the background plausibility is considered for the *rejected* hypothesis, but not for the own position. See my discussion of Reinhard Junker, *Spuren Gottes in der Schöpfung? Eine kritische Analyse von Design-Argumenten in der Biologie* (Studium Integrale; Holzgerlingen: SCM Hänssler, 2009) in Heilig, "Vergleich," 104–106.

Chapter 3

Discourse Context

1. Introduction

In order to maintain the assumption that it was necessary to "hide" criticism, it has to be clarified first in what way Paul's letters were affected by the *rules of public discourse* at all. We thus have to decide on which level of communication the Pauline literature should be located. The question we are thereby trying to answer is with what kind of expectations we are approaching these texts. On which level, if at all, would we expect potential criticism of the Empire – on the surface level of the text or on the subtextual level? The answer to this question is important because it decides whether the lack of explicit polemic in Paul can count as an argument against the existence of critical statements in Paul or not. In analysing the discourse setting of the Pauline letters, I refer to categories which were established by James C. Scott and have been used quite often in relation to the interplay between the NT and its Roman context.[1]

2. James C. Scott's Categories

2.1 The Public Transcript

Communication necessarily takes place wherever individuals interact. But which rules govern these dynamics? And is it possible to make inferences from these rules to what is said, intended and held back? Of particular interest is the question of how communication works between different parties that are divided by a social gap – what influence does the factor of power have?

In his much quoted work *Domination and the Arts of Resistance,* political scientist James C. Scott sheds light on this complex of questions by alerting his readers to different levels of communication between those dominating and the subordinate people. The first level, which is most openly accessible, is called "public transcript" and refers to the open interaction between these

---

[1] James C. Scott, *Domination and the Arts of Resistance: Hidden Transcripts* (New Haven: Yale University Press, 1990).

two groups.² The term is derived metaphorically from a transcript as used in a court situation, which records all statements.³ Scott also classifies nonverbal acts of communication like gestures and rites under this heading.⁴ He criticises the fact that many sociological investigations on the relationship between parties of uneven power focus mainly on the level of the public transcript. He thinks that this inevitably yields wrong results since this discourse is determined by those in power⁵ – with regard to their own behaviour and also with regard to how the subordinate people act. The picture that will emerge from such a methodology is said to inevitably correspond to the account promoted by the power holders in society.

> It is precisely this public domain, where the effects of power relations are most manifest, and any analysis based exclusively on the public transcript is likely to conclude that subordinate groups endorse the terms of their subordination and are willing, even enthusiastic, partners in that subordination.⁶

2.2 The Hidden Transcript

In light of this problematic situation, it is Scott's objective to point out the less obvious elements of discourse, the "hidden transcript." It designates communication that takes place "offstage"⁷ and refers to the internal communication among the subordinate as well as the discourse among those who belong to the ruling class.⁸

The internal communication does not have to be "true" in principle and the public discourse does not have to give a "false" impression of the social interaction within a society.⁹ Nevertheless, the analysis of *both* areas enables the sociologist to gain an advantage of objectivity over against the interacting parties – he or she is the only one who is able to compare the different levels of discourse and to identify potential discrepancies.

---

² Scott, *Domination*, 2.

³ Scott, *Domination*, 2. For a critique of this notion from an anthropological perspective, see Susan Gal, "Language and the 'Arts of Resistance,'" *CulA* 10 (1995): 413–414. Each transcript is itself "a socially constructed artefact, created for definable purposes that depend on the goals of the transcriber" (Gal, "Language," 414). In light of this observation, Scott's claim to objectivity and completeness breaks down.

⁴ Scott, *Domination*, 2, fn. 1. On different non-verbal aspects of a transcript, see Scott, *Domination*, 14.

⁵ Scott, *Domination*, 2. However, as Gal, "Language," 413 remarks critically, Scott underestimates the restrictions the powerful are subject to. Even their public transcript is not self-determined by the individual but develops within the constraints of their social functions.

⁶ Scott, *Domination*, 4.

⁷ Scott, *Domination*, 4.

⁸ Scott, *Domination*, 5.

⁹ Scott, *Domination*, 5.

> The analyst ... has a strategic advantage over even the most sensitive participants precisely because the hidden transcripts of dominant and subordinate are, in most circumstances, *never in direct contact.* Each participant will be familiar with the public transcript and the hidden transcript of his or her own circle, but not with the hidden transcript of the other.[10]

Therefore, this hidden transcript is extremely important for getting a correct idea of society in all its dimensions: "By assessing the discrepancy *between* the hidden transcript and the public transcript we may begin to judge the impact of domination on public discourse."[11] If there is a large discrepancy of power between different groups, this will also result in a larger difference between public interaction and hidden evaluation of the situation. The ultimate goal of Scott's categories is to analyse the effect of domination on political communication by comparing corresponding hidden protocols and contrasting them with the public transcript.[12] Scott argues specifically against the idea that suppressed groups would accept or even support the established inequality. Scott shows that such conclusions usually rest on an analysis of public transcripts and are disproved by an analysis of hidden transcripts.[13]

2.3 The Hidden Transcript and the Public Sphere

How are such insights into the hidden transcripts possible? Are they not inaccessible by definition and restricted from appearing in the public sphere? This is not the case because Scott does not define the hidden transcript primarily by the *social context* in which it takes place,[14] but by its *content*. This content is *shaped collaboratively* by *internal* discourse[15] but can also *become visible externally*. Hidden transcript and public sphere therefore do not exclude each other, as one might think at first sight. In order to avoid confusion it this seems helpful to distinguish two different perspectives, which are (generally) not kept apart by Scott: the public (or hidden) *discourse* (i.e., the communicative act) and the public (or hidden) *transcript* (i.e., the content). The hidden transcript can appear in the realm of public discourse but not in the public transcript, unless it *becomes* part of it.

---

[10] Scott, *Domination*, 15.
[11] Scott, *Domination*, 5.
[12] Scott, *Domination*, 15.
[13] Scott, *Domination*, 70–107.
[14] Which would mean that it can *only* exist in the relation between several proponents of the same social group.
[15] Cf., for example, the explanation of Scott, *Domination*, 8 concerning the furious address of "Mrs. Poyser" towards their landowner in George Eliot's "Adam Bede": "One might say, without much exaggeration, that they had together, in the course of their social interchange, written Mrs. Poyser's speech for her. Not word for word, of course, but in the sense that Mrs. Poyser's 'say' would be her own reworking of the stories, the ridicule, and the complaints that those beneath the Squire all shared."

The fact that the public discourse can get infiltrated by content which originated in a hidden context makes the hidden transcript accessibke. Without this interaction, the hidden transcript would always remain inaccessible to the other party (at least if there are no spies or similar entities).[16] With regard to historical power constellations, this would imply that access to hidden transcripts would remain almost impossible since the internal communication belongs to the past. Especially the transcripts of the dominated would remain unknown to us since they were seldom fixated in written form (as in diaries) but existed most of the time in oral form only and thus have disappeared long ago.[17] It is to the great advantage of the historian that the interplay between the hidden transcript of the dominated and the public interaction with the dominating is much more complex than isolated and parallel communication channels. In what follows, I will shortly summarise the different options for this dynamic as described by Scott.

Firstly, there is the possibility that the *public transcript* of the dominating part of society itself includes expressions of generosity and the like and thereby creates space for the interests of the subordinate people.[18] By these means the aspirations of the subordinate can come to the fore without infringing on the ideology of the dominating class.[19] Secondly, on the other end of the spectrum, there is the *"pure form" of the hidden transcript*. Things cannot be said publicly since there is no space for them in the public sphere, and they would be sanctioned there. They find expression – often in an angry and uncontrolled way – in a social space among the like-minded,[20] in which no negative consequences have to be feared.[21]

Thirdly, between these two extremes, there is the possibility that the hidden transcript steps onto the stage of the public discourse *in a veiled form*. One of Scott's main concerns is the demonstration that this intermediate category exists and is an important key for understanding power relations.[22] This form of reference to the hidden transcript allows dominated people to express their position outwardly but within the limits of a sanction-free realm. Scott assumes that "a partly sanitized, ambiguous, and coded version of the hidden

---

[16] Scott, *Domination*, 15.

[17] Scott, *Domination,* xiif: "If the decoding of power relations depended on full access to the more or less clandestine discourse of subordinate groups, students of power – both historical and contemporary – would face an impasse." Cf. Scott, *Domination*, 19.

[18] Cf. Scott, *Domination*, 18 on the strategy of slaves in the antebellum US South, who did achieve some things in this way.

[19] Scott, *Domination,* 18.

[20] On this, see Scott, *Domination,* 120.

[21] Scott, *Domination,* 18.

[22] Scott, *Domination,* 18–19.

transcript is always present in the public discourse of subordinate groups."[23] He admits that the analysis of this expression of the hidden transcript has some problems since the transcript is veiled.[24] But on the other hand, it allows for access to hidden transcripts, which would otherwise remain inaccessible (especially historical[25] ones).[26]

3. Application to the Pauline Letter

3.1 The Pauline Letters as Hidden Transcript in Veiled Form?

3.1.1 Summary

Some advocates of a counter-imperial interpretation of the NT have employed Scott's categories in order to undergird their position methodologically.[27] In what follows, we will analyse the work of two proponents of this view. Additionally, we will look at the classification suggested by Barclay, a critic of an anti-imperial interpretation of Paul. The focus of this investigation is how Paul's letters can be integrated into Scott's system.

---

[23] Scott, *Domination*, 19. Here, Scott himself distinguishes between the content and the mode of communication: It is the content of the *hidden transcript* that infiltrates *public discourse*.

[24] On the individual means of the veiled expression of the hidden transcripts, cf. the complete sixth chapter in Scott's book (Scott, *Domination*, 136–182).

[25] Scott, *Domination*, 138: "[T]he hidden transcript of many historically important subordinate groups is irrecoverable for all practical purposes. What is often available, however, is what they have been able to introduce in muted or veiled form into the public transcript." As I have explained in the discussion of this section, I would prefer to speak of the hidden *transcript* invading the public *discourse*. I would reserve Scott's wording for the special case in which the subordinate manage to integrate their interests permanently as a publicly recognised and accepted element.

[26] Scott, *Domination*, 19: "Interpreting these texts which, after all, are designed to be evasive is not a straightforward matter. Ignoring them, however, reduces us to an understanding of historical subordination that rests either on those rare moments of open rebellion or on the hidden transcript itself, which is not just evasive but often altogether inaccessible." Cf. also Scott, *Domination*, xii–xiii.: "We are saved from throwing up our hands in frustration by the fact that the hidden transcript is typically expressed openly – albeit in disguised form. I suggest, along these lines, how we might interpret the rumors, gossip, folktales, songs, gestures, jokes, and theater of the powerless as vehicles by which, among other things, they insinuate a critique of power while hiding behind anonymity or behind innocuous understanding of their conduct."

[27] For some, it does not play a decisive role. See, e.g., Wright who mentions the concept of "transcripts" only very briefly in Wright, *Faithfulness*, 1277 and 1314 and apparently mainly because Barclay had brought up the topic.

The classification suggested by Neil Elliott is of interest inasmuch as he makes a case for a counter-imperial *subtext* in Paul.[28] With reference to Scott, he argues that in Paul unsuspicious remarks evoke much more complex apocalyptic scenes, which were known to the readers. Analysing these phrases thus yields insight into the hidden transcript.[29] Elliott thinks this is the case, for example, in Rom 13:1–7, the usual proof text for Paul's high regard for the Roman Empire.[30] This conclusion rests on the assumption that this passage is not what one would expect from the established public transcript. He points to some wordings which are rather suspicious in being quite modest in their affirmation of the Empire.[31] Read against the background of the political rhetoric current at the time when Paul wrote his statement on submission, his comments are said to be "remarkably ambivalent."[32] Elliott points to the fact that the *non-usage* of the "sword" was an important motif of political propaganda. Paul's comment that the state "does not bear the sword in vain" (Rom 13:4) is understood in this context to emphasise the propensity towards violence exhibited by the Roman administration.[33] Elliott thus suspects that in the ear of a Roman official, this kind of language "would have seemed to offer a peculiarly grudging compliance, rather than the grateful contentment of the properly civilized."[34] Hence, according to Elliott, this section is to be located on the level of double entendre, where the hidden transcript comes to the fore in a cautious manner. Thereby, Elliott classifies the Pauline letters as not simply being a form of internal communication. This implies that the hidden transcript is not immediately accessible on the surface of the text but demands a more sophisticated strategy for identification – an approach which is justified by reference to Hays's criteria (see Chapter 2, Section 3.2.2).

3.1.2 Evaluation

But is the category of the veiled hidden transcript the best description for Paul's letters? Or is this terminology not appropriate and hence not useful in our quest for potential criticism? In order to be able to answer this question, we have to examine an important feature of Scott's system, the addressees of veiled hidden transcript. This expression of the hidden transcript is discussed

---

[28] Neil Elliott, "Strategies of Resistance and Hidden Transcripts in the Pauline Communities," in *Hidden Transcripts and the Arts of Resistance: Applying the Work of James C. Scott to Jesus and Paul* (ed. Richard A. Horsley; SemeiaSt 48; Atlanta: Scholars Press, 2004), 97–122. Elliott, "Patience," also applies Scott's work to other early Jewish works.

[29] Elliott, "Strategies," 117–119.

[30] Cf. Elliott, "Strategies," 119–122.

[31] Elliott, "Strategies," 120.

[32] Elliott, "Strategies," 120.

[33] Elliott, "Strategies," 120.

[34] Elliott, "Strategies," 120–121.

in detail in the sixth chapter of Scott's book in all its varieties.[35] It is important to know these techniques by which the hidden transcript infiltrates the public discourse if one does not want to miss it.[36] The various ways of concealment can be divided into two basic strategies: Veiling the message itself or veiling the identity of the message's "sender."[37] The last option is realised, for example, in the case of anonymous graffiti.[38] In a letter that identifies its author only the first option is available (unless the letter is pseudepigraphical). A typical means in this area is the euphemism:[39] Degrading designations from the sphere of the hidden transcript are used in public discourse and thereby evoke negative associations from its original context although they are not established in the official communication and therefore are not subject to sanction.[40] Another relatively safe instrument for the communication of a hidden transcript is "grumbling."[41] A complaint is not formulated clearly but only in passing and allusively. The resentment is expressed, but it still can be denied[42] so that the façade of the public transcript can be maintained.[43] According to Scott, groans, sighs, moans, chuckles, well-timed silence, winks, and staring all fall into this category of means of communication.[44] Scott also introduces more sophisticated forms of disguise[45] like folk tales[46] or the symbolic reversal of social hierarchies.[47] Without discussing these different forms here in detail, what is important for this present work is the following aspect: They are all means of low-threshold *resistance*. And all of these elements are always part of communication processes which are *directed towards superiors* and *discernable by them*. Any kind of disguise that goes so far as to no

---

[35] Scott, *Domination*, 136.

[36] Scott, *Domination*, 138: "If we wish to hear this side of the dialogue we shall have to learn its dialect and codes. Above all, recovering this discourse requires a grasp of the arts of political disguise."

[37] Scott, *Domination*, 139.

[38] Cf. on the option of anonymity Scott, *Domination*, 140–152. In the Roman Empire this option was used sometimes. See, e.g., Champlin, *Nero*, 91 for pasquinades on Nero as murderer of his mother. Frederick H. Cramer, "Bookburning and Censorship in Ancient Rome: A Chapter from the History of Freedom of Speech." *JHI* 6 (1945): 168–169 recounts the situation in the wake of the famine of 6–8 AD: "Rome was flooded with incendiary pamphlets many of which were posted on the walls of the houses, under the protection of darkness and anonymity."

[39] Scott, *Domination*, 152–154.

[40] Scott, *Domination*, 154.

[41] Scott, *Domination*, 154–156.

[42] Scott, *Domination*, 154.

[43] Scott, *Domination*, 155.

[44] Scott, *Domination*, 155.

[45] Scott, *Domination*, 156–172.

[46] Scott, *Domination*, 162–166.

[47] Scott, *Domination*, 166–172.

longer communicate anything overshoots the mark. Sure, such a statement has to be open for two different readings – a provocative and an innocent one.[48] However, it is not the case that the latter is directed towards superordinate people and the first is meant for internal communication only. Rather, *both* elements have to be accessible to the dominating party. The first, in order to achieve the effect of resistance and the second, in order to avoid persecution.[49] Euphemistically expressed threats are only effective if they are understood.[50] Likewise, Scott writes with regard to grumbling:[51]

As with thinly veiled threats expressed in euphemisms, the message must not be so cryptic that the antagonist fails, utterly, to get the point. The purpose of grumbling is often not simply self-expression, but the attempt to bring the pressure of discontent to bear on elites. If the message is too explicit, its bearers risk open retaliation; if it is too vague, it passes unnoticed altogether.

So we are talking about smuggling in some of the content of the hidden transcript into the public discourse.[52] However, this implies that this category is singularly unsuitable as a hermeneutical key for the Pauline letters. Even if Paul really was *expected to respect* the rules of public discourse (whether this really was the case is discussed in the next section), this would not mean that his letters were *part* of the public discourse. They are rather *directed* inwardly and intended for internal communication. For a letter to be meaningfully spoken of as belonging to the category suggested by Elliott, it would have to be addressed to someone from the dominating class, containing critique under a more harmless surface. However, not only is it highly implausible that the letters functioned as provocations directed at outsiders (after all, they are addressed to specific churches and persons and deal with concrete events pertaining to these), but of greater significance for our purposes is the fact that this is not even what Elliott is claiming. Contrary to Scott's veiled hidden transcript, proponents of the counter-imperial interpretation of Paul stress that using the subtext is a way of communicating a message to insiders *without* outsiders being able to understand it. If there really is content critical of the Roman Empire in Paul's letters, it is content written for *other Christians* in encoded form. Although this kind of communication process is hinted at sometimes in Scott's discussion,[53] he does not offer a systematic method for the identification of coded information of this kind. Therefore, Scott's methodological approach does not seem appropriate for our object of study.

---

[48] Scott, *Domination*, 157.
[49] Scott, *Domination*, 157.
[50] Cf. Scott, *Domination*, 153.
[51] Scott, *Domination*, 156.
[52] Scott, *Domination*, 157.
[53] Cf. Scott, *Domination*, 183–184, but cf. again 189.

This does not mean that Scott's work in general or the category of hidden transcripts in veiled form in particular are irrelevant to New Testament studies. It might be quite useful, for example, for the analysis of other biblical material such as the addresses to officials recorded in the New Testament (e.g., before courts).[54] But for the Pauline literature, the category of a disguised hidden transcript cannot simply be appropriated without some modifications and specifications. One more general benefit of Scott's work is, that it emphasises the importance of distinguishing different discourse levels. Hence, we will now move on in our discussion of how Paul's letters are best classified within this taxonomy by taking a look at another proposal, which differs strongly from the one we have just seen.

3.2 Pauline Letters as Hidden Transcript in Pure Form?

3.2.1 Summary

The most extensive interaction with Scott's work from the perspective of NT studies (gospels and Pauline literature) is found in the anthology *Hidden Transcripts and the Art of Resistance* of the year 2004 edited by Richard A Horsley, which also includes the article from Elliott quoted above.[55] In the introduction, Horsley summarises why Scott's focus on less obvious forms of resistance is relevant to New Testament scholars:

Just because Jesus does not lead an armed assault on the temple and the Roman garrison in Jerusalem does not mean that he was not engaged in a message and program of revolutionary change. And just because Paul did not organize attacks on Roman officials or the Ro-

---

[54] For example, Jesus before the high priest (Mark 14:53–65 par) and Pilate (Mark 15:1–5 par) or the speeches of Paul in Acts 23–26.

[55] Richard A. Horsley, ed., *Hidden Transcripts and the Arts of Resistance: Applying the Work of James C. Scott to Jesus and Paul* (SemeiaSt 48; Atlanta: Scholars Press, 2004). Scott's *Domination and the Arts of Resistance* already plays a less important role in Darryl L. Jones, "The Sermon as 'Art' of Resistance: A Comparative Analysis of the Rhetorics of the African-American Slave Preacher and the Preacher to the Hebrews," *Semeia* 79 (=*Rhetorics of Resistance: A Colloquy on Early Christianity as Rhetorical Formation;* ed. Vincent L. Wimbush) (1997): 11–26 and to an even lesser degree in some of the other contributions in the same anthology. There are also references to Scott's categories in the 2008 volume *In the Shadow of Empire* (Richard A. Horsley, ed., *In the Shadow of Empire: Reclaiming the Bible as a History of Faithful Resistance* (Louisville: Westminster John Knox, 2008). Brigitte Kahl, "Acts of the Apostles: Pro(to)-Imperial Script and Hidden Transcript," in *In the Shadow of Empire: Reclaiming the Bible as a History of Faithful Resistance* (ed. Richard A. Horsley; Louisville: Westminster John Knox, 2008), 137–156, for example, searches for a hidden transcript in the pro-(or proto-)imperial transcript of Acts. However, these contributions do not provide many detailed and relevant methodological observations.

man slave system does not mean that he was a 'social conservative' with regard to the Roman imperial order.[56]

This kind of subtle criticism has to be read between the lines of the surface of the text.[57] It is important, then, to decide how the different NT documents relate to Scott's categories.[58] Here, Horsley thinks that NT scholars have an advantage over against other historians since at least some of the texts in the NT are, in his opinion, "evidently records" of a hidden transcript.[59] While some books are said to exhibit a stronger assimilation towards the Roman Empire (Scott explicitly refers to Luke-Acts and the pseudepigraphical Pastorals), he thinks that especially the gospel of Mark, the source Q, and the letters of Paul offer us for straightforward insights into the original early Christian hidden transcript.[60] Horsley makes it clear that, according to his opinion, these texts were explicitly *not* directed towards outsiders.[61] On Paul's letters he writes:

> Read aloud in community gatherings, they address particular circumstances and issues in particular assemblies. As with Mark and Q, Paul's 'texts' were certainly not addressed to outsiders, certainly not the magnates and officials who controlled the Roman imperial order in Greek cities. None figured in open discourse on the public stage of a Thessalonica or a Corinth.[62]

According to Horsley, the Pauline letters thus offer a window onto the hidden transcript emerging in his churches.[63] This transcript is said to have had a

---

[56] Richard A. Horsley, "Introduction: Jesus, Paul, and the 'Arts of Resistance': Leaves from the Notebook of James C. Scott," in *Hidden Transcripts and the Arts of Resistance: Applying the Work of James C. Scott to Jesus and Paul* (ed. Richard A. Horsley; SemeiaSt 48; Atlanta: Scholars Press, 2004), 7.

[57] Cf. Horsley, "Introduction," 11: "Scott thus opens up for New Testament interpreters a whole range of popular political dynamics that often lie hidden (underneath or 'between the lines' of our sources) between passive acquiescence and active revolt."

[58] Horsley, "Introduction," 12: "[S]ome materials in the New Testament were, in their historical origins, representatives of 'hidden transcript,' the politics of disguise, and even more public forms of resistance by subordinated people." Cf. p. 13: "The first step would be to discern whether their sources [of NT scholars] provide a record of the public transcript (nearly all public inscriptions, coins, and most extant documents) or a record of the hidden transcript of the subordinated (e.g. Mark or Paul's letters?) or a record of the hidden transcript of the dominant (e.g. Josephus's *Life*?)."

[59] Horsley, "Introduction," 14.

[60] Horsley, "Introduction," 14.

[61] Cf. Horsley, "Introduction," 14: "Mark and Q were not addressed to outsiders, certainly not the Herodian or high-priestly rulers in Palestine, and none figured in open discourse on the public stage of Tiberias or Jerusalem, even though Mark portrays events in which Jesus publicly confronted the rulers in Jerusalem." Cf. also the remarks on p. 16.

[62] Horsley, "Introduction," 14.

[63] Horsley, "Introduction," 15. Cf. Horsley, "Introduction," 19 on the relation between hidden transcript of the *churches* and the letters of *Paul*.

subversive character since it offers and practices an alternative model for society.[64] For Pauline studies this classification would imply that – contrary to Elliott's assertion – no special strategy is necessary for identifying hidden statements. Since the letters were part of internal communication, potential criticism should be available on the surface of the texts.

Interestingly, this classification is also assumed by John M. G. Barclay, who criticises the counter-imperial interpretation of Paul.[65] In his essay *Why the Roman Empire Was Insignificant to Paul*,[66] Barclay takes up the terminology of Scott as a help in describing coded criticism of the Roman Empire.[67] When summarising the position of those colleagues who argue for a critical assessment of the Empire in Paul, he says that they are locating this criticism in the subtext.[68] He rightly notes that in order to decide how Paul's letters relate to Scott's taxonomy, one has to decide whether they are located "onstage" or "offstage."[69] According to him, Paul's letters are – unlike, for example, Josephus's texts[70] – *not* public documents and only addressed to insiders.[71] Therefore, he concludes that they are hidden transcript *in pure form*:

> There is every reason to think that we have here, in pure form, a Christian 'hidden transcript' – that is, what they said among themselves 'offstage' in freedom and without fear. Thus we should not expect here the kind of dissimulation or disguise associated with Scott's intermediate category; we should find here not coded traces of the hidden transcript, but its full expression, precisely that open and frank language that takes place 'offstage' among those without political power.[72]

---

[64] Horsley, "Introduction," 23.

[65] It is also adopted similarly by Dean L. Pinter, "The Gospel of Luke and the Roman Empire," in *Jesus Is Lord, Caesar Is Not: Evaluating Empire in New Testament Studies* (ed. Scot McKnight and Joseph B. Modica; Downers Grove: IVP Academia, 2013), 109 with regard to the Gospel of Luke. He had previously made similar observations with regard to Paul in Dean L. Pinter, "Divine and Imperial Power: A comparative analysis of Paul and Josephus" (PhD diss., Durham University, 2009), 232 etc.

[66] Barclay, "Empire."

[67] Barclay, "Empire," 382.

[68] Barclay, "Empire," 382.

[69] Barclay, "Empire," 382.

[70] Barclay, "Empire," 382. Cf., e.g., John M. G. Barclay, "Snarling Sweetly: A Study of Josephus on Idolatry," in *Pauline Churches and Diaspora Jews* (ed. John M. G. Barclay; WUNT 275; Tübingen: Mohr Siebeck, 2011), 337–338 with reference to *C. Ap.* 2.73–78 as a kind of hidden transcript in veiled form: Josephus criticises emperor worship but refers (*C. Ap.* 2.74) to "Greeks and some others" in order to reduce the clash with his Roman context.

[71] Barclay, "Empire," 382–383.

[72] Barclay, "Empire," 383.

If we take account of Scott's work, this means that Barclay agrees with Horsley[73] over against Elliott that potential criticism of the Roman Empire would have to be plainly visible on the surface of the Pauline texts. Presupposing this, Barclay emphasises how striking it is that there is no clear rejection of the Roman Empire in Paul. Thus, according to Barclay, the application of Scott's systematisation argues *against* a counter-imperial interpretation.[74]

Have Horsley and Barclay[75] found the best way of relating Paul's letters to public discourse by their use of Scott's categories? This position rests on the assumption that Paul's letters were not only meant for insiders but also not accessible to outsiders. Barclay defends this assumption of purely internal communication by postulating that outsiders would not have tried to get access to early Christian written communication on their own accord.

> [T]he Roman empire was not a police state and, even where voluntary associations were under suspicion, it did not take steps to monitor the written communications of comparatively small groups incapable of launching a political insurrection.[76]

In other words: The correspondence between Paul and his churches was not monitored by the state and hence, there is no reason to assume that this internal discourse was influenced by public standards. Criticism would have been safe and the necessity of hiding it obsolete.

3.2.2 Evaluation

Two critical remarks are in order. First, Barclay demands too much when he limits the presence of threats to *large movements* only. Even though early Christianity was not a phenomenon which could have posed a serious threat

---

[73] Interestingly, Barclay explicitly opposes Elliott's classification, but he does not seem to be aware of the fact that Horsley shares his use of Scott's terminology (although not his exegesis). Barclay, "Empire," 382 refers to Horsley, *Transcripts* but not to his relevant chapter in the book (Horsley, "Introduction").

[74] Barclay, "Empire," 383.

[75] Warren Carter, *Roman Empire and the New Testament: An Essential Guide* (Nashville: Abingdon, 2006), 12 makes a similar decision: "The New Testament writings can, in part, be thought of as 'hidden transcripts.' They are not public writings targeted to the elite or addressed to any person who wants to read them. They are written from and for communities of followers of Jesus crucified by the empire. The New Testament writings assist followers of Jesus in negotiating Rome's world."

[76] Barclay, "Empire," 381. Cf. also Barclay, "Empire," 380: "There is no indication, for instance, that early Christian letters were likely to be intercepted by Roman secret agents ... ." This conclusion is repeated almost verbatim by Pinter, "Gospel," 109: "The Roman Empire was not a police state with secret agents ready to intercept written communications of voluntary associations, religious communities or personal correspondence." And, with other wording, already in Pinter, "Power," 232–233: "It is equally difficult to imagine that the state had access to mechanisms of surveillance needed to track private letters to communities in Philippi or Rome."

to the Empire as a whole, it would have been suspicious enough for Roman authorities if these new groupings were deemed problematic on a local level.[77] And there is a very high plausibility for the assumption that this is precisely what was the case. For outsiders,[78] the Christian assemblies would have looked like *collegia*.[79] For fear of rebellious movements, they were allowed to meet only once a month, whereas Christians, just like Jews,[80] met once a week. This alone would have been suspicious for local authorities.[81] The last thing they wanted were riots and possible intervention and sanction by the Romans.[82] We should also be careful not to underestimate the *Jewish front* as a link between rather marginal Christian communities and local and

---

[77] But see the important remark by Strecker, "Taktiken," 159: "[D]ie paulinische messianische Botschaft [besaß] das Potential, die ideologischen Fundamente der römischen Kaiserherrschaft auf dem Weg der Mikrokommunikation im nichtöffentlichen und halböffentlichen Raum effektiv zu unterspülen."

[78] Markus Öhler, "Römisches Vereinsrecht und christliche Gemeinden," in *Zwischen den Reichen: Neues Testament und Römische Herrschaft* (ed. Michael Labahn and Jürgen Zangenberg; TANZ 36. Tübingen: A. Francke, 2002), 62 correctly specifies: "sowohl staatlich wie gesellschaftlich."

[79] Bruce W. Winter, *After Paul Left Corinth: The Influence of Secular Ethics and Social Change* (Grand Rapids: Eerdmans, 2001), 134–135.

[80] They had special permission for their assembly on each Sabbath (Winter, *Paul*, 134). On the right of assembly, its restrictions, and the situation of the Jews, see Monika Schuol, *Augustus und die Juden: Rechtsstellung und Interessenpolitik der kleinasiatischen Diaspora* (SAG 6; Frankfurt: Verlag Antike, 2007), 95–101.

[81] Winter, *Paul*, 135. Cf. also Paul J. Achtemeier, "Rome and the Early Church: Background of the Persecution of Christians in the First and Early Second Century," in *Foster Biblical Scholarship: Essays in Honor of Kent Harold Richards* (ed. Frank R. Ames and Charles W. Miller; SBLBSNA 24; Atlanta: Society of Biblical Literature, 2010), 238–239 on the restrictive handling of the *collegia* due to their potential threat to the authorities. However, see also Jörg Rüpke, *Religion of the Romans* (trans. Richard Gordon; Cambridge: Polity, 2007), 209 (and the literature cited there) on the more relaxed dealings with the *collegia* already from Tiberius's reign onwards. Tolerance towards religious *collegia* reached its limits where they had the appearance of political subversiveness (Rüpke, *Religion*, 34). Wendy Cotter, "The Collegia and Roman Law: State Restrictions on Voluntary Associations 64 BCE–200 CE," in *Voluntary Associations in the Graeco-Roman World* (ed. John S. Kloppenborg and Stephen G. Wilson; London: Routledge, 1996), 88 similarly concludes: "The very real dangers in belonging to an unrecognized society during the imperial period are usually ignored in any reconstruction of the first-generation Christian reality, as it is in the exegesis of the Christian texts themselves. Yet the clear evidence of Roman prohibition of such societies and the constant threat of their sudden investigation and dissolution must become incorporated into both aspects of our exegetical enterprise." (However, with regard to the hypothesis of a general ban of *collegia,* see Ilias N. Arnaoutoglou, "Roman Law and *collegia* in Asia Minor," *RIDA* 49 [2002]: 27–44 for a more nuanced judgement.) For an overview of the historical development, see Öhler, "Vereinsrecht," 51–61.

[82] Cf. Acts 19:40.

Roman officials.[83] One might exemplarily refer to the incident in Thessalonica, as recounted in Acts 17:1–9, where the Jews were the ones (Acts 17:5) who made the accusations against Paul and his co-workers public charging them to have acted "contrary to the decrees of Caesar, saying that there is another king, Jesus" (Acts 17:7). This troubled (ἐτάραξαν) not only the crowd but also the city authorities.[84] Hence I think that it is not helpful to imagine Paul the tentmaker to have been an ordinary person like the shoemaker who dared to laugh at Caligula (Cassius Dio, *Hist. Rom.* 59.26.8–9).

Second, Barclay also demands more than what is actually needed in order to relate Paul's letters to the *public discourse* in a meaningful way. Internal communication can be affected by rules of public communication without the existence of a central surveillance apparatus. Since Paul's letters were read out loud in the congregations,[85] and we know from 1 Cor 14:23 that the as-

---

[83] Harrill, *Paul*, 80: "Paul's mission to the Gentiles operated without noticeable radicalism *within* the wider Roman culture in part because the Pauline movement was very small, and in part because Paul used specific language that colluded with a particularly Roman discourse of authority. This insight explains why Paul's main adversaries were fellow Jesus followers and apostles – those associated with Paul's tiny subculture closely enough to care about or even to notice it – rather than Roman imperial magistrates." But of course this does not mean that the effects of Paul's statements had to *remain* within the boundaries of initial reception. Cf. the discussion in Judith A. Diehl, "Anti-Imperial Rhetoric in the New Testament," in *Jesus Is Lord, Caesar Is Not: Evaluating Empire in New Testament Studies* (ed. Scot McKnight and Joseph B. Modica; Downers Grove: IVP Academia, 2013), 52–53 for different emphases than my own. On the role of Jewish opposition, see Justin K. Hardin, *Galatians and the Imperial Cult* (WUNT II 237; Tübingen: Mohr Siebeck, 2008), 113–115.

[84] On these politarchs, see Greg H. R. Horsley, "The Politarchs," in *The Book of Acts in Its Graeco-Roman Setting* (ed. David W. J. Gill and Conrad Gempf; vol. 2 of *The Book of Acts in Its First Century Setting;* ed. Bruce W. Winter; Grand Rapids: Eerdmans, 1994), 419–431; on the political situation in Thessalonica, see Robert Jewett, *The Thessalonian Correspondence: Pauline Rhetoric and Millenarian Piety* (Foundations and Facets; Philadelphia: Fortress, 1986), 123–125. On Acts 17:1–9, see also Chapter 4, Section 1.2.2.3.

[85] See, for example, 1 Thess 5:27. Cf. Peter T. O'Brien, "Letters, Letter Forms," *DPL* 550–553: "Most of Paul's letters were addressed to communities of Christian believers and were intended for public use within the congregations." Cf. also how Paul alerts his recipients to the fact tha he is now using his own handwriting in Gal 6:11 and 1 Cor 16:21 (cf. also Col 4:18 and 2 Thess 3:17) which indicates that he composed his letters well aware of the fact that they would be read out loud (Jeffrey A. D. Weima, "Sincerely, Paul: The Significance of the Pauline Letter Closing," in *Paul and the Ancient Letter Form* [ed. Stanley E. Porter and Sean A. Adams; PAST 6; Leiden: Brill 2010], 337–338). The adoption of a "public literary speech style" for his letters is a symptom of this feature (Detlev Dormeyer, "The Hellenistic Letter-Formula and the Pauline Letter-Scheme," in *The Pauline Canon* [ed. Stanley E. Porter; PAST 1. Leiden: Brill, 2004], 69–70). For a concise summary of the evidence for the reading aloud of Paul's letters in the churches, see M. Luther Stirewalt Jr., *Paul: The Letter Writer* (Grand Rapids: Eerdmans, 2003), 141–146. It might be that some letters were originally only addressed to the assemblies in private

semblies were open to outsiders,[86] Paul would have had to consider the possibility that his letters could fall into the wrong hands although they were not addressed to them. This would hold true even if Bruce Winter's intriguing interpretation of the ἄγγελοι in 1 Cor 11:10 as clients of outsiders were incorrect.[87] That Paul encouraged the circulation of his letters further decreased his control over their final recipients.[88] I thus conclude that the Pauline letters, though a form of private correspondence, were *affected* by public scrutiny and the rules of public discourse.[89] The insight we get into aristocratic correspondence through Cicero might offer a useful analogy for this kind of semipublic communication.[90] The fact that the Roman Empire was not a central-

---

house churches. See, for example, on 1 Thess 5:27 Roger W. Gehring, *House Church and Mission: The Importance of Household Structures in Early Christianity* (trans.; Peabody: Hendrickson Publishers, 2004), 178. But even there the focus is most probably on the totality of the believers and not on the house churches (cf. Traugott Holtz, *Der erste Brief an die Thessalonicher* [EKKNT; Zürich: Benziger, 1986], 274). But most importantly, even if this hypothesis were true, there is no reason to assume that the reading of the letters was limited to this context and did not take place in larger, more open meetings.

[86] Cf. Gordon D. Fee, *The First Epistle to the Corinthians* (NICNT; Grand Rapids: Eerdmans, 1987), 684.

[87] Winter, *Paul,* 136–137.

[88] Gal 1:2, 2 Cor 1:1, and Col 4:16. Cf. Schnelle, *Einleitung,* 427. Ephesians might have been an "open" letter "where the superscription might be addressed to a specific person, but intended for a larger audience" (Sean A. Adams, "Paul's Letter Openings and Greek Epistolography: A Matter of Relationship," in *Paul and the Ancient Letter Form* [ed. Stanley E. Porter and Sean A. Adams; PAST 6. Leiden: Brill 2010], 45). For copying of *private* letters, see Stanley E. Porter, "When and How Was the Pauline Canon Compiled? An Assessment of Theories," in *The Pauline Canon* (ed. Stanley E. Porter; PAST 1; Leiden: Brill, 2004), 119 and Jerome Murphy-O'Connor, *Paul the Letter-Writer: His World, His Options, His Skills* (GNS 41; Collegeville: Liturgical Press, 1995), 12–13. For the accessibility of Christian writings on the public market, cf. Christoph Markschies, *Kaiserzeitliche christliche Theologie und ihre Institutionen: Prolegomena zu einer Geschichte der antiken christlichen Theologie* (Tübingen: Mohr Siebeck, 2007), 300–306. An English translation is forthcoming: *Christian Theology and its Institutions in the Early Roman Empire: Prolegomena to a History of Early Christian Theology* (transl. Wayne Coppins; BMSEC 3; Waco: Baylor University Press, 2015).

[89] Similarly Lynn H. Cohick, "Philippians and Empire: Paul's Engagement with Imperialism and the Imperial Cult," in *Jesus Is Lord, Caesar Is Not: Evaluating Empire in New Testament Studies* (ed. Scot McKnight and Joseph B. Modica; Downers Grove: IVP Academia, 2013), 175–176.

[90] Although the distinction between private and public letters was known, it seems that it was the case that even private letters were simply forwarded to people to whom the content might have been of interest: "We also know ... that letters addressed to specific individuals would regularly be circulated among friends and acquaintances ... It seems likely then that much aristocratic correspondence was written with an awareness that it could be distributed more widely beyond the named addressee. Such letters can be classified perhaps as 'semipublic,' although in each case the writer could not be sure exactly

ised police state does not invalidate this conclusion.[91] As Rudich has shown in detail, it is precisely "the *absence* of an institutionalized censorship"[92] at the beginning of the Principate which led to the situation that all statements which were open in principle to the interpretation of being subversive[93] could mean one's downfall:

> [S]ince in Rome censorship as an institution – that is to say, an office or an officer responsible for granting an imprimatur to the work of literature – did not exist, any person influential at court was at liberty to play the censor, to find criminal faults in any piece of writing and draw it to the attention of the Emperor.[94]

3.3 Conclusions

It seems to be unobjectionable in principle to try to locate Pauline letters on the map described by Scott.[95] To be sure, applying the categories of a "subordinate" and a "dominant" party is a problematic tool for demarcating Pauline churches against the backdrop of Roman Imperialism.[96] However, Scott's

---

how many other people would have access to it, or who precisely these additional readers would be." (Jon Hall, *Politeness and Politics in Cicero's Letters* [Oxford: Oxford University Press, 2009], 24–25.) Angela Standhartinger, "Die paulinische Theologie im Spannungsfeld römisch-imperialer Machtpolitik: Eine neue Perspektive auf Paulus, kritisch geprüft anhand des Philipperbriefs," in *Religion, Politik und Gewalt* (ed. Friedrich Schweitzer; VWGTh 29; Gütersloh: Gütersloher Verlagshaus, 2006), 364–382 also refers to Cicero's praxis to justify the assumption of more subtle statements in the letter to the Philippians.

[91] The intentional interception of letters seems to have been a rather rare phenomenon. However, see Cicero, *Cat.* 3.6–13 and Sallust, *Bell. Cat.* 46–47.

[92] Vasily Rudich, "Navigating the Uncertain: Literature and Censorship in the Early Roman Empire," *Arion* 14 (2006): 24; emphasis mine.

[93] Here we are only interested in the social *structures* offering a framework for discourses. On the *content* of what was regarded as subversive, see Chapter 4, Section 1.

[94] Rudich, "Uncertain," 18.

[95] That identifying hidden transcripts in historical situations is more difficult (so the criticism of Christopher Bryan, *Render to Caesar: Jesus, The Early Church, and the Roman Superpower* [Oxford: Oxford University Press, 2005], 114) is clearly stated by Scott himself (see Section 2.3). Nevertheless, I agree completely that such a methodology should be "used only with care" (Bryan, *Caesar*, 113–114).

[96] By referring to different levels of discourse, I am trying to avoid some of the problems associated with talk about "dominant" and "subordinate" parties. Here, more work is needed to ensure that we do not impose anachronistic power structures on the situation of the early Christians (Bryan, *Caesar*, 114). Simply to draw the line with reference to an economic elite (Carter, *Empire*, 8–13) is not sufficient since this would not cohere completely with the boundaries of the Christian church. If one works with a strong notion of elites (e.g., Schreiber, "Paulus," 341), it is of course possible to say that Paul and his churches constituted a "Nicht-Elite-Gruppe." Nevertheless, for a classification of early Christian literature, this demarcation is problematic since many non-Christian non-elite

paradigm emphasises the warranted observation that in the face of power structures there are rules of discourse which can repress public expression of opinion.

Nevertheless, Elliott's classification of Paul's letters has to be corrected inasmuch as Paul's letters are not a veiled hidden transcript in Scott's sense since they are not *directed* towards outsiders but are internal communication. However, he is right insofar as he has recognised that this hidden *transcript* – i.e., the internal content – could not be expressed wholly apart from the rules of public *discourse*. Therefore, we cannot simply assume with Barclay and Horsley that we are confronted with the hidden transcript of the private opinion within early Christian congregations in its pure form.[97]

Again, this is not a sufficient condition for a counter-imperial subtext. However, we have at least dealt with one fundamental objection against this hypothesis.[98] Surely, the way in which the public rules that held in general

---

groups would also fall into this category. And yet these groups (e.g., Jewish communities) would contribute to the localisation of Christian letters within different options of discourse. At the same time, the difficulty of demarcating the Christian transcript by means of socio-economic markers also points to the fact that the *inner*-Christian transcripts have to be taken into account (cf. especially Elisabeth Schüssler Fiorenza, "Paul and the Politics of Interpretation," in *Paul and Politics: Ekklesia, Israel, Imperium, Interpretation: Essays in Honor of Krister Stendahl* [ed. Richard A. Horsley; Harrisburg: Trinity Press International, 2000], 40–57).

[97] Nevertheless, the emphasis on the private nature of church meetings might be of interest with regard to another aspect associated with "hidden transcripts." Since the creation of a hidden transcript requires an isolated, undisturbed social space (see Section 2.2), this raises the question in what way the individual house churches – in contrast to the wider congregation – provided such a context. On this subject, see the classical explanations by Wayne A. Meeks, *The First Urban Christians: The Social World of the Apostle Paul* (New Haven: Yale University Press, 1983), 75–55 and their recent evaluation in Edward Adams, "First-Century Models for Paul's Churches: Selected Scholarly Developments Since Meeks," in *After the First Urban Christians: The Social-Scientific Study of Pauline Christianity Twenty-Five Years Later* (ed. Todd D. Still and David G. Horrell; London: Continuum, 2009), 63–68. The most detailed up-to-date treatment is offered by Gehring, *Church*. Their function as a hotbed for an early Christian hidden transcript, however, has not been discussed sufficiently yet.

[98] In private communication (email from 11.10.2013) Barclay responded to this conclusion (as found in Christoph Heilig, "Methodological Considerations for the Search of Counter-Imperial 'Echoes' in Pauline Literature," in *Reactions to Empire: Proceedings of Sacred Texts in Their Socio-Political Contexts* [ed. John A. Dunne and Dan Batovici; WUNT II 372; Tübingen: Mohr Siebeck, 2014], 73–92) that it was true indeed that outsiders could have had access to Paul's letters, but that he sees "no anxiety" because of this. In other words, Barclay is comparing a Roman public and a hidden Pauline transcript. He does not think that the fact that Paul's letters are influenced by the rules of public discourse restricts Paul in what he wants to say and that his letters would have looked the same if this influence would not have existed. To be sure, this is an important argument that will be

influenced Paul's writing is a larger question, the answer to which also needs to take into account the concrete character of those rules and Paul's personality: Did the rules of public discourse forbid criticism or was it an integral part of the public transcript? And in case of the former, would Paul have even cared? To these questions we now turn.

---

discussed in the next chapter. However, it should also be noted that it presupposes that Paul's letters are *not* hidden transcript in pure form.

Chapter 4

Roman Context

1. The Public Transcript

1.1 Criticism within the Framework of the Public Transcript?

As we have seen above (Chapter 3, Section 3.1), Barclay advocates the position that Paul's letters are best described as hidden transcript in its pure form, viewed from Scott's paradigm. But even if one does not want to follow him in this judgement, Barclay could still argue that locating Pauline literature within the sphere of influence of public discourse does not automatically imply that potential criticism would have to be hidden in the subtext. Hence, in his analysis of the historical situation, Barclay denies that Paul could have formulated his alleged criticism only in veiled form if he wanted to avoid persecution. He argues that there was indeed room in the public transcript for critical remarks on the existing order. Accordingly, Paul could simply have formulated his misgivings about the Roman ruler cults openly if this was something he was concerned about.[1] Barclay judges the claim that Paul could only have expressed his critical attitude towards the Empire in encoded messages to be "without historical foundation."[2] In Scott's terminology, one could say that Barclay attempts to portray the discrepancy between public and hidden transcripts in the Roman Empire as being only small. The examples of criticism within the scope of the public transcript, which Barclay adduces in order to buttress his claim, are diverse. First, he refers to criticism of *pagan gods,* which is said to have been common Jewish property even though pagan gods were supposed to secure the well-being of the Roman Empire. Consequently, it is only natural that it is also found in Paul's letters. *This* criticism was, according to Barclay, the real provocative aspect of Paul's writing. But apparently, it did not keep Paul from expressing it openly.[3] Since Paul is quite outspoken about idol worship, Barclay thinks that it is not plausible that Paul

---

[1] Barclay, "Empire," 381. Of course, the restrictiveness of the public transcript is also only a necessary, not a sufficient condition for the classical subtext-hypothesis. Strecker, "Taktiken," 130, for example, concedes that ancient authors could use code with regard to politically sensitive topics because they feared persecution. Nevertheless, he does not think that the idea of a "coded" criticism describes Paul's approach appropriately.

[2] Barclay, "Empire," 382.

[3] Barclay, "Empire," 381.

would have hidden criticism with regard to other aspects of his pagan environment just because public criticism would have been dangerous. This category, criticism that can actually be found in Paul and the implications of this observation, will be discussed in Chapter 5, Section 2. Here, we want to focus on potential targets that Barclay thinks were open to criticism within the public transcript but which are not mentioned explicitly in a negative way by Paul and, hence, are in the focus of proponents of an anti-imperial interpretation of the apostle.

The first of two areas Barclay mentions is criticism of *Roman officials*. That this was part of public discourse is demonstrably shown, according to Barclay, by statements of both Philo and Josephus.[4] Even Tacitus "in the heart of the establishment" could say through the mouth of the Caledonian general Calgacus that the Roman Empire consisted of "plundering, butchering and stealing" in the name of "peace."[5] Second, with regard to the *emperor cult* as an object of criticism, Barclay refers to Philo's comments in *Legat.* 357, where the Alexandrian Jew admits before a wide audience that he did not sacrifice to Caesar (but only on his behalf).[6] Barclay thinks that it is relevant that even Josephus criticises this cult (*C. Ap.* 2.75).[7] Hence, the fact that the emperor cult could not be accepted from a Jewish perspective was, according to Barclay, a matter of course and nothing Paul would have had to hide.

The question Barclay raises is an important one: "Since he was known to be a Jew what would he need to bury beneath the surface that would not be well known already as a Jewish opinion?"[8] So, would open criticism really have been safe? The answer to this question depends on the precise characterisation of the *object* of criticism.[9] For some of these proposals regarding the

---

[4] He refers to the critical description of Flaccus and other officials in Philo's *Flacc.* and *Legat.* As we have seen in Chapter 1, he rejects the critical subtext that Goodenough had identified in *Somn.* 2.

[5] *Agr.* 30.4 (Barclay); Barclay, "Empire," 382.

[6] Barclay, "Empire," 381. Barclay's summary of *Legat.* 357 is less precise when he says that there Philo denies the divinity of the emperor. Cf. on these events Hans-Josef Klauck, *Herrscher- und Kaiserkult, Philosophie, Gnosis;* vol. 2 of *Die religiöse Umwelt des Urchristentums;* KStTh 9,2; Stuttgart: Kohlhammer, 1996), 44–45. *Legat.* is also adduced as an argument by Cohick, "Philippians," 176 in a similar way: "[Philo] assumes a delegation could present their case and persuade Emperor Caligula of their cause's rightness; there was no need to hide or write private letters in coded message."

[7] Barclay, "Empire," 381.

[8] Barclay, "Empire," 381.

[9] It has to be welcomed that Barclay insists on specifying the allegedly subversive content of Paul's letters. General statements about the danger of "anti-imperial" rhetoric do not help much. See, for example, Diehl, "Rhetoric," 43 (set in italics in the original): "In an empire where leaders had absolute power and in an increasingly hostile environment, explicit language and direct antigovernment or anti-emperor literature would have been

criticised objects, Barclay's thesis seems to be applicable. However, the question is whether his examples really cover all the relevant areas against which criticism of the Empire could have been directed.[10]

1.2 Different Objects of Criticism

1.2.1 Roman Administration and State Ideology

The foundational element of Roman state ideology was the *pax Romana*, the "Roman peace" (or also *pax Augusta*, "Augustan peace").[11] This element is rooted historically in the person of Octavian, who was the adoptive son of Gaius Julius Caesar. After years of bloody conflict, he brought about a state of relative stability with internal peace and external security. This led to palpable relief in many places.[12] The impression of a new era found expression in the motifs of coins and the literary output of writers such as Vergil or Horace, for instance.[13] In this way the *pax Romana* became the programme for the Caesars of the following two and a half centuries.[14]

Given this background, it is beyond dispute that the Roman Empire maintained *as part of the public transcript* the claim of embodying justice. Accordingly, it provided structures that allowed for appeal to higher authorities in cases of injustice.[15] Paul himself made use of this where it worked to his

---

quite dangerous; such writing could have resulted in the death of the ones communicating opposition to the ruling authorities and/or the audience to whom they wrote." To say that *anti*-imperialism would have been quite dangerous in such an – imperial – context only states the obvious. The real question is: What kind of ideas and statements (whether explicitly "anti-imperial" or not) would have been regarded as subversive by Roman authorities and would, hence, have been deemed unacceptable within the public transcript?

[10] On the relevance of Paul's criticism of idol worship Chapter 5, Section 2.1.

[11] Cf. Jürgen Zangenberg, "'*Pax Romana*' im NT," in *Prolegomena, Quellen, Geschichte, Recht* (vol. 1 of *Neues Testament und Antike Kultur;* ed. Kurt Erlemann et al.; Neukirchen-Vluyn: Neukirchener, 2004), 165.

[12] Cf. Zangenberg, "*Pax*," 166. However, this should not hide the fact that this ideal was also accompanied by a strong sense of mission. Cf. Zangenberg, "*Pax*," 164: "Sie [the *pax Romana*] bringt keineswegs das Ende aller militärischer Eroberungen, sondern erfüllt sich dort, wo Völker unter das Dach röm. Zivilisation mit militärischer Sicherheit, unparteiischer Justiz und auf das Gemeinwohl bedachter Verwaltung unter dem einigenden Band des Kaisers gestellt werden ... ." Especially the lower classes had to pay a high price for the Roman peace (see Schreiber, "Paulus," 343).

[13] Zangenberg, "*Pax*," 166. Cf. also the interesting chapter by Dieter Georgi, "Who is the True Prophet?" in *Paul and Empire: Religion and Power in Roman Imperial Society* (ed. Richard A. Horsley; Harrisburg: Trinity Press International, 1997), 36–46, Hardin, *Galatians*, 34–36 and Wright, *Faithfulness*, 298–311.

[14] Cf. Zangenberg, "*Pax*," 165.

[15] Cf. also Barclay, "Empire," 382, fn. 63.

advantage and had no problem in appealing to Roman law.[16] However, sporadic criticism of officials who were not living up to the expectations associated with their administrative function and thereby contradicted their own ideal of the *pax Romana* cannot be equated with the criticism of this keystone of the Empire itself.

The reference to Tacitus certainly seems relevant to our discussion at first sight since here we seem to find criticism directed towards a foundational concept of the Empire's ideology, namely "peace." Although it is true that it reflects an awareness of problematic forms of Roman rule, it does not follow automatically that this is equivalent to questioning Roman propaganda per se. We need to be careful not to see too much of Tacitus's *own* criticism in the speech written by him. If anything, we are dealing here with a hidden transcript *in veiled form* since these explicit words are placed in the mouth of a hostile general.[17] In the speech to his army (*Agr.* 30–32), Calgacus criticises the Roman Empire vehemently indeed. Roman conquests are said to be motivated always by greed and the desire to subdue. The provinces are said to be administered in this spirit. Subjects are said to be exploited and treated like slaves. According to Calgacus, the Roman's nice talk about power ultimately was only a smoke screen for destructive potential (*Agr.* 30.4). Accordingly, Calgacus expresses the view that the subjects submitted only out of fear and the non-Roman parts (Britains, Gauls, Germans) of the army were not motivated by loyalty (*Agr.* 32.3). This speech, which is completely fabricated by Tacitus[18] and may have been attributed to a likewise fictional character,[19] does not at all express the self-image of the early Principate, namely bringing civilisation to subordinates.[20] But Zangenberg is right to note that one should

---

[16] Cf. Acts 16:37–39 (cf. the ironic verse 17:21: ἡμῖν ... Ῥωμαίοις οὖσιν); 21:39; 22:25–29 (!); 23:27; 24:10; 25:11.16. Cf. Nicholas T. Wright, "The Letter to the Romans," in *The Acts of the Apostles, Introduction to Epistolary Literature, The Letter to the Romans, The First Letter to the Corinthians* (vol. 10 of *New Interpreter's Bible*; ed. Leander E. Keck; Nashville: Abingdon, 2002), 721 on Rom 13:6–7: "Paul was always ready to honor the office even while criticizing the present holder. Though of course one hopes that the holder will prove worthy of the office, and one knows that sometimes holders prove so unworthy as to need removing from office, being able to respect the office while at least reserving judgment about the holder is part of social and civic maturity." See Krauter, *Studien,* 90–98 for a good summary of Paul's missionary activity in the context of Roman administration. Although I would evaluate individual events differently, I think he is correct in concluding that Paul's experience was diverse and that sometimes Roman administration was advantageous for him, while at other times he suffered under its rule.

[17] This seems to be the position of Schreiber, "Paulus," 343.

[18] Dylan Sailor, "The *Agricola*," in *A Companion to Tacitus* (ed. Victoria E. Pagán; BCAW; Chichester: Wiley-Blackwell, 2012), 32.

[19] Cf. Sailor, "*Agricola*," 32.

[20] Cf. Sailor, "*Agricola*," 32.

"daraus keine grundsätzliche Kritik an röm. Machtpolitik ablesen."[21] This is confirmed by two literary observations:[22] First, whereas the Roman Empire is bad in itself in the eyes of Calgacus, in *Agr.* Tacitus reports on the life of his father-in-law who confronts this general in combat and who is portrayed as nothing short of a model of *good* administration. Hence, it is evident to the reader that Calgacus is in the wrong in his accusations against the Empire and that – if mediated by the right person – it can produce the good.[23] Second, the mention of the German Usipetes, who are adduced in *Agr.* 32.3 as examples of a people who deserted the Romans, betrays Tacitus's intention. Only shortly before, in *Agr.* 28, Tacitus had already described their fate vividly. Their desertion by ship led to a disaster and ultimately even to the point where they "were reduced to such straits as to eat the weakest of their company, and after them the victims drawn by lot" (*Agr.* 28.2 [Hutton]). Of those who reached land, some were picked up by Germanic tribes and sold as slaves (cf. *Agr.* 28.3). Although there may have been aspects of the Empire which could be unjust in praxis, according to Tacitus, it remained better by far than the alternative: "[H]owever real the injustices done within the framework of the imperial administration, they do not compare to the universal disaster the world would endure in its absence."[24] We can summarise, then, that the reference to Tacitus does not make it plausible that challenging basic principles of the Empire would have been possible in public without resulting in great trouble.[25] Ironically, this is confirmed by the group known as "martyrs," whom Tacitus opposes indirectly in *Agr.* – the very document that Barclay adduces to argue for his position.[26]

---

[21] Zangenberg, "*Pax*," 166.

[22] Cf. Sailor, "*Agricola*," 33.

[23] On the genre of the *Barbarenrede* and its rhetorical function, see Alfons Städele, "Tacitus und die Barbaren," in *Reflexionen antiker Kulturen* (ed. Peter Neukam; KlSL 20; München: Bayerischer Schulbuch-Verlag, 1986), 123–143.

[24] Sailor, "*Agricola*," 33. Cf. Sailor, "*Agricola*," 34 on the Empire in *Agr.* 21: "[I]t destroys freedom; it is the setting for corruption, vice, and injustice; and it is the best of all realizable orders of the world."

[25] Cf. Chester G. Starr Jr., "The Perfect Democracy of the Roman Empire," *AHR* 58 (1952): 7–8 on the control of public expression of opinion.

[26] Cf. Sailor, "*Agricola*," 25 on these persons and Sailor, "*Agricola*," 26–29 on the lifestyle recommended by Tacitus. On Tacitus's remarks about the lack of freedom of expression in his *Ann.* cf. Ronald Mellor, *Tacitus' Annals* (OACL; New York: Oxford University Press, 2011), 78–92. It is also telling that Tacitus himself carefully waited for the death of Domitian before he wrote his critical remarks.

1.2.2 Caesar Cult and Caesar Ideology

1.2.2.1 Introduction

Now we turn to Caesar and his cult(s) as the object of criticism. In order to be in a position to evaluate Barclay's statements regarding the possibility of criticism of the imperial cult, we need to take a quick look at its historical development first. We have to pay special attention to the question of whether and to what extent the criticism which Barclay assumes really did fundamentally challenge the whole of Caesar *ideology*.

1.2.2.2 Historical Overview

The origin of Roman imperial cults is located in the east of the Empire. The historical background for this development was the tradition of scepticism with regard to popular notions of the gods, which progressively depersonalised the divine and, in so doing, elevated outstanding humans to a superhuman level as a counter balance.[27] The increasing shift of power from the *polis* to external rulers caused all existential matters to be concentrated on these figures: "Alles, was positiv von der Macht zu erwarten war, Hilfe, Rettung, Heil, wurde den fernen Inhabern der Macht zugeschrieben."[28] At least since the time of Alexander the Great, the worship of rulers as divine figures was established.[29] Dating from 195 BCE, a temple for the goddess *Roma* is known in Smyrna, a goddess who was worshipped because there was no Roman ruler and because she personified the city Rome.[30] Nevertheless, it did not take long until persons were celebrated in this way after victories. This was the case with the general Pompey, who was venerated in Asia Minor as εὐεργέτης and σωτήρ after his victory against Mithridates.[31]

The rise of Gaius Julius Caesar in the midst of the first century BCE to the position of dictator paved the way for the permanent establishment of the Roman Empire as a monarchy, thereby enhancing the prominence of a single person in the centre of the Empire.[32] Whereas in the east an understanding of

---

[27] Wolfgang C. Schneider, "Herrscherverehrung und Kaiserkult," in *Weltauffassung, Kult, Ethos* (vol. 3 of *Neues Testament und Antike Kultur;* ed. Kurt Erlemann et al.; Neukirchen-Vluyn: Neukirchener, 2005), 210–211.

[28] Schneider, "Herrscherverehrung," 211. For more details, see Simon F. R. Price, *Rituals and Power: The Roman Imperial Cult in Asia Minor* (Cambridge: Cambridge University Press, 1984; repr., Cambridge: Cambridge University Press, 2002), 23–52.

[29] On the evidence for early ruler cults, see Christian Habicht, *Gottmenschentum und griechische Städte* (2nd ed.; München: C. H. Beck, 1970) and cf. Price, *Rituals,* 25–32.

[30] On the varied cults of Roman power, see Price, *Rituals,* 40–47. Cf. Schneider, "Herrscherverehrung," 214.

[31] Schneider, "Herrscherverehrung," 216.

[32] Cf. Karl L. Noethlichs, "Die äußere Entwicklung (Historische Kontexte. Das Imperium Romanum von der Republik zum Prinzipat," in *Prolegomena, Quellen, Geschichte,*

Caesar as "god" is already attested by inscriptions,[33] his honouring in Rome remains vague and controversial.[34] It is commonly assumed that the status of a state deity – accompanied by an own temple with statue, cultic personnel, and regular sacrifices – was awarded only to the late Caesar in 42 BCE.[35] This was preceded by the rise of a comet during the games held in honour of Caesar, which was interpreted as a sign of his deification.[36]

Octavian,[37] the bringer of peace, the "first citizen" *(princeps)*, subsumed his political programme under the motto of the restoration of the Republic although he basically pursued the development of the Empire into a coherent monarchy.[38] People genuinely gave him great credit for his achievement as a peacemaker and he received "echte Dankbarkeit und Verehrung."[39] Correspondingly, he was awarded the title Augustus ("the venerable") taken from the realm of sacred language.[40] However, this did not result in ruler worship along the lines of the Hellenistic model. In Rome itself, the intellectual climate differed from the one just sketched for the east. Here, the idea of the divine within the human was more alien.[41] Even after the civil wars, the exceptional position of Augustus was still rooted in the sacrality of the *imperium* itself.[42] Since now the *imperium* was focused on the *imperator* alone and since he thus became the "maßgebliche Träger des öffentlichen Wohlergehens und der Garant des Sieges,"[43] his person became cultically relevant.[44]

Recht (vol. 1 of *Neues Testament und Antike Kultur;* ed. Kurt Erlemann et al.; Neukirchen-Vluyn: Neukirchener, 2004), 147.

[33] Cf. Manfred Clauss, *Kaiser und Gott: Herrscherkult im römischen Reich* (Stuttgart: Teubner, 1999), 47 and Klauck, *Kaiserkult,* 46.

[34] Cf. Klauck, *Kaiserkult,* 46–47.

[35] But cf. Clauss, *Kaiser,* 48–51 on earlier veneration of Caesar as divine.

[36] Cf. Klauck, *Kaiserkult,* 48.

[37] On the divinity of Augustus and his cult, see Karl Galinsky, "Continuity and Change: Religion in the Augustan Semi-Century," in *A Companion to Roman Religion* (ed. Jörg Rüpke; BCAW; Blackwell: Chichester, 2007), 80–82.

[38] Cf. Erich S. Gruen, "Augustus and the Making of the Principate," in *The Cambridge Companion to the Age of Augustus* (ed. Karl Galinsky; CCCl; Cambridge: Cambridge University Press, 2005), 33–51. Cf. also Starr, "Democracy," 5–6, who shows how Augustus endeavoured not to give the impression of an imposed monarchy and comments subsequently: "Yet beneath the surface, and more openly after his death, one can detect a realization of the fact that the Principate was essentially the rule of one man."

[39] Klauck, *Kaiserkult,* 52.

[40] Klauck, *Kaiserkult,* 52.

[41] Schneider, "Herrscherverehrung," 215.

[42] Schneider, "Herrscherverehrung," 216. Cf. also the section "Die religio des Imperium Romanum" in Wolfgang C. Schneider, "Politik und Religion," in *Prolegomena, Quellen, Geschichte, Recht* (vol. 1 of *Neues Testament und Antike Kultur;* ed. Kurt Erlemann et al.; Neukirchen-Vluyn: Neukirchener, 2004), 27 for the concepts underlying cult and state.

[43] Schneider, "Herrscherverehrung," 216.

[44] Schneider, "Herrscherverehrung," 216.

This found expression, among other ways, through his inclusion in the Roma-cult and the instatement of his own priesthood.[45] On this basis, aspects of the Hellenistic conception of the emperor developed in Rome also.[46] The deification of Caesar as *divus Iulius* in 42 BCE enabled Augustus to be called *divi filius,* "son of the deified (Caesar)." The distinction between a deified person *(divus)* and a god in the full sense *(deus)*[47] was not followed in the east and Augustus was understood simply to be a "son of god."[48] From Egyptian texts we also know the designation "god from god" for this adoptive relationship.[49] In accordance with this notion, temples in honour of Augustus soon developed throughout Asia Minor.[50]

In a very detailed study, Price was able to point out the dynamic behind this development. According to him, the Hellenistic ruler cult already was an attempt of the cities to integrate power "which was external and yet still Greek"[51] by means of incorporating it into the traditional pagan cults.[52] Confronted with the rule of the Roman emperors, the people in the east similarly chose to use their "traditional symbolic system," which enabled them to understand the emperor "in the familiar terms of divine power."[53] This perception of the divinity of the emperor in the east and the cult(s) resulting from it,[54] thus were not a centralised imposition by Rome but a deeply Greek reac-

---

[45] Schneider, "Herrscherverehrung," 216.

[46] Schneider, "Herrscherverehrung," 216.

[47] Cf. Klauck, *Kaiserkult,* 46. Galinsky, "Continuity," 80 says this distinction soon became "no more than a semantic nicety." For a different perspective on *divus* and *deus,* cf. Ittai Gradel, *Emperor Worship and Roman Religion* (Oxford Classical Monographs; Oxford. Oxford University Press, 2002), 61–69.

[48] *Divi filius* could only be translated as υἱὸς τοῦ θεοῦ. Cf. Klauck, *Kaiserkult,* 47 and Price, *Rituals,* 75. For more details on the linguistical and conceptual aspects associated with Latin and Greek terminology, see Simon R. F. Price, "Gods and Emperors: The Greek Language of the Roman Imperial Cult," *JHS* 104 (1984): 79–95.

[49] See P.Oxy. 1453.10–11 (ὀμ[ν]ύομεν Καίσαρος θεὸν ἐκ θεοῦ) and *OGIS* 655.1–2 (Καίσαρος Αὐτοκράτορος θεοῦ ἐκ θεοῦ).

[50] See Clauss, *Kaiser,* 63–64. Cf. Noethlichs, "Entwicklung," 148.

[51] Price, *Rituals,* 30.

[52] On the forms of imperial cults in the context of traditional ritual praxis, see Angelos Chaniotis, "Der Kaiserkult im Osten des Römischen Reiches im Kontext der zeitgenössischen Ritualpraxis," in *Die Praxis der Herrscherverehrung in Rom und seinen Provinzen* (ed. Hubert Cancik and Konrad Hitzl; Tübingen: Mohr Siebeck, 2003), 3–28.

[53] Price, *Rituals,* 248.

[54] Steven J. Friesen, "Normal Religion, or, Words Fail Us: A Response to Karl Galinsky's 'The Cult of the Roman Emperor: Uniter or Divider?,'" in *Rome and Religion: A Cross-Disciplinary Dialogue on the Imperial Cult* (ed. Jeffrey Brodd and Jonathan L. Reed; SBLWGRW 5. Atlanta: Society of Biblical Literature, 2011), 24 thinks that it would be more appropriate to speak of a plurality of "imperial cults" in anaology to other religious cults in order to avoid the wrong impression of a special phenomenon and in order to enable a more nuanced understanding of it. Although I am not sure whether this linguistic

tion towards Roman rule.[55] Out of consideration for the traditional religious ideas in Rome, Augustus accepted cultic veneration of his person even in the east on a rather small scale.[56] In Rome itself, Augustus exhausted all possibilities with regard to "numinoser Überhöhung seiner Stellung,"[57] all the while being careful not to cross any borders – presumably under the impression of Julius Caesar's recent fate.[58] What was worshipped during his lifetime was his *genius,* his guardian spirit, and the divine power in him, the *numen.*[59] His final inclusion among the state gods took place only after his death in 14 CE.[60] The precedence set by his case became the foundation for the deification (apotheosis) that was from then on a standard feature of all other emperors except for those who were especially unpopular. It happened on the basis of a witness who testified before the Senate that he had seen how the soul ascended from the funeral pyre to the sky.[61]

Another qualitative step[62] in the developing emperor cult took place during the time of Caligula,[63] who "erstmalig versucht, direkt in Konkurrenz zu althergebrachten Gottheiten zu treten."[64] Whereas it was customary until then

---

shift is necessary (of course we can speak collectively about "the" Dyonisus cult), the point he wants to express by means of this suggestion is no doubt correct. Cf. on this Mary Beard, John A. North, and Simon R. F. Price, *A History* (vol. 1 of of *Religions of Rome;* Cambridge: Cambridge University Press, 1998), 318. See also the poignant comments by Wright, *Faithfulness,* 313–314.

[55] However, this does not mean that this form of expression was not also seized upon by Rome (sometimes mediated through the governor; Price, *Rituals,* 70–71) and that the emperor was not involved personally. See on this the very important discussion Price, *Rituals,* 53–77. We even know that sanctions from Rome had to be feared quite early on for incorrectly executing the cults to which one had freely devoted oneself (Price, *Rituals,* 66).

[56] Schneider, "Herrscherverehrung," 216. Cf. Klauck, *Kaiserkult,* 49 on the ambivalent relationship between Augustus and his worship. On the specific honours, see Klauck, *Kaiserkult,* 50–51.

[57] Klauck, *Kaiserkult,* 49.

[58] Klauck, *Kaiserkult,* 49.

[59] Cf. Klauck, *Kaiserkult,* 52. On the importance of attributing *numen* to Augustus, see Clauss, *Kaiser,* 68–69.

[60] Klauck, *Kaiserkult,* 49.

[61] Clauss, *Kaiser,* 74–75. Cf. Klauck, *Kaiserkult,* 48.

[62] Clauss, *Kaiser,* 90 thinks Caligula "zog ... aus den seit Caesar und Augustus im Westen geduldeten und/oder gesteuerten Vorstellungen von der lebenden Gottheit die eigentlich logische Konsequenz."

[63] On Tiberius, his predecessor, see Clauss, *Kaiser,* 76–89, who concludes (p. 88): "Letzten Endes konnte Tiberius auch auf kultischem Sektor nicht mehr hinter die Ehren zurückfallen, die für Augustus gegolten hatten."

[64] Klauck, *Kaiserkult,* 55. Cf. Suetonius, *Cal.* 22.

to sacrifice *on behalf of* the emperor only and not *to* the emperor himself,[65] Caligula demanded to be treated like other gods. This not only contradicted Jewish practice (as is sometimes claimed) but the procedure as established in general.[66] Caligula's intention to erect a statue of himself in the Jewish temple – which certainly would have caused huge riots in the population – was never implemented because Caligula was assassinated beforehand in 41 CE.[67]

Claudius was more reluctant to accept cultic honours than his predecessor,[68] and the demands of Nero also remained within the usual framework, being characterised by a special association with the sun god Sol.[69] After the general Vespasian was proclaimed emperor by his soldiers after Nero's death in 69 CE,[70] the imperial cult was a welcome tool in order to legitimate his rule by establishing continuity with his Julio-Claudian predecessors – due to lacking physical descent.[71] As a result he played a significant role in introducing the emperor cult to the west.[72] Domitian, who followed his brother Titus[73] (69–81 CE; both were sons of Vespasian), allowed himself to be called "lord and god"[74] and encouraged the imperial cult.[75] It is debated, however, whether he joined Caligula in overstepping the existing boundaries.[76] At least part of the later tradition can be attributed to the subjectivity of the sources, which

---

[65] Where sacrifices were made to the emperor directly, he was usually incorporated into a range of other gods (usually in a more prominent position) or deified predecessors. See on this issue the discussion of Price, *Rituals,* 210–220).

[66] Cf. also the extensive discussion in Hardin, *Galatians,* 102–114, which builds on the work of Miriam Pucci Ben Zeev and Tessa Rajak. He demonstrates that – contrary to the frequent assumption – there was no official exception for the Jews as a *religio licita* and that sacrifices *to* the emperor were also not standard in the non-Jewish world. On supposedly "approved" religions, see Rüpke, *Religion,* 35: "A term such as *religio licita,* 'approved' religion(s), which the Christian writer Tertullian uses of the Jews in the Roman empire …, had no official standing. There was no register of associations that listed all those that had been approved by the authorities. Decisions about what was alien and dangerous were made from case to case, triggered by a particular incident against the background of specific ideas about what constitutes a threat."

[67] Klauck, *Kaiserkult,* 56.

[68] Klauck, *Kaiserkult,* 56. For more details regarding Claudius, see Clauss, *Kaiser,* 94–98.

[69] Cf. Clauss, *Kaiser,* 98–111.

[70] Klauck, *Kaiserkult,* 58.

[71] Klauck, *Kaiserkult,* 59.

[72] Klauck, *Kaiserkult,* 59. See also his comments on the integration of Vespasian's rather sceptical sounding last words into this framework.

[73] On Titus, cf. Clauss, *Kaiser,* 117–119.

[74] Cf. Clauss, *Kaiser,* 120.

[75] Klauck, *Kaiserkult,* 60.

[76] Klauck, *Kaiserkult,* 60.

tried to make Domitian the negative foil for Trajan (98–117 CE), whose modesty with regard to cultic veneration they wanted to emphasise.[77]

1.2.2.3 Jews in the Public Transcript

So far the historical summary. Because of their religion, it was not an option for devout Jews to participate in the traditional pagan cults – nor in the imperial cult, which was an integral part of the former.[78] Naturally, this rejection of pagan gods, the divinity of the emperor, and associated cults cast a poor light on them in the eyes of others. Nevertheless, speaking generally, it did not cause too much danger for them as Lightstone summarises: "As much as detractors may have criticized Jews for their non-participation in the pagan cults of their respective cities, Roman authorities recognized and accepted this non-participation and regularly provided dispensation from the pagan-cult involvements."[79] However, we also have to be careful not to paint too tolerant a picture. Although it is unlikely that central sanctions existed for refusing to participate in imperial (and other pagan) cults, this by no means means that such an attitude was met with enthusiasm locally.[80] After all, we should not forget that, for non-Jews also, the pressure to participate – though (largely) non-central – was present nevertheless due to fellow citizens who

---

[77] Cf. Klauck, *Kaiserkult*, 60–61. See also Clauss, *Kaiser*, 133–138.

[78] Cf. Jack N. Lightstone, "Roman Diaspora Judaism," in *A Companion to Roman Religion* (ed. Jörg Rüpke; BCAW; Blackwell: Chichester, 2011), 360–362 for a short summary of Jewish monotheism in the Diaspora. For the few indications of Jewish participation in non-Jewish cults (outside Egypt) see John M. G. Barclay, *Jews in the Mediterranean Diaspora from Alexander to Trajan (323 BCE–117 CE)* (Edinburgh: T&T Clark, 1996), 321–323.

[79] Lightstone, "Judaism," 361. Cf. also Hardin, *Galatians*, 107, whose basic statement corresponds to Barclay's thesis: "[P]articipation in imperial celebratory processions was not a viable alternative to many Jews in the Diaspora, as imperial processions were regularly linked with the worship of the pagan gods. ... Because there had been long-standing toleration for Jews not to worship Greek and Roman deities, it can safely be assumed that Jews were not compelled to participate in imperial processions that were linked to pagan worship. ... [A] refusal to participate in imperial processions was not seen as politically seditious."

[80] Cf. Chapter 5, Section 2.1 on the reactions towards Jewish refusal to participate in pagan cults.

cared about this issue.[81] Imperial festivals, in particular, involved the whole city.[82]

Yet even more importantly, the fact that the Jews rejected the aspects mentioned by Lightstone should not detract from the fact that, even so, they were part of the system of ruler ideology and were expected to express their loyalty in other ways. Accordingly, they sacrificed in Jerusalem *to* their god YHWH *on behalf* of the emperor. Since this corresponded to the praxis of the non-Jewish nations, we can assume that this sufficed as a demonstration of allegiance.[83] In this sense we may say, as some do, that the Jews "participated" (within the range of their piety) in the imperial cult, thus defining this term rather loosely.[84] However, it might be less misleading to speak of their rejection of imperial cults that were associated with pagan rites and of their acceptance of or at least submission to a certain ruler ideology.

The biggest conflict between the Jewish rejection of certain forms of imperatorial ideology and the Roman Empire took place under Caligula. As we have seen, his *demand* for divine honours and direct sacrifices contradicted not only the established public transcript for dealing with the Jews but also Roman praxis in general.[85] Consequently, Philo does not mince words when, in *Legat.*, he criticises Caligula heavily for overstepping the mark.[86] Howev-

---

[81] On the role of imperial cults for the self-conception of cities and the resulting participation of the *whole* city, see Price, *Rituals*, 107–114 on communal festivals. The social pressure for pagans who became Christian is also emphasised by Stephen Mitchell, *The Rise of the Church* (vol. 2 of *Anatolia: Land, Men and Gods in Asia Minor;* Oxford: Clarendon, 1993), 10. Cf. Hardin, *Galatians*, 42–46 on the expectations towards the individual citizen.

[82] E.g., by means of sacrifices in front of the house, accompanying the procession (see Price, *Rituals,* 112; cf. Price, *Rituals,* 107–114).

[83] Cf. James S. McLaren, "Jews and the Imperial Cult: From Augustus to Domitian," *JSNT* 27 (2005): 271–273. By means of the temple tax the individual Jew in the diaspora contributed to this expression of loyalty (Hardin, *Galatians,* 108). In addition to these sacrifices there were many inscriptional dedications honouring the emperor (Hardin, *Galatians,* 108–109). Cf. also Hans Leisegang, "Philons Schrift über die Gesandtschaft der alexandrinischen Juden an den Kaiser Gaius Caligula," *JBL* 57 (1938): 392: "Die Juden aber hatten sich tatsächlich an diesem mit den Caesaren getriebenen Kultus so weit beteiligt, dass sie sich rühmen konnten, hierin nicht hinter den anderen Völkern zurückzustehen." On the crucial importance of this, see Josephus, *B.J.* 2.197.

[84] So, for example, Hardin, *Galatians,* 105.

[85] Hardin, *Galatians,* 105: "[T]he crazed emperor was not merely demanding that Jews step beyond their special exemption; with regard to imperial veneration, he was transgressing the *modus operandi* of his predecessors. ... [T]he Jewish concern during Gaius's reign represented a broader phenomenon."

[86] He is said to have "no longer consented to remain within the bounds of human nature," a border which Philo presupposes as self-evident (*Legat.* 75 [Smallwood]). Philo says that he crossed this line and "aspired to being regarded as a god" (*Legat.* 75). In what follows, Philo describes in detail how Caligula's self-perception increased more and more

er, even this text, which Barclay adduces as an example of blatant criticism of the *divinity* of the emperor, Caligula is accompanied by very high esteem for other emperors, especially Augustus. Philo's respect for them is not even diminished by the fact that other cultures met them with divine honours (as long as they did not force the Jews to join them in doing so).[87] Philo's critique of how Caligula breached this taboo thus should not be interpreted as criticism of the rule of Caesar in general: "Gaius wird ... als die große Ausnahme unter allen Caesaren dargestellt, so dass durch seine Verurteilung die kaisertreue Gesinnung als solche nicht in Frage gestellt wird."[88]

We thus conclude that, on the one hand, this example truly demonstrates that criticising the divinity of the emperor and excessive cultic demands was possible (with the exception of Caligula).[89] On the other hand, this case

---

until he fancied himself to be a demi-god. He compares pejoratively the achievements of those persons worshipped as demi-gods with Caligula's own achievements (*Legat.* 78–92). In *Legat.* 93 he then begins his description of the next step in Caligula's development: "Gaius' madness, his wild and frenzied insanity, reached such a pitch that he went beyond the demi-gods and began to climb higher and to go in for the worship paid to the greater gods, Hermes, Apollo, and Ares, who are supposed to be of divine parentage on both sides." With pungent sarcasm, Philo demonstrates the distance between the nature these gods are assumed to have and Caligula's own nature (*Legat.* 94–114). Philo subsequently (*Legat.* 116) complains that the population of the Empire supported this "vanity" and only the Jews did not do so because they believed "that the Father and Creator of the universe is one God" (*Legat.* 115; Kohnke better: "daß e i n Gott sei, der Vater und Schöpfer der Welt"). In their eyes, Caligula's behaviour was "the most horrible of blasphemies" (*Legat.* 118) because he did not respect the border between God and humanity. See also Chapter 4, Section 2.2.2.

[87] Philo contrasts Caligula's behaviour with that of other emperors when he denounces Caligula for setting up images of himself in Jewish synagogues in Alexandria (cf. *Legat.*134–140). Augustus's reign is described in length (*Legat.* 143–159). How he ended the civil war is praised in glowing terms (*Legat.* 144). Therefore, Philo thinks: "[I]f ever there was a man to whom it was proper that new and unprecedented honors should be voted, it was certainly fitting that such should be decreed to him." Among other accolades, he considers him to be "the first and greatest universal benefactor" (*Legat.* 149 [Smallwood]). Accordingly, Philo writes that Augustus was honoured by the whole world as evidenced by the many and beautiful temples (*Legat.* 150–151). This high respect notwithstanding, it is recounted that the Jews left their synagogues unchanged (*Legat.* 152). Nevertheless, Philo says, the Jews could always be certain that the emperor would respect their customs (*Legat.* 153; 155–158). Yes, Philo even claims that Augustus himself "did not approve of any one's addressing him as master or god, but if any one used such expressions he was angry" and that he even shared the Jews' opinion about the inappropriateness of such behaviour (*Legat.* 154 [Yonge]).

[88] Leisegang, "Schrift," 395.

[89] Philo's criticism of Caligula was possible because the emperor had offended general conventions of the public transcript – not only with regard to the Jews but in general. At the same time, this work is a typical example of a *hidden transcript in veiled form* (cf. Chapter 3, Section 2.3). Philo admittedly writes "a document addressed to a wide audi-

should not be used as evidence for the view that open criticism of the imperatorial rule and honour itself was possible. Hence, we have to conclude that Barclay's assertions with regard to emperor ideology are only partially true. Indeed, it was possible for monotheistic Judaism to reject the *divinity* of the emperor and resulting *cults* (which were also objectionable because of their integration into other pagan cults). This behaviour, together with its rationale, was generally known as part of the public transcript and was not sanctioned in most cases, at least not from the official side.[90] However, it is important to note that the Jews had to express their loyalty through other means. This demonstrates that emperor ideology cannot be reduced to the emperor cult[91] (or that one needs to define the imperial cult more broadly).[92] This is Bar-

---

ence" (Barclay, "Empire," 381), but it is not at all addressed to Caligula himself. Rather, *Legat.* is meant for Claudius (or maybe Nero): "Philo will not directly present the new emperor with a lecture on ideal kingship, but he devotes several pages to such a lecture directed to Gaius by Macro, and shows how Gaius' perversion of true kingship was one of the causes of his downfall." (Erwin R. Goodenough, *An Introduction to Philo Judaeus* [2nd ed. Oxford: Blackwell, 1962], 60.) On the dating of the text: The reference to Claudius in *Legat.* 206 necessitates the assumption that he is already dead. Cf. Leisegang, "Schrift," 399 and Goodenough, *Introduction,* 60. We find a similar orientation in Seneca, *Clem.* for Nero. Although this work naturally is more positive towards its recipient, there nevertheless remains a discrepancy between historical realities and the ideal presented, which results in a parenetic function (cf. Krauter, *Studien,* 64–67).

[90] In this regard, Acts 17:1–9 has long been of interest as a possible exception. Does the charge of acting against "Caesar's decrees" (οὗτοι πάντες ἀπέναντι τῶν δογμάτων Καίσαρος) have anything to do with the imperial cult? The traditional answer that behind this incident lies the charge of treason was effectively criticised by Edwin A. Judge, "The Decrees of Caesar at Thessalonica," *RTR* 30 (1971): 71–78 (reprinted in Edwin A. Judge, *The First Christians in the Roman World: Augustan and New Testament Essays* [WUNT 229; Tübingen: Mohr Siebeck, 2008], 456–462). From my perspective, the most important counter-argument is that this charge would probably have been discussed before the proconsul (Justin K. Hardin, "Decrees and Drachmas at Thessalonica: An Illegal Assembly in Jason's House [Acts 17.1–10a]," *NTS* 52 [2006]: 32). (As regards the conviction that "it is unlikely that two rather unimportant Roman citizens in the Greek East would have been charged with treason" [Hardin, "Decrees," 33], I am not convinced.) Hardin, "Decrees," 33–38 has shown that the alternative proposal of Judge is also problematic, according to which the background for the conflict was the regulation that predicting the death of the emperor was not allowed (cf. Cassius Dio, *Hist. Rom.* 56.25.5–6), and Paul's proclamation of the coming lord Jesus implied such a statement. Hardin, "Decrees," 38–49 himself argues convincingly that the problem was the framework of imperial regulations against voluntary associations (*collegia*; cf. Chapter 3, Section 3.2.2).

[91] E.g., Justin Meggitt, "Taking the Emperor's Clothes Seriously: The New Testament and the Roman Empire," in *The Quest for Wisdom: Essays in Honour of Philip Budd* (ed. Christine E. Joynes; Cambridge: Orchard Academic, 2002), 151–153.

[92] Hardin, *Galatians,* 102–110. I would prefer the first approach, see above.

clay's mistake when he speaks only of divinity and cult with regard to emperor ideology and thus limits the range of options inappropriately:[93]

[W]hat would he need to bury beneath the surface that would not be well known already as a Jewish opinion? That Caesar is neither God nor son of God? Philo said so at length in a document addressed to a wide audience (his *Legatio*), indeed more or less directly to the emperor's face (*Legatio* 357). That one should not take part in the imperial cult? That was a well-known Jewish stance, and Paul says it clearly enough in his blanket ban on worshipping 'idols.'

Such a move fails to recognise the true nature of the postulate of the divine nature of the emperor as a specific expression of the underlying ideology in a specific cultural environment.[94] Hence, this form was easier to criticise – for people with a different cultural/religious background – than the ideology itself. It is beyond question that Caesar had to be recognised as saviour and absolute lord, for example, and was pictured as such by state propaganda. It would have been a great provocation to disagree publicly at such a fundamental level – regardless of whether Jews accepted the specific interpretation of his role as divine or not.

A helpful analogy for this differentiation are the *non-Jewish* intellectuals of the Roman Empire. Their rejection of excessive cultic honours for emperors (especially when still alive) was given expression without questioning the role of Caesar within the Empire itself.[95] Seneca's *Apocolocyntosis* is an extremely waspish parody of Claudius's apotheosis (*Apocolocyntosis (divi) Claudii* literally means "The Gourdification of (the Divine) Claudius"[96]). Seneca definitely had a personal axe to grind with the late Emperor, who was responsible for his exile, and took advantage of the general climate after the Emperor's death to express his own frustration (cf. Seneca, *Apoc.* 1.1). Relentlessly, he mocks Claudius's weaknesses like his limping (*Apoc.* 1.2; 5.2), his sicknesses (*Apoc.* 3.1–2), his love for gambling (*Apoc.* 12.3; 14.4–15.1), and – as a running gag – his slurred pronunciation (*Apoc.* 5.2–3; 6.2; 7.1–2; 7.4). Seneca's criticism is certainly not trivial but indirectly accuses Claudius of tyranny (*Apoc.* 5.3; 6.2; 13.4–14.2) even through the mouth of the deified Augustus (*Apoc.* 10.3–11.5). But this by no means implies that Seneca questioned the emperorship per se. Nero, in contrast, is described very positively

---

[93] Barclay, "Empire," 381.

[94] See also Galinsky, "Cult," 3–4.

[95] Cf. Hubert Cancik, *Römische Religion im Kontext: Kulturelle Bedingungen religiöser Diskurse* (vol. 1 of *Gesammelte Aufsätze;* ed. Hildegard Cancik-Lindemaier; Tübingen: Mohr Siebeck, 2008), 227–245 on the negative evaluation of the ruler cult by Tacitus and the qualifications on pp. 237–238.

[96] On the title, see Otto Schönberger, *Apocolocyntosis divi Claudii: Einführung, Text und Kommentar* (Würzburg: Königshausen und Neumann, 1990), 28–30.

by his tutor (*Apoc.* 4).⁹⁷ Autocracy was not the problem, personality was. Claudius could be criticised (posthumously (!) and not in the *laudatio funebris,* which was also written by Seneca⁹⁸) because, in the public perception, he was not a good emperor but a tyrant. Nor is Seneca opposed to traditional belief in the gods. Rather, he thinks that the deification of tyrants like Claudius is so ridiculous that it does harm to true piety (cf. *Apoc.* 11.4). However, Price has shown⁹⁹ that the assumption that writings like Seneca's *Apoc.*¹⁰⁰ "mock the whole institution of imperial apotheosis" and that such jokes¹⁰¹ are "evidence for the total rejection of the imperial cult on the part of the élite" simply "rests on a naive view of the significance of jokes and satire."¹⁰² Instead, jokes are made about "those things that matter most," and accordingly, *Apoc.* "is better seen as directed specifically against the apotheosis of the wholly implausible figure of Claudius, rather than against apotheosis in gen-

---

⁹⁷ Marion Altman, "Ruler Cult in Seneca," *CP* 33 (1938): 202–203. Of course, this also includes a hortative aspect (Schönberger, *Apocolocyntosis,* 23–24 and 27). But cf. also Edward Champlin, "Nero, Apollo, and the Poets," *Phoenix* 57 (2003): 273–283, who argues quite convincingly that the idea of the "New Age of Apollo" did not emerge before the latter half of 59 CE and that the description of Nero in *Apoc.* 4 should be regarded as a later insertion.

⁹⁸ Tacitus, *Ann.* 13.3.

⁹⁹ Price, *Rituals,* 114–117.

¹⁰⁰ Often reference is also made to Plutarch, e.g., *Mor.* 170E: "As he [the superstitious man] hates and fears the gods, he is an enemy to them. And yet, though he dreads them, he worships them and sacrifices to them and besieges their shrines; and this is nothing surprising; for it is equally true that men give welcome to despots, and pay court to them, and erect golden statues in their honour, but in their hearts they hate them and 'shake their head.'" Cf. the claims of Kenneth Scott, "Plutarch and the Ruler Cult," *TAPA* 60 (1929): 117–135 with Price, *Rituals,* 201 and Christopher P. Jones, *Plutarch and Rome* (Oxford: Clarendon, 1971), 123–124. On Plutarch's political thought, cf. also Parrott, "Thought," 143–162.

¹⁰¹ The most famous probably is the self-ironic statement by Vespasian when dying (Suetonius, *Vesp.* 23.4 [Rolfe]): "Woe's me. Methinks I'm turning into a god." (But, for a different evaluation of Vespasian's last words, see Clauss, *Kaiser,* 116–117.) For other humorous statements, see Kenneth Scott, "Humor at the Expense of the Ruler Cult," *CP* 27 (1932): 322–328, who lists many intriguing examples but whose final conclusion is affected by Price's judgement: "Our evidence seems to point to the existence of a reading public which had no genuine religious faith in the ruler cult, and we can hardly be mistaken in thinking that the most cultivated Greeks and Romans had as much belief in the apotheosis of a ruler as the same educated class would have today. That some of these same people doubtless observed or officially encouraged the worship of the ruler as an act of political allegiance is quite another matter. True religious belief in the divinity of the king or emperor is to be sought among the more ignorant lower classes, especially among barbarian peoples and in the eastern provinces of the Roman Empire."

¹⁰² Price, *Rituals,* 115.

eral."[103] Hence, it is not surprising that Seneca supported deification in those cases where, from his perspective, emperors really deserved it.[104]

The potential for conflict when questioning basic elements of emperor ideology becomes even more apparent when we consider one element that is completely missing from Barclay's Jewish examples: a competitor. We should not forget that the proclamation of *another* lord lends additional explosive power to the challenge of imperatorial priority. Jesus or analogous (e.g., messianic) figures do not appear in Barclay's discussion of the possibility of public criticism.[105] Of all things, this neglects what constitutes the Christian movement, its character as a messianic group who claimed that the king of the Jews had appeared and was alive.[106] In this regard, it is also interesting to note that divine honours for other individuals ceased with the exaltation of Augustus. Apparently, even less problematic human "competition," which could have been integrated into the system quite easily, was not tolerated.[107]

---

[103] Price, *Rituals*, 115. Similarly Altman, "Cult," 200: "In no place does he condemn deification as such; in fact, it is very evident that he approved of the apotheosis of Augustus ... Augustus was his idea of the perfect prince with all the qualities of a Stoic sage. Therefore, it seems that his satire was meant to be an attack not on the state religion but on the deification of unworthy emperors." Contra Scott, "Humor," 326: "Seneca clearly had no more admiration for the ruler cult than he had for Claudius who had banished him to Corsica, and the satire, coming from the pen of so distinguished a personage, must have caused a sensation among court circles at Rome. Can we suppose that Seneca's opinions varied greatly from those of the reading public of the day?"

[104] Seneca, *Clem.* 1.10.3. Schönberger, *Apocolocyntosis*, 25 and 31 (but cf. also Altman, "Cult," 200, fn. 10).

[105] The same criticism can be levelled against Harrill, *Paul*, who finds almost no potential for conflict between Paul and the Roman Empire. He only remarks (p. 94): "[Paul] was not a pacifist in the modern sense, either. Indeed, Paul expected the imminent coming of a divine empire ruled by Christ and God. He thus was not completely comfortable with Roman imperial rule or ideology." But he does not develop the latter thought further.

[106] As correctly noted by Heike Omerzu, "Paulus als Politiker? Das paulinische Evangelium zwischen Ekklesia und Imperium Romanum," in *Logos – Logik – Lyrik: Engagierte exegetische Studien zum biblischen Reden Gottes: Festschrift für Klaus Haacker* (ed. Volker A. Lehnert and Ulrich Rüsen-Weinhold; ABIG 27; Leipzig: Evangelische Verlagsanstalt, 2007), 275: Paul's gospel "bildet ... in jedem Fall einen inhaltlichen Gegensatz zur 'Heilserwartung' der Pax Romana. Schließlich verkündet Paulus das Evangelium eines politischen Aufrührers, der von den Römern wegen seines Widerstands gegen das Imperium gekreuzigt wurde." On the Roman handling of messianic movements which "von den zuständigen Behörden als Störenfriede der *pax Romana* eingeschätzt wurden, gegen die eingeschritten werden musste" (Christoph Riedo-Emmenegger, *Prophetisch-messianische Provokateure der Pax Romana: Jesus von Nazaret und andere Störenfriede im Konflikt mit dem Römischen Reich* [NOTA/SUNT 56; Göttingen: Vandenhoeck & Ruprecht, 2005], 313–314) see Riedo-Emmenegger, *Provokateure*, 245–312.

[107] See Chapter 6, Section 3.2.

1.2.2.4 Censorship in the Early Principate

It is one thing to say that there was no place for criticism of emperor ideology in the Roman public transcript and another, to evaluate the consequences of speaking one's mind out loud. Accordingly, it is in order to ask whether public criticism – though not appreciated – would really have resulted in acute danger.[108]

In the Latin of Paul's day, there was no term for what we call "censorship" today.[109] But it would be completely wrong to conclude on this basis that such a phenomenon did not exist. After all, the early Empire was characterised by a big discrepancy between linguistic representation and the real life.[110] Accordingly, it is not especially helpful to limit the discussion of the public transcript to legal requirements: "[C]oncentration on the legal vocabulary and the like, with the purpose of elucidating the predicament of the period's literati, does not seem to me especially profitable ... ."[111] From the time of the Republic we know of only one case of censorship of an author,[112] so that Rudich concludes that the system "allowed the free flow of thought within confines not much different from modern standards."[113] But this changed dramatically with the Principate: "[I]t cannot be denied that with its arrival the very principle of intellectual exchange, be it in oral or written form, ceased to be taken for granted and became increasingly an object of abuse at

---

[108] Cf., e.g., Cohick, "Philippians," 175: "In sum, the rise of imperial rule was questioned and resisted even at the highest level, which undermines the notion that silent resistance was the only option for those who opposed imperial power."

[109] Rudich, "Uncertain," 7. On the role of the *censor,* see Rudich, "Uncertain," 8. Hence, Jacob Taubes, *Die Politische Theologie des Paulus* (2nd ed.; München: Wilhelm Fink, 1995), 27 goes too far when he writes with regard to the beginning of Romans (Rom 1:3–4: "Ich will betonen, daß das eine politische Kampfansage ist, wenn an die Gemeinde nach Rom ein Brief, der verlesen wird, von dem man nicht weiß, in wessen Hände er fällt, und die Zensoren sind keine Idioten, mit solchen Worten eingeleitet wird, und nicht anders."

[110] Cf. the very illuminating remarks of Rudich, "Uncertain," 7–8. Although the adherence to the values of the Republic was only superficial, it nevertheless could be strong enough to create some space for the expression of unwelcome opinions. See, e.g., Cramer, "Bookburning," 158 on the education system which remained the matter of the *pater familias* – at least for some time (see Cramer, "Bookburning, 170 for the later development).

[111] Rudich, "Uncertain," 10. Cf. Rudich, "Uncertain," 9–10. Cf. also Rudich, "Uncertain," 15: "This review makes even more dramatic the recognition that all our efforts to determine the legal grounds of the policies – which included what we call censorship – aiming at the abolition of *libertas,* that is, freedom of speech, are ultimately irrelevant to the realities of the early Empire."

[112] Gnaeus Naevius, who had to go to prison around 204 BCE. Cf. Rudich, "Uncertain," 12.

[113] Rudich, "Uncertain," 13.

the hands of the authorities."[114] During the time of Augustus, such curtailment of the freedom of expression could take the form of exile and (later, after the crisis in 6 AD) of book burning[115] – in the city and outside (Tacitus, *Ann.* 4.35 mentions that this was done by the *aediles;* outside Rome, it was done by the municipal magistrates, cf. Cassius Dio, *Hist. Rom.* 56.27.1 and 57.24.4).[116]

The lèse-majesté *(laesa maiestas),* which was meant to protect the people from insult and oppression during the Republic, was transferred to the *princeps* during the time of Augustus,[117] which basically meant that "any action or behavior construable as subverting the authority of the Emperor"[118] ran the risk of entailing a charge. All that was needed was a person willing to denounce someone.[119] The degree of criticism in the statements under scrutiny was relatively irrelevant,[120] and the denial of the charge almost always a lost cause.[121] From now on, cases of censorship of writers and other publicly relevant figures did not stop. We know of many incidents during the reign of

---

[114] Rudich, "Uncertain," 14. Cramer, "Bookburning," 191 speaks poignantly of a "slow, but steady strangulation of the freedom of speech and writing in the early decades of the Roman principate."

[115] Cramer, "Bookburning," 157–178 gives a fascinating and detailed account of the development. It can be summarised in one sentence (Cramer, "Bookburning," 177): "From a relatively liberal policy in the matter of freedom of speech and writing, Augustus progressed, if progress it can be called, towards one of greater severity and stricter curbs."

[116] Cf. Cramer, "Bookburning," 171.

[117] Karl Christ, *Geschichte der römischen Kaiserzeit* (6th ed.; München: C. H. Beck, 2009), 187. Cf. Rudich, "Uncertain," 11.

[118] Rudich, "Uncertain," 16.

[119] See Cramer, "Bookburning," 180: "In such, as in all other criminal cases, prosecution was begun by private individuals. For Rome did not know any public prosecutors. An action that ended with the defendant's conviction brought handsome rewards to the man who had taken the time and trouble as well as the risk of bringing a criminal to justice." Cf. also Tacitus, *Ann.* 4.30 on the "denouncers" *(delatores).*

[120] Cf. Rudich, "Uncertain," 17–18: "Under these circumstances what actually mattered was not the problem of legality, but the properties of the written material construable as offensive, and the interest of persons ready to exploit it to the benefit or detriment of the author. The record shows that, in principle, any text dealing even remotely with public life could be charged with subversion ... . Furthermore, since in Rome censorship as an institution – that is to say, an office or an officer responsible for granting an imprimatur to the work of literature – did not exist, any person influential at court was at liberty to play the censor, to find criminal faults in any piece of writing and draw it to the attention of the Emperor. Within the paranoid ambience of the regime, this type of interpreter threatened to achieve paramount importance. (Being slightly facetious, one may suggest that this was how reader-response criticism came to be born.)"

[121] Look, for example, at the desperate attempt of Ovid, *Tr.* 2 to protest his innocence (cf. Rudich, "Uncertain," 19).

Augustus although they did not result in executions yet.[122] Tiberius began quite liberally but became increasingly strict so that under his reign the first executions happened (affecting astrologers first and later also simple authors) and pardon became very rare.[123] Now the short advice, given in a play, "to bear the follies of the reigning prince with patience" (Scaurus, *Atreus;* following Euripides, *Phoen.* 393; cf. Tacitus, *Ann.* 6.29; Cassius Dio, *Rom. Hist.* 58.24.4) could mean the end – even though Augustus had originally approved of the play.[124] Similarly, and even more absurdly, a history of the Augustan era (which apparently also was acceptable to this emperor) was presented as a reason for charging its author, Cremutius Cordus (FRHist 71), with treason (for personal reasons):

> He was accused of having praised Cassius and Brutus, and of having assailed the people and the senate; as regarded Caesar and Augustus, while he had spoken no ill of them, he had not, on the other hand, shown any unusual respect for them. This was the complaint made against him, and this it was that caused the death as well as the burning of his writings.[125]

We know of similar cases from Caligula,[126] Nero,[127] and even Vespasian.[128] In this climate, it is quite common for an author to use a code for critical remarks.[129] Rudich notes that today we might sometimes find it difficult to

---

[122] Rudich, "Uncertain," 14 and 20. For Julius Caesar's ambivalent behaviour, see Cramer, "Bookburning," 158–159.

[123] Rudich, "Uncertain," 15, 19, and 21–22. Cf. Cramer, "Bookburning," 178–188 for the development which was driven by quite unassuming causes. Tiberius's stance is summarised drastically by Cassius Dio, *Rom. Hist.* 57.23.1–3.

[124] Cramer, "Bookburning," 190.

[125] Cassius Dio, *Rom. Hist.* 57.24.3–4. On Cremutius Cordus and Tacitus's use of "figured speech," see Mary R. McHugh, "Historiography and Freedom of Speech: The Case of Cremutius Cordus," in *Free Speech in Classical Antiquity* (ed. Ineke Sluiter and Ralph M. Rosen; Mn.S 254; Leiden: Brill, 2004), 391–408.

[126] Rudich, "Uncertain," 16. He did, however, start out by trying to make a good impression by being more tolerant than his predecessor (Cramer, "Bookburning," 194–195).

[127] Rudich, "Uncertain," 15–16 and 22–23. On the persecution of intellectuals under Nero in general, see Vasily Rudich, *Political Dissidence under Nero: The Price of Dissimulation* (London: Routledge, 1993), and Vasily Rudich, *Dissidence and Literature under Nero: The Price of Rhetoricization* (London: Roudledge: 1997).

[128] Rudich, "Uncertain," 20. According to Mellor, *Annals,* 90, Claudius was the only emperor of the Julio-Claudian dynasty from whose reign we do not know of censorship of writers.

[129] E.g., Schreiber, "Paulus," 342. Rudich, "Uncertain," 18: "One must add that, because of the need for dissimulation, men of letters did sometimes resort to a sort of 'code,' drawing on the traditional fields of reference, so that they could express dissident sentiments with little or no fear of immediate harassment. This made their texts polytelic and polyvalent, each of them pursuing a variety of goals and capable of being viewed on different levels. To illustrate: a retelling of the well-known story about an atrocity committed by some ancient or mythological tyrant could purport to display the author's skill at emula-

detect these statements but that there were many not well-disposed contemporaries who obviously did not have such problems and identified many, sometimes too many, subversive encoded messages.[130] Even a very weak suspicious fact could be interpreted in such a way (and could result in exile or execution) so that even "a discourse dealing with abstract virtues and vices, typified in the figures of animals and the like" could be interpreted as a personal attack on the Praetorian Guard Sejanus.[131] Whether these subversive – or rather subversively interpretable – remarks were oral or written[132] and stated in large or small circles was irrelevant.[133] Rudich describes this situation of lacking legal protection as giving rise to an "omnipotence of the reader."[134] Of course, the situation in the east was much more relaxed than in Rome itself,[135] but the early Christians were certainly confronted with parties who would have readily played the role of the omnipotent and unfavourable reader.[136]

1.2.2.5 Results

As far as the divinity of Caesar is concerned, we can conclude that, at least in the time frame relevant for Paul, negative remarks about his supposed nature and associated worship probably were possible within the public transcript without risking persecution. Nevertheless, the precise reconstruction of how the relationship between the Christians and the Roman emperor developed

---

tion, his sense of drama, or – covertly – his disapproval of the current Emperor's reign of terror. Conversely, it could be read with attention paid solely to its rhetoric and style, or as inviting."

[130] Rudich, "Uncertain," 19.

[131] Cf. Rudich, "Uncertain," 21.

[132] Rudich, "Uncertain," 20: "In examining the potential for subversion, in terms of the activities that were at risk of being censored, it is not always possible, or even necessary, to distinguish fully between an action and an utterance, or between an oral and written statement ... ."

[133] To give an example: Clutorius Priscus, a Roman knight, got money for a poem he had written in occasion of the death of Germanicus. When Tiberius's son (Drusus the Younger) was sick, Clutorius Priscus prepared a similar poem which he recited within his circle of friends. Whereas things ended well for the patient – he recovered – they did not for the poet – these lines cost him his life. See Tacitus, *Ann.* 3.49–51. Cassius Dio, *Rom. Hist.* 57.20.3 (Cary) says that, hearing of his death, Tiberius "was vexed at this, not because the man had been executed, but because the senators had inflicted the death penalty upon a person without his approval." Cf. on the more general issue of private utterances Rudich, "Uncertain," 24–25.

[134] Rudich, "Uncertain," 24.

[135] Cf. Whitmarsh, "Resistance," 61.

[136] Cf. Acts 17:7; 25:7–8.

under Nero is difficult.[137] In any case, this tolerance should not be overemphasised. A factor neglected by Barclay is the stance from which criticism was formulated. What was possible for someone who was known to be a loyal Roman citizen might have been too much from a person associated with this strange new movement, not least represented by Paul himself.[138] Also, things could change quickly as later developments show.[139] Additionally, *local* dynamics could vary significantly. Local pressure to be a good member of society could easily escalate. In any case, the situation was safer as long as the followers of the Messiah Jesus remained and were seen as part of Judaism whose special beliefs were known and hence not automatically associated with the impression of disloyalty.[140] Where Christians came to be regarded as a distinct movement, expectations and corresponding danger increased.[141] Questioning imperatorial rule, by contrast, would have been perceived has highly provocative – especially if Caesar's claims were being attributed to another person.[142]

---

[137] It is telling to see how differently two important German books on Paul evaluate the historical setting of Rom 13:1–7. Michael Wolter, *Paulus: Ein Grundriss seiner Theologie* (Neukirchen-Vluyn: Neukirchener Theologie, 2011), 314 writes: "Dass es auch Träger politischer Gewalt gibt, die nicht das Böse bekämpfen und das Gute fördern ... wird von Paulus hier nicht bedacht." Schnelle, *Paulus,* 335–336 entertains the possibility that Suetonius, *Nero* 16.2 reflects a contemporary situation and that "der Römerbrief ... diese Entwicklung in ihren Anfängen [bezeugt]" (Schnelle, *Paulus,* 336), which seems to me to be a plausible development after Claudius's edict in 49 CE (cf. p. 335). The more tensions arose between Roman authorities and this strange new movement, the more critically statements would have been judged, which might have been tolerated if coming from someone else.

[138] Correctly Hans-Josef Klauck, "Des Kaisers schöne Stimme: Herrscherkritik in Apg 12,20–23," in *Religion und Gesellschaft im frühen Christentum: Neutestamentliche Studien* (WUNT 152; Tübingen: Mohr Siebeck, 2003), 265: "Sodann dürfte es nie klug gewesen sein, einen römischen Kaiser direkt zu kritisieren, dazu noch aus der Position einer marginalisierten, beargwöhnten Minderheit."

[139] Cf. Barclay himself in Barclay, "Snarling Sweetly," 337, fn. 9, where he refers to *C. Ap.* 2.73–78 with great sensitivity for the specific situation of the time of composition: "This issue [the religious status of the emperor] was of special sensitivity in the Domitianic era (during, or soon after which, *c. Apion.* was written) with an increased Flavian emphasis on imperial religious honours."

[140] This is the basic argument of Hardin, *Galatians,* who thinks that the motive of the agitators was to ensure the label of the Jewish community for the Galatian churches in order to remove ambiguity regarding their social status and the expectations connected with it (see p. 112). The problem of the "Entfremdung" between Jews and Christians as an intensifier of the conflict between the Empire and Christians is also recognised by Öhler, "Vereinsrecht," 62. He thinks that this new classification can be assumed "[s]pätestens seit Nero." Cf. Tacitus, *Ann.* 15.44.

[141] On the expectations of fellow citizens, see above, Section 1.2.2.3.

[142] This conclusion runs counter to the position of Harrill, *Paul,* 89.

1.3 Conclusions: Modification of the Object of Criticism

We are now in the position to make some well-founded observations. First, Barclay is only partially correct when he questions the danger of publically criticising aspects of the Roman Empire. Where such statements would have affected fundamental aspects of *Roman ideology,* especially with regard to the identity-establishing figure of the emperor, Barclay's argument is not applicable. So it is very reasonable to assume that it would have been dangerous indeed for Paul to state *such* criticism on the surface of the text of his letters.[143] Speaking of "Roman" ideology should not imply that Romanisation is the process of simply imposing a foreign culture onto a native one. That this is not the case is most obvious in the various forms the imperial cults take (see Chapter 4, Sections 1.2.2.2 and 2.2.1).[144] Nevertheless, there does not seem to be a problem with the assumption that, from the perspective of a Jew like Paul, there would have been elements (e.g., military ones) that would have been classified as typical expressions of the Empire.[145] It goes without saying that the term "ideology"[146] is being used here as "not in the narrow sense of political ideologies, but in the broader concept of beliefs about how the world should be organized."[147] Of course, there was a plurality with regard to these "concepts and beliefs."[148] Nevertheless, this should not hide the fact that there is a fundamental unity which may legitimately be subsumed under the modern notion of such a belief system.[149] Even the term

---

[143] Similarly, e.g., Schreiber, "Paulus," 342: "Es ist aber offensichtlich, dass es in der frühen Kaiserzeit nur unter Einsatz des eigenen Lebens möglich war, grundlegende Kritik am Kaiser und seiner Regierung öffentlich zu äußern."

[144] Harrill, *Paul,* 79 correctly points out that "Roman" identity is "a social and cultural construct composed of various and competing forms."

[145] With regard to local authorities, one has to be careful indeed to see "Rome" behind everything. See Matthew V. Novenson, "What the Apostles Did Not See," in Reactions to Empire: Proceedings of Sacred Texts in Their Socio-Political Contexts (ed. John A. Dunne and Dan Batovici; WUNT II 372; Tübingen: Mohr Siebeck, 2014), 55–72. Cf. below Chapter 4, Section 2.2.2.

[146] Karl Galinsky, "In the Shadow (or Not) of the Imperial Cult: A Cooperative Agenda," in *Rome and Religion: A Cross-Disciplinary Dialogue on the Imperial Cult* (ed. Jeffrey Brodd and Jonathan L. Reed; SBLWGRW 5; Atlanta: Scholars Press, 2011), 219 finds fault with the uncritical use of the term "ideology" (or even "propaganda") in this context: "[W]hat is meant by ideology? Is the New Testament ideological, too? How so? 'Propaganda' has now generally been discarded, and 'ideology' has crept in to fill some of that void, but it needs definition."

[147] With Louise Revell, *Roman Imperialism and Local Identities* (Cambridge: Cambridge University Press, 2009), 13.

[148] Rightly emphasised by Galinsky, "Shadow," 220.

[149] Revell, *Imperialism,* 109 concludes – after having emphasised the variegated experience of the person of the emperor in the Empire – with the statement that "the emperor and the ideology legitimating his position were one of the social structures which determined

"propaganda" can be used in a helpful way in our context[150] if we are careful not imply anachronistic connotations of a central *Gleichschaltung*.

Second, it seems plausible that the use of a critical subtext would have been a safe – or at least safer – alternative. The effective history of these letters itself demonstrates that counter-imperial statements are not easily detectable in Paul, and scholars still have problems to identify them with enough certainty, their historical background knowledge notwithstanding. This allows for the conclusion that the use of the subtext for critical remarks would have been a relatively safe option for Paul although the risk of being interpreted as subversive (whether justifiably so or not) could never be ruled out.

This leads us naturally to the question of whether it is reasonable to assume that Paul had such a critical attitude, which he somehow tried to express. This question is deeply connected with an analysis of Paul's worldview and personality, to which we will turn in the next chapter. But before we do so, we have to consider an even more fundamental question, still referring to the historical situation during the early Principate: Were there enough points of contact between Paul's ministry and public representations of Roman ideology to allow for the conclusion that he probably took a conscious stance (whether positive or negative) towards this entity?

---

peoples' understanding of being Roman" and at the same time "also one of the factors through which this experience differed across the empire." For a very detailed proposal of an ideology, which was internalised in times of peace, as a foundation for the long existence of the Roman Empire, see the work of Clifford Ando, *Imperial Ideology and Provincial Loyalty in the Roman Empire* (ClCT 6; Berkeley: University of California Press, 2000). One should note however, that Ando stresses the voluntary receptiveness at the cost of real constraints set by Rome. Cf. critically Michael Peachin, review of C. Ando, *Imperial Ideology and Provincial Loyalty in the Roman Empire, AHR* 107 (2002): 922. Revell, *Imperialism,* 191–192 gives a balanced and plausible summary of the dynamic: Roman power was not the only means of diffusion of Roman ideology. Both parties were involved with their interests, but a clear disparity existed. For good discussions of the use of the concept of ideology with regard to Paul and Empire, see Harrison, *Paul,* 37–40 and Strecker, "Taktiken," 141–144. For an excellent summary of Roman imperial ideology in the context of empire studies, see Greg Woolf, "Inventing Empire in Ancient Rome," in *Empires: Perspectives from Archaeology and History* (ed. Susan E. Alcock et al.; Cambridge: Cambridge University Press, 2001), 311–322.

[150] For a recent rejection of the term "propaganda" see Harrill, *Paul,* 78–79. For a more relaxed attitude towards this term, see Olivier Hekster, "The Roman Army and Propaganda," in *A Companion to the Roman Army* (ed. Paul Erdkamp; BCAW; Malden: Blackwell, 2007), 340.

2. Roman Ideology in the Environment of Paul

2.1 Introduction

It can still happen that classes on the historical context of the New Testament include much information about the Jewish dimension of the world of the NT writers but that the Greek element is only mentioned briefly and the Roman aspect neglected completely.[151] At at least to some extent, this tendency to focus on the Jewish *Umwelt* of the NT authors is justifiable, simply because it is more than that, it is their *Mitwelt*.[152] Where the Roman influences are considered, however, one often gets the impression that, whereas we know how to evaluate the significance of Jewish backgrounds because the rootedness of the NT authors in this traditions is so obvious the Roman foreground is somehow more difficult to grasp. Often cultural elements are simply listed in a quite neutral, archaeological fashion when describing Paul's context.[153] But what do these lists imply? Is this what *we* see as people interested in Roman history? Or is this what a Jew like *Paul* would have perceived in entering a city in Asia Minor or Greece in the first century? To put it very basically: What follows from taking into account our historical knowledge of the Roman Empire – is it friend or foe of counter-imperial interpretations of Paul? The answer to this question depends mainly on our decision to what extent Paul was confronted with imperial references on a daily basis.

---

[151] Of course, today there are also many textbooks which try to bring to light the interwovenness of the New Testament writings and its Graeco-Roman context. See, for example, Gary M. Burge, Lynn H. Cohick, and Gene L. Green, *The New Testament in Antiquity: A Survey of the New Testament within Its Cultural Contexts* (Grand Rapids: Zondervan, 2009).

[152] Roland Deines, "Historische Analyse I: Die jüdische Mitwelt," in *Das Studium des Neuen Testaments* (ed. Heinz-Werner Neudorfer and Eckhard J. Schnabel; 2nd ed.; Wuppertal: R. Brockhaus, 2006), 100. Moreover, such an emphasis is legitimate in light of the former neglect of the Jewish roots of Christianity in earlier scholarship according to which Paul almost became the inventor of a Hellenistic mystery cult. The fascinating discoveries of the Dead Sea Scrolls rightly reinforced this tendency which has led to a "third quest" in the *Leben-Jesu-Forschung* and to a "new perspective" on Paul.

[153] To give a random example: This is at least the tendency in Eckhard J. Schnabel, *Paul and the Early Church* (vol. 2 of *Early Christian Mission;* Downers Grove: InterVarsity, 2004), in which one easily finds information on all the cults – including imperial ones – in the cities Paul visited. There certainly is a justifiable reason for books which offer such encyclopaedic information. But how are students of the New Testament expected to be able to evaluate the relevance of this information and to integrate it into their interpretation of specific Pauline letters?

2.2 Imperial Cults as an Expression of Imperial Ideology

2.2.1 Pervasiveness

Was "Rome" present in the daily lives of the apostle and the members of his churches? There is no question that Paul had many problems with local authorities and addressed many aspects of Graeco-Roman culture – but it is doubtful that he would have blamed the Emperor for all this.[154] Hence, the question needs to be raised whether Paul had more direct contact with Rome – a question that is usually affirmed with regard to the imperial cults, which were spread throughout the whole Empire. The importance of this assessment is made perfectly clear by Miller when he says with regard to a counter-imperial interpretation of the apostle's writings: "[T]o the extent that this interpretation of Paul is dependent on the ubiquity of the imperial cult, it begs the question of how widespread the cult actually was *in Paul's time, and in the places where Paul worked.*"[155] In discussing Paul's access to Roman ideology, reference is indeed most often made to the public impact of imperial cults, which are said to have been a prominent feature in the cities he visited and where he founded his churches. Horsley, for example, writes: "[H]onors and festivals for the emperor were not only widespread but pervaded public life, particularly in the cities of Greece and Asia Minor, the very area of Paul's Mission."[156] It is true that imperial festivals were events that

---

[154] The comment by Samuel Vollenweider, "Politische Theologie im Philipperbrief?" in *Paulus und Johannes: Exegetische Studien zur paulinischen und johanneischen Theologie und Literatur* (ed. Dieter Sänger and Ulrich Mell; WUNT 198; Tübingen: Mohr Siebeck, 2006), 468–469 is noteworthy: "[D]er Apostel [bezieht sich] dabei meist gar nicht auf die Gesamtgestalt des römischen Reichs oder auf seinen Repräsentanten, den Kaiser, sondern auf näher liegende, mikropolitische Strukturen, vornehmlich auf die *Stadt,* handle es sich nun um die klassische griechische Polis oder um eine römische Kolonie. Dies ist nicht weiter auffällig. Gerade im Raum des östlichen Mittelmeers bleibt die Stadt zur Zeit des frühen Prinzipats die hauptsächliche Referenzgrösse politischer Prozesse wie politischer Reflexion." On the tendency to see Caesar behind every power structure Paul encountered, see Novenson, "Apostles." (Carter's approach to Matthew builds on this assumption; cf. Joel Willitts, "Matthew," in *Jesus Is Lord, Caesar Is Not: Evaluating Empire in New Testament Studies* [ed. Scot McKnight and Joseph B. Modica; Downers Grove: IVP Academia, 2013], 89–90.) Maybe Vollenweider's objection can be countered in part by the notion that the cities themselves constituted "das Rückgrat des römischen Imperiums" (Strecker, "Taktiken," 158).

[155] Colin Miller, "The Imperial Cult in the Pauline Cities of Asia Minor and Greece," *CBQ* 72 (2010): 316.

[156] Richard A. Horsley, "General Introduction," in *Paul and Empire: Religion and Power in Roman Imperial Society* (ed. Richard A. Horsley; Harrisburg: Trinity Press International, 1997), 4.

involved the whole city and surrounding areas[157] for several days and characterised the public atmosphere.[158]

However, Miller accuses some Pauline scholars of overemphasising how pervasive the imperial cults were. Among others, he quotes Crossan and Reed as claiming: "In any city that Paul visited, evidence of emperor worship appears repeatedly in present excavations."[159] Miller has tried to point out that NT scholars often misread the map provided by Price on the distribution of imperial cults. In his article, Price's map – which collects evidence from several hundred years – is analysed with regard to the cities Paul probably visited and with regard to the relevant time frame of his ministry. Miller concludes that imperial cults played only a very marginal role in these areas.[160] Of the 156 buildings listed by Price, only 18 are said to have existed with certainty before the death of Nero in 68 CE. If one also considers buildings with merely possible connections to imperial cults, the number increases to 57.[161] If the resulting list is compared to cities of Pauline activity,[162] then, in Asia Minor, only Ephesus and Hierapolis remain as cities which certainly featured imperial cults, and Tarsus, Pisidian Antioch, Ancyra, and Pessinus as cities which might have had such cults.[163] In Greece, the situation is said to be similarly sparse: In the relevant timeframe, Miller says, only Athens and Corinth exhibited imperial cults – but he thinks that there was none in Philippi or Thessalonica.

Unfortunately, the picture Miller paints is distorted by a deficient methodology. As far as I know, this has not been sufficiently recognised in the literature so far.[164] Miller only looks for remains of temples but fails to take into

---

[157] See, e.g., Price, *Rituals,* 107. This alone relativises the following statement of Miller, "Cult," 322: "There is no evidence for the cult in any period at Corinth's port city of Cenchreae."

[158] See Price, *Rituals,* 101–114.

[159] Crossan and Reed, *Search,* 143.

[160] Miller, "Cult," 315.

[161] Miller, "Cult," 318.

[162] Miller, "Cult," 317–318.

[163] On the problem of reconstructing Paul's missionary journeys with regard to the Galatian cities, see Miller, "Cult," 318.

[164] Diehl, "Empire," 225–226 simply reproduces his findings. In another article, Diehl, "Rhetoric," 54 even accepts Miller's conclusions – quite an alarming sign of the state of the discussion in my opinion: "There is a recent debate as to the extent to which the people of Asia Minor were participating in the imperial cult at the time of Paul's letters. Recent archaeology, investigating the ruins of large cities in Asia Minor, has determined that the adoption of the imperial cult did not develop as rapidly as once thought. ... In Philippi there is no evidence of emperor worship before the second century. Verification of the imperial cult in Thessalonica appears to be late, dating from 238 CE." It is especially surprising that a scholar like Fantin, *Lord,* 43, who writes on a closely associated subject, simply notes that "Miller's article is helpful as a discussion of imperial cults proper in

account other evidence. This is fatal since often we have very good reasons (e.g., on the basis of literary evidence and general knowledge of Roman politics)[165] to assume that there were imperial cults in a city although we have not found any ruins yet. Sometimes this is even certain on the basis of inscriptions. As a result, we get the impression that the imperial cults were surprisingly widespread right at the beginning of the Roman Empire. To get an impression of the distorted picture that emerges from Miller's deficient approach, let us consider what he says with regard to Philippi:

> Philippi became a 'neokorate' city only in the early second century, and there is no evidence of the cult before then. Moreover, the silence of the archaeological record regarding the existence of the cult in this Roman colony appears very loud indeed. How widespread and constituent a part of city life could the cult have been in Paul's day if such a major center of *Romanitas* lacked it?[166]

This would be an impressive argument indeed if its assumptions were not wrong. Inscriptions, however, clearly show that this analysis, which is based

---

Paul's time and as a corrective to some excessive claims." The only problem that he seems to have with Miller's article is that it does not consider other forms of "imperial presence." (To be fair, in a short review of Miller's article, Joseph D. Fantin, review of Colin Miller, "The Imperial Cult in the Pauline Cities of Asia Minor and Greece," *BSac* 168 [2011]: 98–99 at least mentions Miller's problematic discussion of the evidence regarding Corinth.) Rosemary Canavan, *Clothing the Body of Christ at Colossae* (WUNT II 334; Tübingen: Mohr Siebeck, 2012), 76 also does not seem to find anything objectionable in Miller's paper. Even Schnelle, *Einleitung,* 190 refers to Miller's argument. Other scholars apparently do not really know how to treat these results. John A. Dunne, "The Regal Status of Christ in the Colossian 'Christ-Hymn': A Re-Evaluation of the Influence of Wisdom Traditions," *TJ* 32 (2011): 17, for example, notes, citing Miller: "Recently there has been some question as to whether Paul's counter-Imperial language would also include reference to the Imperial cult. Miller argues that the evidence suggests that the Imperial cult was 'marginal' in Paul's day and thus it is anachronistic to speak in terms of a widespread religious phenomenon." But then he only continues by saying: "Perhaps new evidence will continue to point in this direction despite the claims of previous scholars that the Imperial cult was vibrant by the middle of the first century." He then cites, among others, no less than Price, *Rituals* – the very basis of Miller's argument. Richard S. Ascough, "Comparative Perspectives: Early Christianity and the Roman Empire," *ARG* 14 (2013): 333 recognises that Miller's conclusions go "against findings by others," but he thinks that his "call for caution in positing the predominance of emperor worship within the myriad of civic religious practices in the pre-Flavian period is worth heeding." Wright, *Faithfulness,* 1273 notes correctly that Miller's thesis is "insupportable" and refers to his reconstruction of the apostle's Roman context, but he also does not explain *how* it is that Miller reaches wrong conclusions.

[165] See, for example, the poignant discussion of Antioch in Syria in Warren Carter, "Roman Imperial Power: A New Testament Perspective," in *Rome and Religion: A Cross-Disciplinary Dialogue on the Imperial Cult* (ed. Jeffrey Brodd and Jonathan L. Reed; SBLWGRW 5; Atlanta: Scholars Press, 2011), 139–140.

[166] Miller, "Cult," 322.

on archaeological remains of cultic sites, is wrong.[167] Similarly confusing is Miller's treatment of Thessalonica, about which he writes: "Thessalonica, it seems, became a city of the imperial cult only very late, under the emperor Gordian sometime after 238 CE."[168] Here again Miller errs on the basis of the lack of archaeological remains since a temple from the reign of Augustus can be assumed due to the epigraphic evidence (*IG* X 2.1, no. 31), which is also supported by numismatic data (*RPC* 1, nos. 1554–1555).[169] Miller wants to incorporate numismatic evidence into his argument, but he clearly misinterprets the work of Barbara Burrell, who refers only to "the temple that made the city neokoros," not to imperial cults in general.[170] Miller's other source[171] focuses on the cultic activity of the *Thessalian koinon* (not the city Thessalonica!) and does not support Miller's claim either. Even where Miller acknowledges imperial cults during the time of Paul, his assessment lacks precision. This is the case, for example, in his analysis of the situation in Corinth. Miller acknowledges imperial cult in Corinth[172] but emphasises that it was not "without competition."[173] In light of the many temples, especially of Olympian deities,[174] he concludes: "Thus, here as elsewhere, we must see the imperial cult in its proper context: alongside many other gods in the city life and by no means demanding exclusive loyalty."[175] The second part of this statement is completely uncontroversial. However, Miller somehow seems to deduce from this observation that the imperial cult becomes almost invisible in this context:

---

[167] See Lukas Bormann, *Philippi: Stadt und Christengemeinde zur Zeit des Paulus* (SNT 78; Leiden: Brill, 1995), 41–60. For an extensive catalogue of inscriptions which can be searched and is updated online (http://www.philippoi.de/) see Peter Pilhofer, *Katalog der Inschriften von Philippi* (vol. 2 of *Philippi;* 2nd ed.; Tübingen: Mohr Siebeck, 2009). On the relevance of the imperial cult in Thessalonica, see recently Harrison, *Paul,* 55–56.

[168] Miller, "Cult," 322.

[169] Cf. Ioannis Touratsoglou, *Die Münzstätte von Thessaloniki in der römischen Kaiserzeit: 32/31 v. Chr. bis 268 n. Chr.* (AMUGS 12; Berlin: de Gruyter, 1988), 140–144 for this series and p. 25, fn. 2 on the plausible connection to the building of the temple.

[170] Barbara Burrell, *Neokoroi: Greek Cities and Roman Emperors* (CCSNS 9. Leiden: Brill, 2004), 199 (a passage that Miller, "Cult," 322, fn. 25 erroneously locates on p. 191 and adduces as support for his thesis).

[171] Kaja Harter-Uibopuu, "Kaiserkult und Kaiserverehrung in den Koina des griechischen Mutterlandes," in *Die Praxis der Herrscherverehrung in Rom und seinen Provinzen* (ed. Hubert Cancik and Konrad Hitzl; Tübingen: Mohr Siebeck, 2003), 211–214.

[172] Miller, "Cult," 329–330.

[173] Miller, "Cult," 330.

[174] It is, by the way, surprising that Miller, "Cult," 331 thinks that the evidence for an imperial cult in Corinth "is a bit dicey and fragmentary" and "slightly less conclusive than we would desire" (p. 332). One wonders how he would judge the evidence for other cults in Corinth.

[175] Miller, "Cult," 330–331.

The lack of evidence in Corinth for the imperial-cult-saturated environment is perhaps more striking as well as more historically telling than for any other Pauline city. ... In other words, even though Corinth was about as loyal a Roman colony as one could expect, this loyalty apparently did not translate into a central position of the emperor in the city cults. Insofar as generalizing across the ancient world is ever helpful, it may be useful to ask: If the imperial cult did not take center stage in veteran-and-Roman-citizen-populated Corinth, where did it?[176]

Just compare these statements with the summary of DeMaris, which takes the perspective of an ancient visitor:[177]

An axis projected from Temple E divided the forum temples, left and right. As one approached the west end of the forum, the temple of the imperial cult stood above a monumental set of stairs, elevated by a podium, and flanked by the smaller forum temples below it. This cluster of forum temples drew the eye to the west end of the forum, but they also pointed beyond themselves to the larger, higher temple looking down on the forum. If Olympian deities dominated the center of Corinth in the Roman era, they did so in the service of the imperial cult. ... If the Archaic Temple had once dominated the city center because of its elevation and size, the Romans undid its dominance by blocking it off from the forum and turning its face westward ... Now Temple E, a Roman creation, controlled the forum. The imperial cult was, therefore, the new religious focal point of Roman Corinth. In this way, Corinth did indeed conform to what we would expect of a traditional Roman colony. It was not, as Pausanias presented the city, a museum of the glorious Greek past.

Comparable things could be said with regard to Miller's analysis of other cities. But even if Miller's assessment were true to the extent he claims, its significance would become doubtful as soon as one took a deeper look and analysed the ideological meta-level beneath the imperial cults. As Miller himself stresses with recourse to Price, emperor worship was an attempt to integrate the external power of Roman rulers into the local worldview by drawing upon suitable categories that already had been used in a similar way under Hellenistic rulers, namely cults of traditional deities.[178] While Miller points to this deep structure in order to show that imperial cults were nothing special, it also demonstrates that the building of temples and shrines was only one concrete expression of a far greater matter, namely how to deal with Roman power, focussed on the person of the emperor. If one accepts Price's

---

[176] Miller, "Cult," 331.

[177] Richard E. DeMaris, "Cults and the Imperial Cult in Early Roman Corinth," in *Zwischen den Reichen: Neues Testament und Römische Herrschaft*; ed. Michael Labahn and Jürgen Zangenberg; TANZ 36; Tübingen: A. Francke, 2002), 82. Most scholars today believe that Temple E should be associated with Octavia or Gens Julia. Of course, much more could be said beyond Temple E; cf. Bruce W. Winter, "The Enigma of the Imperial Cultic Activities and Paul in Corinth," in *Greco-Roman Culture and the New Testament: Studies Commemorating the Centennial of the Pontifical Biblical Institute* (ed. David E. Aune and Frederick E. Brenk; NovTSup 143; Leiden: Brill, 2012), 62–68.

[178] Miller, "Cult," 319–320.

explanation for the use of divine categories for the Roman ruler (as Miller does), there is no reason why the emperor should not have been understood within this framework from the beginning. That the integration into existing cultic forms happened smoothly – as Miller emphasises – only serves to confirm the *intuitive* connection between external power and divine attributes and honours in the native worldview. Hence, it should be concluded that Miller not only fails to demonstrate that imperial cults were not widespread from the beginning of the Principate, but he also does not give any reason to deny the assumption that the interpretation of Augustus as in some sense "divine" was an integral component of Anatolian and Greek worldviews from the beginning.

2.2.2 Perceptibility

Would Paul have been able to perceive the imperial cults that existed in his environment as distinct phenomena, and would he have been able to react to them as such? To be sure, it is correct that Miller emphasises that the imperial cult was only "one cult alongside many others"[179] designed in correspondence to other traditional cults.[180] There might even be some truth in his conclusion that, in the perception of a hypothetical contemporary in Asia Minor or Achaia, the imperial cult might have been only "one cult among many and often ... indistinguishable from the cult of any other god"[181] and "nothing particularly new or exciting."[182] However, this seems to be too simplistic a framework for understanding Paul. True, on the one hand, Price has demonstrated that the imperial cults did not supersede the allegedly degenerated traditional cults.[183] This is reflected by the fact that more money was still being spent on traditional cults than on imperial cults.[184] On the other hand,

---

[179] Miller, "Cult," 316. For a strong critique of an alleged special status of imperial cults in comparison to their religious environment, see also Galinsky, "Cult," 4–5.

[180] Miller, "Cult," 319–320. Cf. Galinsky, "Cult," 4–5, who also emphasises the embeddedness of imperial cults in traditional ones.

[181] Miller, "Cult," 320.

[182] Miller, "Cult," 320.

[183] Price, *Rituals,* 163–165 against, e.g., Hans Lietzmann, *Die Anfänge* (vol. 1 of *Geschichte der Alten Kirche;* 3rd ed.; Berlin: de Gruyter, 1953), 174: "Im westlichen Kleinasien lehren uns noch heute die Ruinen, daß seit der Kaiserzeit im wesentlichen nur noch Kaisertempel gebaut werden. Die alten Götter müssen sich mit dem begnügen, was ihnen der Glaube früherer Jahrhunderte beschert hat, und nur den Heilgöttern weiht der wohl begründete Volksglaube Tempel, die mit Kliniken verbunden sind." Meggitt, "Clothes," 145–148 describes the impact of the imperial cult without the necessary comparative perspective on other pagan cults. When he turns to this aspect (Meggitt, "Clothes," 148–149) he exaggerates the competitive dimension of the imperial cult by focussing on exceptions.

[184] Price, *Rituals,* 165. Of course, how striking this proportion really was in the eyes of the observer largely depends on how different cults were grouped together: Imperial vs.

though, does this mean that there was nothing distinctive about the imperial cults? One could argue[185] that, at least in some cities,[186] imperial cults were more visible through the building of *new* and often quite impressive temples in prominent locations.[187] Also, one should not underestimate that the "numbers and spread" of imperial cults gave them "a supra-local dimension."[188] As Ando observes, "the position of Augustus atop the empire allowed the Mediterranean world to share a deity for the first time."[189] Accordingly, the imperial cult constituted a "religiöses Phänomen, das, wo immer Paulus auch hinkam, eine Konstante bildete und das selbst bei größtem Desinteresse und größter Abneigung nicht zu übersehen oder zu ignorieren war."[190]

At least as important as this general counterargument, however, is the fact that we cannot simply deduce from the integration of the imperial cults into the traditional ones that *Paul* (unlike Miller's hypothetical person) would not have paid special attention to the imperial cult when being confronted with it on his journeys.[191] First, we have to note that Miller's argument only works if

Olympian cults? Augustus vs. Zeus? Imperial cults (of different emperors/members of the imperatorial family) vs. cults of individual traditional deities like Artemis? Especially in the latter scenario, the rise of the imperial cults would have been perceived as an extraordinary phenomenon.

[185] See, e.g., Hardin, *Galatians,* 41 for this kind of argument.

[186] E.g., Zanker, *Augustus,* 295 emphasises the continuity with traditional temples *as well as* the impressive nature of (many) imperial temples: "Die neuen Kaiserheiligtümer waren oft größer und monumentaler als die der alten Götter, unterschieden sich aber in ihrer äußeren Erscheinung von diesen in der Regel nicht." This point is applied too generally by Meggitt, "Clothes," 146.

[187] Price, *Rituals,* 136–146.

[188] Galinsky, "Cult," 9.

[189] Ando, *Ideology,* 407.

[190] Krauter, *Studien,* 113. Cf Ando, *Ideology,* 408: "A century after Augustus ... [a] traveler could recognize at least one temple in every city he visited and would know the prayers for one divinity in every ritual he witnessed; he could identify the dates of imperial holidays in any civic calendar as shared with every municipality in the empire." Cf. Zanker, *Augustus,* 302, who even speaks of "Gleichschaltung" with regard to emperor worship in the east of the Empire. I think that, in light of these considerations, the comment by Schnelle, *Einleitung,* 190 that Paulus "bewegt sich ... mit seiner Mission nicht in 'dem' Imperium Romanum, sondern immer in Sub-Kulturen (Judentum, hellenistische Städte, Provinzen, Landschaften)" becomes less relevant. This bolsters the conclusion by Strecker, "Taktiken," 158: "Für den Apostel war die Welt offenbar weithin mit dem Gebiet des Imperium Romanum identisch."

[191] Cf. Miller, "Cult," 332. Harrison, *Paul,* 35 responds to a similar objection raised by Galinsky, who also emphasises the embeddedness of imperial cults in the context of other cults, that "the Julio-Claudian conception of rule" distinguished this cult from others. However, since cults for other deities also represented an attempt to integrate power that felt alien, it seems doubtful that this really was a striking difference from the perspective of a native person. If one wanted to pursue this line of argument one could maybe argue that, *for Paul,* the first category of power was simply an illusion whereas he recognised the

it is directed against a position which claims that Paul dealt *primarily* with the imperial cult and that it played a special role for him far above all other pagan cults. Such a view seems problematic indeed in light of the textual evidence of the Pauline letters, in which idol worship seems to be understood quite broadly and a good argument can be made that ruler cults are sometimes included. This is probably the case in 1 Cor 8:5. Here the "so called gods" in heaven and on earth are mentioned together (καὶ γὰρ εἴπερ εἰσὶν λεγόμενοι θεοὶ εἴτε ἐν οὐρανῷ εἴτε ἐπὶ γῆς). So, if reference to imperial cults was intended by mentioning "lords," it is not seen as an isolated phenomenon. In light of the differentiation in the next clause (ὥσπερ εἰσὶν θεοὶ πολλοὶ καὶ κύριοι πολλοί), it seems quite plausible that imperial cults could be explicitly in view here as one subcategory of idol worship.[192] This is very much in line with Rom 1:23, where the image of the mortal human (ὁμοιώματι εἰκόνος φθαρτοῦ ἀνθρώπου ...) is aligned with other idols (... καὶ πετεινῶν καὶ τετραπόδων καὶ ἑρπετῶν). There is no good reason to assume that images of the emperor should not be included here.[193] Additionally, a similar argument can be made for Gal 4:8–9. According to Witulski, τὰ ἀσθενῆ καὶ πτωχὰ στοιχεῖα (Gal 4:9) explicitly refer to emperor worship – and, at the same time,

---

second as distinct since it was real – although exaggerated – power. However, reducing the Roman Empire in relation to Paul to the level of *power* takes away its specific *Roman* aspect. In this context the argument of Novenson, "Apostles" seems valid to me.

[192] Fee, *Epistle,* 373 thinks that the second group of the "lords" refers to deities of the mystery cults. Wolfgang Schrage, *Der erste Brief an die Korinther: 1Kor 6,12–11,16* (EKK 7,2; Solothurn: Benziger, 1995), 240–241 thinks this differentiation between traditional and oriental cults is anachronistic. He thinks that the division is only preparatory for 1 Cor 8:6. From my perspective, the option of "lords" as reference to the emperor cult is often too easily dismissed. At least it has the advantage of making sense of the first half of the verse: ὥσπερ, which connects 5a and 5b introduces the experiential illustration of what is said before: There are so called (λεγόμενοι = not true) gods 1) in heaven and 2) on earth (ἐπὶ γῆς), namely human figures. The latter correspond to the many "lords" which are manifest (εἰσίν) – in person and in the form of statues. Similarly Wright, *Faithfulness,* 1284. See Winter, "Enigma," 71 for a change in the imperial cult as background for these verses. (On imperial cults in Corinth in general, cf. Chapter 4, Section 2.2.1.) I do not think that the plural is a counter-argument (so Schrage, *Brief* [II], 240) against imperial references since the current emperor was not the only imperial deity (see Chapter 4, Section 1.2.2.2). I do also not think that the distinction between "übermenschliche[n] Wesen" and their "irdische[n] Repräsentanten" (Schrage, *Brief* [II], 240) makes sense in this context. Interestingly, even Barclay, "Empire," 374 thinks that the emperor might well be included here, but emphasises that they are lumped together with the rest of pagan idolatry: "The Gods 'in heaven and on earth' might well include the objects of the imperial cult, but if so, Paul is not concerned to spell out their Roman profile, nor does he give this form of idolatry any special emphasis or heightened attention."

[193] Cf. Robert Jewett, *Romans: A Commentary* (Hermeneia; Minneapolis: Fortress, 2007), 49.

are associated very closely with the former pagan lifestyle of the Galatians.[194] Accordingly, the mere fact that imperial cults belonged to the same main-category as other traditional cults, by no means implies that Paul would not have been able to perceive them as a clearly distinguishable sub-category also.[195] Even if he did not do so explicitly in his letters, this does not mean that he would not have been able and willing to do so in a fitting situation.[196] Second, we should not forget that perception is determined to a large degree by categories presupposed by a particular worldview.[197] From a Jewish perspective, all pagan cults were a breach of the first(/and second) commandment of the Decalogue (Exod 20:3 + 4–6 and Deut 5:7 + 8–10) and in conflict with the belief of monotheism.[198] But the deification of a human being also

---

[194] Thomas Witulski, *Die Adressaten des Galaterbriefes: Untersuchungen zur Gemeinde von Antiochia ad Pisidiam* (FRLANT 193; Göttingen: Vandenhoeck & Ruprecht, 2000). However, I am not convinced that the "elements" really have to be a new entity, different from earlier deities, cf. p. 143.

[195] Against John M. G. Barclay, "Paul, Roman Religion and the Emperor: Mapping the Point of Conflict," in *Pauline Churches and Diaspora Jews* (ed. John M. G. Barclay; WUNT 275; Tübingen: Mohr Siebeck, 2011), 355: "He recognizes that there are 'many gods' and 'many lords' (1 Cor 8.5), but he shows no interest in their differing identities, lumping them together into a single category." Johannes Woyke, *Götter, 'Götzen,' Götterbilder: Aspekte einer paulinischen 'Theologie der Religionen'* (BZNW 132; Berlin: de Gruyter, 2005), 454, who is quite reluctant to see references to imperial cults in the passages he analyses, concludes that it is "[b]emerkenswert ... dass *Paulus religionsphänomenologische Differenzierungen geläufig zu sein scheinen*" (italics original). Paul was a careful observer of his pagan environment and we should not underestimate his ability with regard to imperial cults.

[196] I think the sobering comments by Wright, *Faithfulness*, 382 on our textual evidence hit the nail on the head.

[197] For the relevance of the category of worldview for NT studies, see Nicholas T. Wright, *The New Testament and the People of God* (COQG 1; Minneapolis: Fortress, 1992), 31–144. For a non-Jewish example, see Pausanias's description of Hadrian's temple of Zeus in Athens (Pausanias, *Descr.* 1.18.6–9). The juxtaposition of imperial and traditional motifs does not hide the fact that there is a subtle critical subtext marking out the local-Greek over against the imperial-Roman (Whitmarsh, "Resistance," 62–68).

[198] Of course, one has to be careful not to imagine Jewish monotheism in too abstract a way. Barclay, *Jews*, 429–434 has rightly emphasised that Jewish monotheism was largely defined on the level of *worship*. Accordingly, he argues that the monotheism of Jews in the Diaspora is better described in negative terms by rejection of (a) the "alien cult," (b) the "pluralist cult," and (c) the "iconic cult." Goodenough, *Politics*, 110–115 goes further when arguing that Philo's *real* problem in *Legat.* 118 is not Jewish monotheism (or detestation of images) but most importantly Jewish particularism and patriotism. But I think he overestimates the "divinity" attributed by Philo to the patriarchs and especially to Moses. See on this Larry Hurtado, *One God, One Lord: Early Christian Devotion and Ancient Jewish Monotheism* (2nd ed.; repr.; London: T&T Clark, 2005), 59–63; Louis H. Feldman, *Philo's Portrayal of Moses in the Context of Ancient Judaism* (CJAn 15; Notre Dame: University of Notre Dame Press, 2007), 332–348. Also, he underestimates the one dis-

implied the more specific transgression of the border between human creature and creator. A mortal simply was not to perceive of himself as divine (cf. 2 Macc 9:12: μὴ θνητὸν ὄντα ἰσόθεα φρονεῖν). Even though all pagan cults ultimately constitute a common category from a Jewish-Christian perspective, we should be careful not to deduce from this, as Miller does, that there is a one-to-one correspondence between the de facto presence of cults as accessible via the archaeological record and the respective significance a contemporary Jew would have attached to it. Miller's argument would be very effective if he were able to show that Paul really was not able to recognise imperial cults as such. But this is not what the historical evidence suggests. It rather makes it very plausible that a Jew in the first century was well-aware of the imperatorial deifying hubris and of the resulting conflict with his or her faith. We have already discussed one important example, Philo's criticism of Caligula, especially in *Legat.* 118 (Smallwood), which defines the "most horrible of blasphemies" as the fundamental "apparent transformation of the created, destructible nature of man into the uncreated, indestructible nature of God." The fact that the constant danger of such a sacrilege sharpened Philo's *perception* of such cults in general is demonstrated by Philo's eloquent description of Augustus's cults (*Legat.* 149–151 [Smallwood]):[199]

[T]he whole world voted him honours equal to those of the Olympians. Temples, gateways, vestibules, and colonnades bear witness to this, so that the imposing buildings erected in any city, new or old, are surpassed by the beauty and size of the temples of Caesar, especially in our own Alexandria. There is no other precinct like our so-called 'Augusteum,' the temple of Caesar, the protector of sailors. It is situated high up, opposite the sheltered harbours, and is very large and conspicuous; it is filled with dedications on a unique scale, and is surrounded on all sides by paintings, statues, and objects of gold and silver. The extensive precinct is furnished with colonnades, libraries, banqueting-halls, groves, gateways, open spaces, unroofed enclosures, and everything that makes for lavish decoration. It gives hope of safety to sailors when they set out to sea and when they return.

Josephus also expresses the conviction of an unbridgeable divide between God and human beings, e.g., in *A.J.* 18.256 or in *C. Ap.* 2.75–76. In the first, the fact that Caligula deified himself (ἐκθειάζων ἑαυτόν) is described as a transgression of human boundaries (ἐξίστατο τοῦ ἀνθρωπίνως). On the latter, Barclay comments: "Josephus insists on a clear distinction between humanity and God, with the implication that even emperors cannot cross this line."[200] In

---

cussed with regard to Caligula. The *rationale* Philo gives for why Caligula's behaviour constituted the worst sacrilege (ἀσέβημα) seems entirely plausible (even if one prefers to detect hidden motives). Nevertheless, the aspect of disdain for specifically *Roman* hubris might well have played a role in Paul's evaluation of imperial cults in comparison to other pagan cults (see Chapter 5, Section 1.4.3).

[199] On this, see the last chapter, Chapter 4, Section 1.2.2.3.

[200] John M. G. Barclay, *Flavius Josephus: Against Apion* (FJTC 10; Leiden: Brill, 2007), 208.

the NT itself, this separation of human and divine sphere (which is also presupposed, e.g., in John 10:33) is most vehemently emphasised in Acts 12:21–23, where the blurring of this line (12:22: Θεοῦ φωνὴ καὶ οὐκ ἀνθρώπου) is equated with not giving honour to God (οὐκ ἔδωκεν τὴν δόξαν τῷ θεω) and judged immediately (both 12:23).[201] Since this conviction is deeply rooted in Jewish creational monotheism itself,[202] we have every reason to assume that it was also an important lens through which Paul perceived his environment. This is all the more true because we can assume that Caligula's attempt to erect an image in the temple in Jerusalem[203] evidently came as a shock (just like the ἔκπληξις in Philo, *Legat.* 189) that left its mark on early Christianity for decades.[204] Hence, it seems very plausible historically to attribute to Paul the same sensitivity we do not deny his contemporaries to have had.

Additionally, as a follower of the Messiah Jesus, the Lord and Saviour[205] of the whole world, Paul's attentiveness to exaggerated imperial claims probably was even heightened in comparison to his fellow Jews. Once we recognise the specifically *christological* character of Paul's apocalyptic epistemology,[206] we discover that it functions in quite the opposite way Barclay says it does. When Paul agrees with the Corinthians that "an idol in this world is nothing" and that "there is no god but one" (οὐδὲν εἴδωλον ἐν κόσμῳ καὶ ὅτι οὐδεὶς θεὸς εἰ μὴ εἷς; 1 Cor 8:4), he would have been still aware of an important difference between imperial and other pagan statues. While the idol is nothing (1 Cor 10:19), demonic forces are connected with it (1 Cor 10:20). But Paul would have known perfectly well that *imperial* statues did represent

---

[201] Cf. Josephus, *A.J.* 19.343–350. Cf. Klauck, "Stimme," 251–267 who thinks that the motif of the "voice" is an indirect criticism of Nero.

[202] Travis B. Williams, "The Divinity and Humanity of Caesar in 1Peter 2,13," *ZNW* 105 (2014): 143 muses with regard to 1 Pet 2:13 "why an ontological distinction would be drawn at this point, given that it would amount to a misrepresentation of the actual practices and beliefs surrounding the cult of the emperor." Although I fully appreciate Williams's recognition of recent scholarship on the imperial cult, I do not think that we should assume first-century Jews to have had a similarly nuanced perception. It is Jewish creational monotheism, not "Christian-Platonism," which is the lens through which claims of divinity with regard to the emperor are regarded as blasphemous.

[203] Tacitus, *Hist.* 5.9; Josephus, *A.J.* 18.256–309 and *B.J.* 2.184–203.

[204] Most scholars assume that this conflict is reflected in Mark 13:14: (τὸ βδέλυγμα τῆς ἐρημώσεως ἑστηκότα ὅπου οὐ δεῖ) and Matt 24:15 (τὸ βδέλυγμα τῆς ἐρημώσεως ... ἐν τόπῳ ἁγίῳ). Cf. also 2 Thess 2:4.

[205] "Saviour" is not a frequent Pauline designation for Christ. But it is striking that the only time it occurs in the undisputed letters, namely in Phil 3:20, it is used in the context of a reference to the "citizenship" (πολίτευμα).

[206] Cf. also Barclay, "Paul," 358.

a very concrete person sitting in Rome.[207] The message both kinds of cults conveyed were equally pretentious, but in some sense the latter were to be taken more seriously since they at least pointed to a concrete rival of the Messiah Jesus.[208] There is good reason to assume that even for pagan citizens there was a difference between the traditional gods and Augustus as the bringer of the new age.[209] How much more would Paul – not only a Jew with great eschatological hopes but also a follower of the Messiah Jesus who believed that these hopes had been fulfilled in him – have perceived this claim? If we agree with Barclay's judgement on Paul's emotions, according to which the apostle spoke of idol worship only with "aggression in his voice,"[210] we should also not underestimate his sensibility with regard to emperor worship as a special provocation.

Nevertheless, while this discussion does counter the argument which denies that Paul would have perceived the imperial cult as such, there is still a note of caution we ought to heed, resulting from this discussion: Whether a specific Pauline expression (e.g., "son of god") refers to the imperial cult or not has to be evaluated in each individual case. It has to be decided carefully whether the wording in question refers to (a) the pagan cultic realm in general, (b) the cult of a specific deity, (c) the imperial cults, or (d) something else completely.[211]

2.3 Other Expressions of Imperial Ideology

We have already pointed out several times that it is not pertinent to restrict the potential conflict that Paul might have perceived between his message and his Roman context to certain buildings like temples. Miller himself is quite aware of the limited focus of his work:[212]

> I am concerned here only with the imperial cult, that is, with the ritual worship of living or dead emperors, most commonly in the form of animal sacrifice (but also in other forms, such as the offering of incense, etc.). This is the subject of Price's research, and this is what Pauline scholars mean when they refer to the 'imperial cult' that supposedly made up the fabric of society. My aim is to modify and often deny what others have argued. I am not, however, concerned with the much greater issue of views of the emperor or the empire generally, or with the many other complex subjects that traditionally fall under the subject

---

[207] Similarly Wright, *Faithfulness*, 1284: "Paul can think of the Olympians on the one hand, and know that they are fiction; of Caesar on the other hand, and know that his theological claims are false."

[208] I thus cannot agree with the conclusion of Krauter, *Studien*, 124 that the lack of clear criticism of emperor worship demonstrates "dass er für ihn eine Frage von untergeordneter Bedeutung war."

[209] See, e.g., Witulski, *Adressaten*, 149.

[210] Barclay, "Paul," 356.

[211] Cf. Chapter 6, Section 3.2.

[212] Miller, "Cult," 317.

of 'Roman imperial ideology.' Thus, prayers for the emperor's genius, the portrayal of a deified Augustus on coins, or the inscriptional propagation of the emperor's virtues, though related to the imperial cult, will not be discussed.

Hence, in order to appropriately assess the presence of imperial ideology, it is necessary to widen the focus from concrete imperial cults to other forms of expressing the status of the Empire and of its personification, the emperor. Interestingly, following the statement quoted and "disproven" by Miller, Crossan and Reed also clarify what they mean by "emperor worship," which they believe was present in "any city that Paul visited": "Archaeologists find inscriptions for the imperial cult, usually. They find statues of the imperial family, usually. They find emperors on coins, always."[213] Hence, they already have a wider focus compared to Miller's analysis, which means that he is, in effect, discussing a straw man.

We have already noted that concrete ritual acts are based on an understanding of the divinity of the emperor, which is a reaction to the experience of external power. This consistent claim to power was expressed in a number of different ways, which were accessible to Paul.[214] The transformation of public space was not limited to imperial temples but also expressed by non-cultic statues.[215] The reconfiguration of public space also influenced locations of leisure like the theatre.[216] The image of the emperor was especially present through the minting of coins. Coins used a pictorial language that was easy to understand and widespread.[217] They were not just neutral representations of

---

[213] Crossan and Reed, *Search,* 143.

[214] Cf. on this also Meggitt, "Clothes," 151–153 and Strecker, "Taktiken," 137–141.

[215] See, for example, Hardin, *Galatians,* 30–32. However, in his discussion he does not focus specifically enough on the period relevant to Paul. For the reorganisation of public spaces begun by Augustus, see above all Paul Zanker, *Augustus und die Macht der Bilder* (5th ed.; München: C. H. Beck, 2008).

[216] Hardin, *Galatians,* 31: "These structures not only enhanced the city's appearance and civic pride, but the forms of leisure that attended them were often occasions for imperial sacrifices and festivals. Even when cultic rites were not being celebrated, the structures themselves were continual reminders of the emperor's greatness. The overwhelming imperial statues postured behind the stage of theatre on the colonnaded façade *(scaenae frons),* for example, gave the impression that the rulers in Rome were actually present." However, the theatre was not only a means for dissemination of imperial ideology, but also an opportunity to negotiate it critically (see Jeff Jay, "The Problem of the Theater in Early Judaism," *JSJ* 44 [2013]: 218–253). On the transformation of public space in the cities of Asia Minor, see also Jürgen Süss, "Kaiserkult und Urbanistik: Kultbezirke für römische Kaiser in kleinasiatischen Städten," in *Die Praxis der Herrscherverehrung in Rom und seinen Provinzen* (ed. Hubert Cancik and Konrad Hitzl; Tübingen: Mohr Siebeck, 2003), 249–281.

[217] Cf. Peter Herz, "Emperors: Caring for the Empire and Their Successors," in *A Companion to Roman Religion* (ed. Jörg Rüpke; BCAW; Blackwell: Chichester, 2011), 311. On religious motifs on Roman coins in general, see Jonathan Williams, "Religion and Roman

the emperor but often conveyed specific claims of Caesar.[218] It has often been noted that the representation of the emperor on coins was a true novelty, which began with Augustus. Before him, almost no Roman had been pictured on a coin whereas images of Augustus on coins are known from approximately 200 cities.[219] Because of their use in everyday situations, coins were "[e]ines der wirksamsten Mittel antiker Propaganda" and were able to communicate "Herrscher-Ideologien bis in die entlegendsten Teile eines Landes."[220] Mark 12:13–17 demonstrates this impressively even for the time frame relevant to our discussion.[221]

Imperial ideology also influenced the temporal dimension. Fixing New Year's Day to the 23rd of September, the birthday of Augustus, probably is the best known example in this category (see above all *OGIS* 458). This was a significant intervention in the everyday reality of the population. As Price notes, humans often have the tendency "to conceive of the calendar not as arbitrary divisions of a continuum, but as actually regulating time itself."[222]

Coins," in *A Companion to Roman Religion* [ed. Jörg Rüpke; BCAW; Blackwell: Chichester, 2011], 143–163). For an example of the integration of coinage material into the larger context of evidence for the imperial cults, see Barbette S. Spaeth, "Imperial Cult in Roman Corinth: A Response to Karl Galinsky's 'The Cult of the Roman Emperor: Uniter or Divider?,'" in *Rome and Religion: A Cross-Disciplinary Dialogue on the Imperial Cult* (ed. Jeffrey Brodd and Jonathan L. Reed; SBLWGRW 5. Atlanta: Scholars Press, 2011), 61–82.

[218] Cf., for example, Hardin, *Galatians,* 29 or the contribution of Larry J. Kreitzer, *Striking New Images: Roman Imperial Coinage and the New Testament World* (JSNTSup 134; Sheffield: Sheffield Academic, 1996), 69–98 on apotheosis. Fergus Millar, "State and Subject: The Impact of Monarchy," in *Caesar Augustus: Seven Aspects* (ed. Fergus Millar and Erich Segal; Oxford: Clarendon, 1984), 45 advises against calling the conveyed message "propaganda" and says instead: "What we have is once again a set of visible and incontrovertible examples of how people construed the world in which they lived; or, to put it another way, of the symbols which they thought it appropriate to display publicly." However, see also the emphasis of Price, *Rituals,* 172–173 who argues that – all local initiative notwithstanding – the emperor himself was involved in the choice of motifs. See Andrew Burnett, "The Augustan Revolution Seen from the Mints of the Provinces," *JRS* 101 (2011): 1–30 for a recent defence of relative provincial freedom with regard to the motifs.

[219] Millar, "State," 44–45. Cf. recently Burnett, "Revolution," 21. On non-imperial portraits, see p. 22.

[220] Rainer Riesner, "Geographie, Archäologie, Epigraphik und Numismatik," in *Das Studium des Neuen Testaments* (ed. Heinz-Werner Neudorfer and Eckhard J. Schnabel; 2nd ed. Wuppertal: R. Brockhaus, 2006), 208.

[221] Cf. Riesner, "Geographie," 208–209. Cf. also the suggestions by Kreitzer, *Images* for numismatic evidence as a background for other NT passages.

[222] Price, *Rituals,* 106. He points to an amusing modern analogy: "Even in this century, admittedly in the House of Lords, one can find a protest that the change of summer time resulted in a drought and flood by tampering with the natural order of things."

Accordingly, Augustus's birthday became part of the "natural order" and his achievements were brought to collective consciousness annually.[223] This effect was reinforced by imperial festivals in shorter intervals.[224] The idea of a golden age established by Augustus was also vividly portrayed and promoted by the authors Vergil and Horace.[225] However, we must be careful not to postulate direct dependence too quickly. Wright, for example, uses Roman literature to extract quite a detailed Roman *Heilsgeschichte*.[226] It is certainly important to reconstruct Roman ideology as found in the literary sources in order to know what we are looking for. But it would also be necessary to show as a next step how this narrative could have been communicated to Paul – either in written form or by means of symbols.[227] Written sources that should not be underestimated in that regard are honorific inscriptions, which Paul would have been able to read in many places.[228]

In light of these means, the general assumption that Paul came into contact with Roman ideology in many diverse ways seems well-founded. And even

---

[223] Price, *Rituals*, 106.

[224] For imperial festivals, see Price, *Rituals*, 101–132, who also demonstrates that they were not only the elite's business but that the whole population was involved and that they also affected the surrounding region. The implication of a larger radius is not taken seriously enough by Miller, "Cult" (see Section 2.2.1).

[225] As mentioned above (Chapter 4, Section 1.2.1), see on the role of literature especially Georgi, "Prophet," Hardin, *Galatians*, 34–36 and Wright, *Faithfulness*, 298–311. As with all our sources for imperial ideology, we need to ask the critical questions whether (a) they could have been known to Paul in some way or (b) they could reflect widespread ideas that could have been accessible to Paul in other form. For a balanced discussion on the question whether Paul could have had contact with Vergil's *Aeneid* (with negative answer) see Harrison, *Paul*, 25–26.

[226] Wright, *Faithfulness*, 298–311. What can certainly be assumed is an awareness of a conflict beetween two versions of a "fundamentale Zeitenwende" in the history of the world (Strecker, "Taktiken," 157–158).

[227] There is a certain tension between the comment of Wright, *Faithfulness*, 294 on the complexity of Roman literary ideology and the idea that Paul was aware of it in a way comparable to Wright's own summary. The latter conviction is expressed, for example, on p. 306): "Though the components of this great narrative are so radically different from the great single story in which the apostle Paul believed himself to be living, the overall shape, and indeed the very *idea* of there being such an overall shape to a centuries-long story, would I think have been recognized at once." Can we assume that Paul had comparable insights into Roman literary culture or that other forms of expression, like coins, could convey these rather complex ideas?

[228] Harrison, *Paul*, 25. However, the exact *value* of this evidence has to be judged carefully. There is the intriguing possibility that Paul knew the *Res gest. divi Aug*. This might be of interest for the interpretation of the verb θριαμβεύω in 2 Cor 2:14 (cf. *Res gest. divi Aug*. 4.1).

though ca. 90% of the addressees of his letters probably were illiterate,[229] the apostle probably could assume basic knowledge of Roman ideology among his congregations "derived through reading or, more likely, by other means (aural, visual, theatre)."[230] Also, we should not overrate the significance of the ability to read in light of what we have learned with regard to Paul's use of the Greek translation of the Hebrew Bible. Pauline research has established a multitude of, often very subtle, scriptural references – independent of the question to what degree Paul's readers would have been able to identify and understand these quotes, allusions and echoes.[231]

2.4 Conclusions

Our willingness to accept critical subtexts should depend upon the degree to which the object subject to potential criticism was not only under a taboo (Chapter 4, Section 1) but also prominent in the context of the writer in question. I fully appreciate the cautionary note not to overemphasise the influence of imperial motifs – especially cultic rites – on Paul's writing. Nevertheless, I think it is reasonable to conclude with Galinsky that there is "[n]o question ... that early Christians had experience with the cult of the emperor and, on a far larger scale, the Roman system in general, and they engaged with it."[232] However, this result is quite vague and no conclusions regarding specific elements of imperial ideology are possible on this basis. In order to establish specific intertextual links between Roman propaganda and Pauline wordings, it is not enough simply to refer to a very general "Romanisation" of the city Paul is writing to or from. Rather, it is indispensable to demonstrate the accessibility of the specific motif in question to Paul and/or his readers. Hafemann, for example, argues in detail that θριαμβεύω with the direct object was used as a terminus technicus for leading captives in a triumphal procession and was almost synonymous with "to lead sb. to death"[233] and that this is the

---

[229] Cf. the discussion in Harrison, *Paul*, 20–22 with occasionally more optimistic evaluations depending on location.

[230] Harrison, *Paul*, 20.

[231] Cf. Hays, *Echoes*, 29, who distinguishes between implied and actual reader. For a thought-provoking discussion of the reading abilities of the audience of Paul's letters, see Christopher D. Stanley, *Arguing with Scripture: The Rhetoric of Quotations in the Letters of Paul* (New York: T&T Clark, 2004), 38–61.

[232] Galinsky, "Cult," 10.

[233] Scott J. Hafemann, *Suffering and the Spirit: An Exegetical Study of 2 Cor 2:14–3:3 within the Context of the Corinthian Correspondence* (WUNT II 19; Tübingen: Mohr Siebeck 1986), 39.

intended meaning in 2 Cor 2:14. However, he does not demonstrate that the execution of captives was a well-known part of this rite for Paul.[234]

The hypothesis of a *counter*-imperial subtext in Paul rests not only on the assumption that Paul had contact with elements of Roman ideology but also on the assumption that he judged them negatively. Thus, we turn next to the question of how these aspects probably were integrated into Paul's worldview (Roman context → Paul) and what kind of constraints his personality would have placed on the way he would have expressed such thoughts (Paul → ecclesial context).

---

[234] So also Larry J. Kreitzer, *Images*, 128. Kreitzer thinks that the numismatic evidence supports Hafemann's claims. Although this is the correct procedure, I do not think that the material Kreitzer cites can bear that weight.

Chapter 5

Pauline Context

1. Counter-Imperial Attitude?

1.1 Introduction

This chapter deals with the question whether it is possible to substantiate that Paul had a critical attitude towards the Empire. In the last chapter, we briefly discussed whether the claims of imperial propaganda were accessible, and we concluded positively that this assumption is generally plausible. But is there any evidence that this ideology of the Empire was also picked up critically by Paul? What is needed, then, is an analysis of Paul's *worldview* with regard to such a critical attitude.[1] This task also includes taking into account the *literary context* of his letters, especially the remarks in Rom 13:1–7, which deal explicitly with the state. We will need to ask whether they can be integrated into a coherent sketch of Paul's worldview.

We will begin with a look at N. T. Wright's suggestion for integrating the Empire into the whole of Pauline theology found in his book *Paul: In Fresh Perspective*. We will then compare it to John M. G. Barclay's outline, which makes explicit reference to Wright's contribution and aims to correct it. We will then evaluate the strengths and weaknesses and suggest an own synthesis.

1.2 N. T. Wright: The Empire as Oppressor of God's People

As we have seen, Wright in his work briefly introduces Hays's method for identifying echoes and argues for its applicability to counter-imperial echoes in Paul (for a summary, see Chapter 2, Section 3.2.1). He then provides an

---

[1] Schreiber, "Paulus," 343 asks this question with regard to the early Christian attitude towards Rome in general. Since the Christians did not belong to the elite, which was generally more critical towards the Roman Empire, and since the Christians would have been regarded with enmity by their fellow citizens, he thinks that "eine kritische Wahrnehmung der politischen Verhältnisse seitens der ersten Christen" is probable. With regard to Paul, I think that we can have a more precise reconstruction of his attitude by considering the place of Rome in his worldview.

1. Counter-Imperial Attitude 111

overview of the Roman context of Paul's proclamation[2] followed by a detailed exposition of the Jewish tradition in which the apostle stood.[3] According to Wright, already the Old Testament evidence demonstrates a certain ambivalence:

> The rulers are wicked and will be judged, especially when they persecute God's people. But God wants the world to be ruled, rather than to descend into anarchy and chaos, and his people must learn to live under pagan rule even though it means constant vigilance against compromise with paganism itself.[4]

Wright traces this double strand through the whole intertestamental period within a wide stream of early Judaism.[5] He argues that this position is ultimately based on two cornerstones of the Jewish worldview: creation and covenant. The god YHWH, who created the world, one day will also redeem it from evil. In the meanwhile, it is his will that the world is administered in an orderly way. Thus, even pagan governments can partially anticipate God's recreational work.[6] Nevertheless, the stewards are themselves responsible to God and one day will be held accountable. Then the people of God will be freed from their oppressors because the covenant God will be faithful to his promises.[7]

---

[2] Wright, *Perspective*, 62–65 begins his argument with a sketch of the ideology underlying the Roman Empire. It was construed around the pillar values of the Republic: Freedom, Justice, Peace, Salvation (Wright, *Perspective*, 63). These concepts are brought into focus in the one person of the emperor who guaranteed their reality (Wright, *Perspective*, 63). The proclamation of this achievement was "good news" (Wright, *Perspective*, 64). In the works of the historians and poets this relationship between Roman rule and cosmic order became an eschatological narrative which found its climax in the present (Wright, *Perspective*, 64). This ideology was made visible in the whole Roman Empire by impressive symbols, such as the depiction of the imperial family on coins: "From Spain to Syria, everybody knew about Rome, what it stood for, what it did, and who was in charge of it." (Wright, *Perspective*, 64). The integrating factor of this ideology was the ruler cult which was based on the post-mortem apotheosis of the former ruler by which the new emperor became "son of god" (Wright, *Perspective*, 64). Especially in the east of the Empire, where the worship of rulers as divine was common, the cult flourished. Festivals in honour of the emperor were celebrated, priesthoods installed, statues of the imperial family adorned with motifs of the pantheon (Wright, *Perspective*, 65). According to Wright, this is the cultural context in which Paul proclaimed *his* gospel (Wright, *Perspective*, 65). Compare my own summary of the Roman context in Chapter 4.

[3] Wright, *Perspective*, 65–69.

[4] Wright, *Perspective*, 66.

[5] Wright, *Perspective*, 67–68. This summary rests on the analysis of Wright, *New Testament*, 145–338

[6] Wright, *Faithfulness*, 381 also emphasises this positive aspect.

[7] Cf. Wright, *Perspective*, 68–69. Wright's procedure of focussing on *pagan* (not simply Roman) foreign rule over the Jews is a methodological advantage over against Krauter, *Studien*, 104–110, for instance, who gives a good summary of the diversity of stances

Wright argues that, as a Jewish thinker, Paul can also be located in this framework. Accordingly, the role the Roman Empire played for Paul, can be understood in relationship to the basic elements of the Jewish worldview.[8] The conviction that a creator God exists demands belief in a future intervention and restoration; the belief in a covenant implies the liberation of God's people from pagan oppression. This framework, which Paul held as a devout Jew, was then modified by his experience of the Messiah and the Spirit of God. Paul's *messianic* theology confesses Jesus as king, Lord, and Saviour. His apocalyptic theology interprets Jesus's death and resurrection as the revelation of the faithfulness of God.[9] In contrast to his Jewish predecessors and contemporaries, Paul thus thinks that death is already defeated and the reign of God has already begun. This also means that with the defeat of death the strongest weapon of those who suppress has been disarmed:[10]

> It is the inauguration of God's new world, the new creation with the unstoppable power of the creator God. The resurrection of the crucified Messiah thus functions in Paul's thought both as history, as theology, and (not least) as symbol, the symbol of a power which upstages anything military power can do.[11]

The *Christusereignis* plays an important role in Wright's system – but only as a modifying element of a thoroughly Jewish theology. Bringing together the product of this modification with Caesar's claim would lead us to expect just what, according to Wright, we do in fact find in Paul's letters, i.e., that Jesus is Lord and Caesar is not[12] – a claim that Wright then tries to substantiate through his exegesis of the Pauline letters.[13]

Although in this paradigm Paul is very sceptical of non-Jewish foreign rule, it nevertheless allows room for a positive evaluation of governmental structures that ensure order in a fallen world. Therefore, the explicitly positive evaluation of the Roman Empire, which can be found on the surface of the text in Rom 13:1–7, makes sense (cf. "Thematic Coherence").[14] In contrast to other proponents of a counter-imperial reading of Paul, Wright thus does not have to suggest a special interpretation of this passage.[15] Instead, the

---

towards Roman rule but in my mind does not address the underlying Jewish ideological structures which shaped this perception.

[8] The other elements of this worldview are discussed earlier in the book: creation, covenant, Messiah, and apocalyptic (Wright, *Perspective*, 21–39 and 40–58).

[9] Cf. Wright, *Perspective*, 69.

[10] Wright, *Perspective*, 69.

[11] Wright, *Perspective*, 70.

[12] Wright, *Perspective*, 69.

[13] Wright, *Perspective*, 69–79.

[14] Wright, *Perspective*, 78–79. Cf. also his more detailed discussion of this passage in Wright, "Letter," 715–723.

[15] Cf. Barclay, "Empire," 372.

demand for a peaceable civilian attitude constitutes a "dialectic counterpart"[16] to the more implicit critical sideswipes against imperial ideology: "[I]t is important that his readers do not take his covert polemic against the imperial ideology as a coded call to a Christian version of the so-called fourth philosophy."[17]

1.3 John M. G. Barclay: The Empire as a Consciously Ignored Peripheral Phenomenon

John M. G. Barclay has directed some important questions at Wright's suggestion. He locates the Empire at the periphery of Paul's theology and interests. According to him, it is not even an autonomous entity. What *is* foundational to Paul's worldview is the battle between different cosmic powers – spirit and grace on the one side and sin, death and flesh (sometimes also Satan and demons) on the other.[18] In this cosmic spiritual battle, the Roman Empire only plays a subordinate role:

> In fact, Paul's most subversive act, vis-à-vis the Roman empire, was not to oppose or upstage it, but to relegate it to the rank of a dependent and derivative entity, denied a distinguishable name or significant role in the story of the world … Paul's language of 'powers' thus denotes comprehensive features of reality which penetrate (what we call) the 'political' sphere, but only as it is enmeshed in larger and more comprehensive forcefields.[19]

This means that the Empire is not recognised *as such,* and accordingly, we should not expect Paul to interact with its claims explicitly, since the *Christusereignis* is happening at a much more encompassing frontline.[20] For Barclay, this does not mean that Paul's gospel is *apolitical*. Elements which *we* would attribute to the Roman Empire might have belonged to Paul's categories of flesh, sin, and death.[21] The Roman Empire is not the enemy, but it can include evil elements. At the same time, Rom 13:1–7 demonstrates that political authority is not located solely in the realm of sin but partially also in the realm of divine power.[22] Barclay deduces that we should not expect con-

---

[16] Barclay, "Empire," 372.
[17] Wright, "Letter," 719.
[18] Barclay, "Empire," 383. Similarly McKnight and Modica, "Conclusion," 212, although from a different perspective: "[T]he New Testament writers affirm that Jesus is Lord, not with the sole intent of debunking Caesar and his empire, but to offer a stark contrast between the kingdom of God and the kingdom of Satan."
[19] Barclay, "Empire," 383–384.
[20] Barclay, "Empire," 385. Cf. Barclay, "Empire," 387.
[21] Barclay, "Empire," 385.
[22] Barclay, "Empire," 385. Similarly Harrill, *Paul,* 77: "Matters are much more complicated than simply asking an either/or question – whether Paul was for or against the Roman Empire – because he likely was both."

crete criticism of the Empire in Paul since talking about it explicitly would have been too much acknowledgement already.[23]

1.4 Evaluation: What is the Real Plight?

1.4.1 Apocalyptic Mindset as Sufficient Proof?

The dialogue between Wright and Barclay points to the decisive question: What is the real frontline in God's *heilsgeschichtlichem* drama? In what follows, we will discuss the character of the fundamental "plight" of God's people as seen by Paul and how it relates to the Roman Empire.[24]

Joel R. White tries to solve this problem by analysing Paul's tradition-historical context. White, who argues *against* specific counter-imperial echoes in Paul, nevertheless thinks that it can be shown that Rome played quite a central (and negative) role in Paul's worldview. On the one hand, White criticises the imperial background that is often assumed for some *christological* statements,[25] and by means of exegeting select prime examples of counter-imperial subtexts (1 Thess 4:13–17; 1 Thess 5:3; Phil 3:20), he tries to demonstrate that the assumption of a counter-imperial intention does not shed light on the meaning of the passages.[26] On the other hand, White thinks that it is very plausible historically that Paul's gospel had traits subverting imperial ideology.[27] He justifies this position by arguing that Paul's worldview was deeply rooted in Jewish – especially Danielic – eschatology in which the "fourth kingdom" was equated with Rome and in which God's liberating action was expected.[28] He concludes:

First century Jews believed they were living during the time of Daniel's fourth kingdom, which they identified with Rome. They eagerly awaited the end of Rome's hegemony and its replacement by God's eternal kingdom and were convinced that the time allotted by God for Daniel's fourth kingdom was drawing to its conclusion.[29]

---

[23] Barclay, "Empire," 386.

[24] Over thirty years ago Parrott, "Thought," 225–254 recognised the importance of the context of Paul's wider theology. He also correctly noted the Jewish attitude towards Gentiles (p. 226) and the transformation of Paul's Jewish worldview by the Christ event (p. 226–227). However, he failed to track the modification of this Jewish stance towards foreign rule but turned instead to other modifications in Paul's theology. Hence, his discussion lacks precision with regard to the subject matter.

[25] See his discussion of imperial vocabulary, especially κύριος (White, "Subtexts," 308–311). In the categories of Hays, one could say that he is criticising the claim that the "volume" is high.

[26] Cf. White, "Subtexts," 311–315.

[27] White, "Subtexts," 315.

[28] White, "Subtexts," 316–325.

[29] White, "Subtexts," 325.

He demonstrates carefully that Paul presupposes this tradition in 1 Cor 15:24–28, 1 Cor 6:2, 1 Cor 7:29–31, Rom 13:11–12a, Rom 16:20a, and 2 Thess 2:3–4. Accordingly, Paul shared the eschatological expectation of Jewish apocalypticism that YHWH would intervene in the course of history in order to end the suppression of his (in Paul's eyes newly defined) people by the last Danielic (Roman) kingdom.[30] For White, this implies that the "the subversive quality" of the Pauline gospel cannot be denied:

> Daniel was well-known and broadly accepted by Jews in the Second Temple period, not least among them Paul, who demonstrates familiarity with this narrative and implicitly affirms it at several points. This is one clear area of continuity between first-century Judaism and the Apostle or, to put it another way, between the pre-Damascus Saul and the post-Damascus Paul. While the standard Jewish apocalyptic framework was thoroughly modified by the Apostle to account for the central place he came to assign Christ in God's plan of salvation, its basic structure remained essentially the same.[31]

However, I am under the impression that the evidence White adduces cannot bear the weight of his conclusions. After all, reference to and use of Danielic *language* does not automatically imply that the *content* of the concepts thus designated also was in continuity with the Jewish tradition.[32] Even if one were willing to accept the notion that in Paul's eyes the structure of the eschatological conflict basically remained the same before and after Paul's *Damaskuserlebnis*, it would not follow that the different roles were still filled by the same cast.[33] After all, God's people are redefined also. Why not their enemy, too? White does not demonstrate that the correlation between God's enemy and the Roman Empire can still be presupposed. The entity that is explicitly mentioned as the "last enemy" *is not Rome but death*.[34] It is certainly true that, for Paul, however "universal" his new conception of the conflict

---

[30] White, "Subtexts," 325–333.

[31] White, "Subtexts," 333.

[32] This is analogous to the way some modern Christian circles use biblical apocalyptic language but take it to mean something decidedly different than originally intended."

[33] Krauter, *Studien,* 103 correctly remarks that labelling Paul a "Jew" does not help much in this regard but that the decisive question is "was für ein Jude Paulus vor und nach seinem Damaskuserlebnis war." Cf. Krauter, *Studien,* 101 on apocalyptic themes which, he says, are christologically orientated. This implies that it is wrong to speak "von einer bruchlosen 'Übernahme.'" Accordingly, I think that Omerzu, "Paulus," 277 misses part of the story when she writes that the Roman Empire takes the place of the "Erfahrungen der Diadochenherrschaft" of Jewish apocalypticism and that the significant difference between the early Jewish and early Christian apocalyptic mindset is "dass aus christlicher Perspektive mit Kreuzigung und Auferstehung Jesu das Eingreifen Gottes und die Erneuerung des Gottesvolkes bereits begonnen haben." This is certainly not wrong. However: What happened to the definition of the "Gottesvolk" and what does this imply for its enemy? I think that here the discontinuities within a continuous apocalyptic framework need to be considered in more detail.

[34] 1 Cor 15:26; Cf. White, "Subtext," 327.

at the heart of this world may have been, the expected reign of the Messiah from the parousia onwards would automatically have ended the "Roman world order" and that the new world order Paul was waiting for was "non-Roman."[35] But was this only a side effect of God's victory won at a totally different front,[36] or had Rome itself become God's enemy in Paul's view? It seems that White is trying to establish the latter position by reference to the effective history of Danielic eschatology in early Judaism and in Paul's letters. However helpful these observations may be, they cannot serve to prove this point. What he really demonstrates is merely the fact that the wordings and deep structures used, stem from a certain tradition. Whether Paul would have filled these concepts in the same manner as his contemporaries did and as he did himself before his encounter with the Messiah is a question that is not answered bur rather reinforced by White's work.

1.4.2 The Redefined Enemy of God

In chapter nine of his *magnum opus,* Wright offers some very helpful thoughts on the relationship between "plight" and "solution" in Paul's worldview.[37] At least since the reformation, this interpretative problem had been resolved by saying that Paul had an afflicted conscience because the law was accusing him. It was appeased by his encounter with the grace of the risen Christ on the way to Damascus. In this paradigm, the plight precedes the solution in the perception of Paul. From Sanders onwards, many scholars have argued that this might have been the sequence in Luther's search for a gracious God but that it would be anachronistic to attribute the same mindset to Paul. Sanders turned the sequence on its head. According to him, Paul was a self-confident Jew who lived in the sense of Phil 3:4–6 without any self-doubt according to Torah. It was only the experience on his way to Damascus which made it clear to him that, in light of God's intervention and in light of this radical *solution,* there also had to be a corresponding problem.[38] Wright's own approach steers a middle course. He argues convincingly that Paul, like every other Jew rooted in his tradition, definitely had an awareness of some

---

[35] White, "Subtext," 333.

[36] Similarly also Omerzu, "Paulus," 283–284.

[37] I think Douglas Moo, "Review of N. T. Wright, *Paul and the Faithfulness of God,*" n.p. [accessed on 5 December 2013]. Online: http://thegospelcoalition.org/book-reviews/review/paul_and_the_faithfulness_of_god) is spot on when he says that Wright's solution to the plight-solution problem is "utterly convincing."

[38] Ed P. Sanders, *Paul and Palestinian Judaism: A Comparison of Patterns of Religion* (London: SCM, 1977), 443 in a section entitled "[t]he solution as preceding the problem": "It appears that the conclusion that all the world – both Jew and Greek – equally stands in need of a saviour *springs from* the prior conviction that God had provided such a saviour. If he did so, it follows that such a saviour *must* have been needed and then only consequently that all other possible ways of salvation are wrong."

1. Counter-Imperial Attitude

kind of problem. The problem was: Why is this world still influenced by so much evil although it was created by a good creator God? And why is Israel still suppressed by her enemies although she has these promises from her covenant God? This Jewish perception of the plight arose directly from Jewish monotheism, one important element in Paul's theology – although modified around the Messiah and the Spirit. This modification also led to a modification of the "plight":[39]

> What happened to Saul of Tarsus on the road to Damascus can be put, from one angle, like this: there was revealed to him an 'answer' to a question which was like the questions he had had but much, much more complex. He was provided with a 'solution' to a problem far deeper and darker than the problem he had been addressing. It was like someone trying to figure out how to draw an accurate circle and then, suddenly, being shown how to construct a perfect sphere. Following his Damascus Road vision, Saul of Tarsus was not thinking, 'Well, I've had this problem for a long time, and now I have the solution to it.' Nor was he thinking, as Sanders and others have suggested, 'Well, I didn't know I had a 'problem,' but if this is a 'solution' there must have been a problem of some sort.' He was asking himself (scrolling through his well-remembered scriptures as he did so): what does *this* 'solution' (the resurrection of the crucified Jesus) have to say to *these* 'problems'? Paul was like a man who, on the way to collect a prescribed medication, studies the doctor's note and concludes from the recommended remedy that his illness must be far more serious than he had supposed.[40]

If the messiah was a *crucified* one, this meant the solution could not simply be equivalent to Israel bringing light into the darkness of the pagan nations by means of her Torah piety.[41] Otherwise, the death of the Messiah would have been completely in vain (Gal 2:21). Wright demonstrates that for Paul the cross implied that the Jews had themselves become part of the problem they originally were meant to solve. The *risen* Messiah, on the other hand, emphasised the cosmic dimension of the solution and gave an insight into God's intended future, a restored creation, in which death would be defeated completely.[42] The transformative work of the Spirit revealed the depth of the human and hence Jewish problem since the Law alone was not able to mediate this life-giving power.[43] The Spirit as an eschatological entity had burst

---

[39] Other discussions of the Damascus experience remain on the level of "solutions" themselves. Paul, being called apart from any "works of the law," recognised that grace in Christ was the real *soteriological* basis (see, e.g., Jörg Frey, "Paul's Jewish Identity," in *Jewish Identity in the Greco-Roman World/Jüdische Identität in der griechisch-römischen Welt* [ed. Jörg Frey, Daniel R. Schwartz, and Stephanie Gripentrog; AJEC 71; Leiden: Brill, 2007], 319). This does not follow Luther in his view of Judaism but still assumes a relative continuity regarding the "plight" that the pre- and post-Damascus Paul would have imagined.

[40] Wright, *Faithfulness*, 751.
[41] Wright, *Faithfulness*, 752–755.
[42] Wright, *Faithfulness*, 756–758.
[43] Wright, *Faithfulness*, 758–764.

into the present and was renewing the "people of God," who were the means of God's action in the world he had never given up. This reworked "people of God," who were characterised by the Spirit even in the present, were not a complete novelty, they were the answer to Israel's exile. Yet at the same time, they constituted an extended, worldwide family of God.[44]

The continuity between the original and modified plight in Paul's worldview thus is a substantial continuity. Sin and death had been the problem from the beginning in a certain sense, and God's covenant with Abraham had always been the intended solution, even though the faithful Israelite – Jesus – was necessary to achieve what Israel could not do through Torah.[45] However, there is also a clear discontinuity in the *perception and classification* of this plight between Paul and his contemporaries and between the Paul before and after his call as an apostle. For Paul, a notion of the plight in which ethnic Israel has to be liberated from her pagan enemies is a reductionistic view of the real problem. As the redefinition of "Israel" (most obviously in Gal 6:16; cf. Rom 2:26.29 and Phil 3:3) shows, the categories referred to by Paul's language differ from those ideas of his contemporaries – even though, from Paul's later perspective, there probably was a continuous connection between both conceptions: The new people of God are nothing but the people of God that God had always intended by means of ethnic Israel – the one large family of Abraham defined by faith.[46]

Even if one does not want to follow Wright in his reconstruction of Paul's redefinition of the people of God (via the promise to Abraham and Jesus as the faithful Israelite), the new understanding of what constitutes the boundaries of God's people – namely faith, not circumcision – requires us to rethink another aspect.[47] These observations sensitise us to the difficulty of integrating the old enemies of Israel, the old "plight," into this modified Jewish worldview. Which role could the Roman Empire as a concrete historical phenomenon still play? Wright himself emphasises that the plight, which was now perceived to be more dire than thought before, also had consequences in this regard:

The resurrection itself demonstrated that the real enemy was not 'the Gentiles,' not even the horrible spectre of pagan empire. The real enemy was Death itself, the ultimate anti-

---

[44] Wright, *Faithfulness*, 761.
[45] Cf. above all Rom 3:22. Cf. Wright, *Faithfulness*, 836–851.
[46] See the detailed justification in chapter 10 in Wright, *Faithfulness*, 774–1042 and 1128–1258.
[47] Cf. Schnelle, *Paulus*, 449–450 for a different route with the same result: The crucified Jesus Christ crossed the boundaries of traditional Jewish ideas, and Paul modified the *Gottesvolkbegriff* in order to solve this tension (cf. Schnelle, *Paulus*, 650–653, where this is explicated but where he also assumes a "neu[e] Vision" in Romans).

creation force, with Sin – the personified power of evil, doing duty apparently at some points for 'the satan' itself – as its henchman.[48]

He continues:

Paul thus came to believe that in and through the death, resurrection and enthronement of Jesus and the outpouring of the spirit *the true nature of the enemy, of 'the problem,' had itself finally been revealed*. Just as Isaiah, in a moment of sharp clarity, saw that Assyria was not the real and ultimate problem facing Israel, but that Babylon would be, so Saul of Tarsus, as part of what was 'revealed' on the road to Damascus in the unveiling of the risen Jesus as Messiah and Lord, realised that Rome itself, and paganism in general, was not the real problem. ... The real problem was Sin and Death – enemies which could be tracked, in a way that so far as we know had not been done before then, all the way back to Adam. If Sin and Death had been defeated in the unexpected messianic victory, then they had been the real problem all along.[49]

The continuity with the Jewish context is provided by the fixed *arrangement* of roles:[50] Creation in general and the people of God in particular are in need of salvation in view of God's enemies, and God himself is the saviour in this situation. But the *cast* of the characters is discontinuous in part. The creator God and his creation are still there although the first concept is modified around the experience of the Messiah and the Spirit. But the people of God are no longer defined ethnically nor are their enemies. In some sense, there still is an element of continuity since the recasting is not akin to a second attempt but represents the original cast of choice by God, the director. From the beginning, it was his aim to defeat sin and death which would not affect ethnic Israel alone since they were always meant to become the one worldwide family of Abraham. The Roman Empire can no longer take its prominent place in this widened horizon. It cannot be equated with the real plight, nor can it be interpreted as its real manifestation.[51]

1.4.3 Synthesis: Paul's Multi-Layered Reality

Against this background, it might seem surprising that in his direct interaction (in chapter twelve) with Barclay, Wright draws the following conclusion: He agrees with Barclay that the real conflict for Paul was not simply the national oppression of Israel but that the "plight" as he saw it after the solution that he

---

[48] Wright, *Faithfulness*, 761.
[49] Wright, *Faithfulness*, 762.
[50] Schnelle, *Paulus*, 449 correctly notes that there is an ineluctable continuity between the God of Israel and the Father of Jesus Christ: "Ihm war es unmöglich, das Heilshandeln Gottes in Jesus Christus von der Geschichte Israels zu lösen. Es gibt nur eine Geschichte Gottes, die von Anfang an durch die Schöpfungs- und Heilsmittlerschaft Jesu Christi bestimmt wird."
[51] Cf. this analysis with Carter, *Empire*, 16–18, who in his section "The Empire is of the Devil" does not give any Pauline references.

encountered at Damascus indeed took the form of sin and death.[52] Nevertheless, he insists on interpreting the apocalyptic victory of Jesus on the cross not only as a defeat of abstract powers but also with regard to concrete referents:

> I am following what I take to be a first-century understanding in which all previous narratives – the story of 'the powers' as well as of Israel! – come to their climax. And just as Jesus is no mere cipher for Israel's narrative, but the very son of the covenant god, so Rome is no mere irrelevant or insignificant political entity, but the final Monster in whom precisely the power of 'death' itself has been unleashed on to that 'son of god.'[53]

According to Wright, Rome was still relevant to Paul as such because it was *the* expression of destructive forces which culminated in his own time in the climax of human history and *Heilsgeschichte* in the crucifixion of Jesus. So, in the end, the Roman Empire still is the fourth Danielic kingdom.[54]

This move seems quite astonishing and one could get the impression that Wright jeopardises here what he has earlier gained in order to defend his interpretation of Paul's engagement with imperial ideology.[55] After all, if Rome is not the real enemy of God, can it still be equated with the fourth Danielic kingdom?[56] The logic of 1 Cor 15:24–26 – which alludes to Dan 2:44 – does not point in this direction.[57] Similarly, when Paul alludes to Dan 7:22 in 1 Cor 6:2–3, he seems to think of something more comprehensive

---

[52] Wright, *Faithfulness*, 1286–1288 with reference to Eph 6:12.14–17, 1 Thess 5:8, and 1 Cor 15:25–26 and 56. See also Wright, *Faithfulness*, 1311 and 1318.

[53] Wright, *Faithfulness*, 1311

[54] Wright, *Faithfulness*, 1311 and 1316.

[55] He still insists (Wright, *Faithfulness*, 1318): "The key to it all, then, as to so much else, is to understand the Jewish context from which Paul came, and then to understand the nature of the change in Paul's Jewish understanding caused by his belief in the crucified and risen Messiah."

[56] Wright, *Faithfulness*, 1298–1299 convincingly shows that for Paul – contrary to his Jewish tradition – the climax of God's story has already occurred. However, I do not see why this should make his insistence on Paul seeing Rome as the fourth Danielic empire more plausible. Sure, Rome was in charge when this climax occurred in the death of Jesus, sure, Rome was Satan's henchman in crucifying the Messiah. But does this also imply that it *is* the fourth kingdom?

[57] This is especially the case if we regard 1 Cor 15:26 as the apodosis of the double protases in 1 Cor 15:24 (and understand τὸ τέλος there adverbially; this makes perfect sense as a justification for ἐν τῷ Χριστῷ πάντες ζῳοποιηθήσονται in 15:22):

> [24] Then, in the end,
>   when he hands over the kingdom to God the Father,
>   when he has brought to an end all rule and all authority and power,
>   ([25] for he must reign until he has put all his enemies under his feet)
>   [26] the last enemy to be destroyed is death.

But the point remains valid even if we do not accept this solution on syntactical grounds (see Fee, *Epistle*, 756–757 for a discussion of this).

than the Roman Empire. What Wright writes about Paul's political theology (rulers are God's way of ordering the world and will be held accountable in the future)[58] is certainly right, but it seems doubtful that, for Paul, these beliefs are still *located* in the framework of eschatology in the strict sense. However, even if we allowed for the moment that Paul still regarded Dan 2 and 7 as pointing to Rome as the kingdom under which the climax of God's *Heilsgeschichte* would take place, we would do so only because the notion of the "fourth kingdom" would have lost its importance as the enemy of God. This seems to be the only possible way to combine Wright's insistence both on the reconfiguration of the enemy of God as well as the identification of Rome with the fourth kingdom. But under this assumption Wright's constant references to Rome as the fourth kingdom would equally lose their relevance, no longer proving Paul's critical assessment of Rome in his eschatological framework. The only internally consistent solution I can see to save Wright's argument would be to insist on a stronger notion of the fourth kingdom, associating it very closely with God's ultimate enemy after all. But then we would run the risk of downplaying the transformation that took place within Paul's Jewish mindset and that Wright rightly and eloquently describes.

Be that as it may, such a return to the plight of the pre-Christian Paul does not seem *necessary* in order to counter Barclay's criticism. Rather, I think that Barclay's proposal not only is compatible with Wright's broader suggestion for solving the plight-solution-enigma,[59] but also does not in any way exclude the possibility of a counter-imperial subtext.[60] When Barclay empha-

---

[58] Wright, *Faithfulness*, 1318.

[59] An explanation I find very persuasive. In contrast to other proposals that also do not follow a caricature of Second Temple Judaism as a "legalistic" religion, Wright rightly stresses the importance of Paul's perception of the *plight* as a crucial factor for his theology. Wolter, *Paulus*, 23–30, on the other hand, also wants to emphasise that Paul's conversion-call should not be understood in an individualistic, Lutheran manner, but he thinks that the main paradigm shift Paul experienced near Damascus was the realisation "dass den Völkern durch Jesus Christus der Weg zur Teilhabe an Gottes Heiligkeit eröffnet worden ist – und zwar ohne dass sie sich der Beschneidung unterziehen und ihr Leben an der Tora orientieren müssen" (Wolter, *Paulus*, 28). However, Wolter's reconstruction of Paul's deduction is incomplete. It does not seem plausible that the most important shift in Paul's worldview took the indirect route of recognising that (a) the people whom he was persecuting were right and that (b) since they were not acting according to his zeal for Torah, obviously the observation of the laws was (c) no longer how the people of God were marked and hence (d) mission to the Gentiles was mandatory (cf. Wolter, *Paulus*, 27). It seems far more plausible to assume that when Paul had to accept the insight that the "solution" he had advocated obviously was not the right one, he concluded that this also changed his view of the plight *itself* (no longer simply the holiness of Israel!) and hence allowed for a broadened perspective.

[60] Hence, it should be emphasised that I am *not* arguing for a purely "spiritual" interpretation of Paul (cf. Wright, *Faithfulness*, 1288).

sises that for Paul the real frontier is a cosmic battle, this is probably correct. It would be wrong to negate this and to try to attribute this role to the Roman Empire. Instead, the really important question is whether Paul's perception of everyday reality was multi-layered or not. Just because he would have agreed with Barclay that the most important conflict is the one between sin and the Spirit, does not mean that it does not affect ordinary decisions and behaviour on a lower level. The foundational conflict in Gal 5:17, for example, is followed in 5:19–26 by very concrete expressions of this battle. Similarly, the book of Acts gives us a good impression of the various local complications of Paul's mission through his contemporaries, and nevertheless, without further explanation, he is able to say in 1 Thess 2:18[61] that it was Satan who hindered him from visiting the church.[62] Hence, it would be wrong to say that these "ordinary" things were only peripheral to Paul. The concrete, contemporaneous circumstances do not just float around in space without evaluation just because Paul has a cosmic perspective. Rather, he interprets the events and conditions confronting him within such a wider framework.

We thus have to argue, against Barclay, that Paul's concrete judgements of specific contemporaneous phenomena as expressions of cosmic forces result from his theological interpretation of the world and do not contradict it at all.[63] On the contrary, if we assume the latter, we should also expect the former, wherever contemporary figures claim roles (saviour of the world etc.)

---

[61] 1 Thess 3:1 tells us that it was from Athens that Paul wanted to visit the young church. Acts 17:13–15 describes Paul's problems in Berea and his reason for going to Athens but not explicitly what caused him to stay there. I think it is likely that Paul is still referring to the events described in Acts 17:1–9, which had also caused him to leave and created a situation that was still ongoing (so, e.g., Frederick F. Bruce, *1 & 2 Thessalonians* [WBC 45; Waco: Word Books, 1982], 55). The concrete circumstances certainly belong to that which was expounded by the deliverer of the letter (Charles A. Wanamaker, Charles A. *The Epistles to the Thessalonians: A Commentary on the Greek Text* [NIGTC; Grand Rapids: Eerdmans, 1990], 122).

[62] Cf. the passive in Rom 1:13 and 15:22 (cf. also Gal 5:7–8 on ἐγκόπτω; Jewett, *Romans*, 922–923 gives a good summary of the obstacles behind Rom 15:22 although it does not influence his exegesis of 1:13 in Jewett, *Romans*, 129). Whatever the σκόλοψ τῇ σαρκί in 2 Cor 12:7 is, it probably also belongs into this category since most interpretations argue for a concrete reference (illness etc.). Paul himself is also able to spell out his troubles in a very concrete way: 2 Cor 11:23–28.

[63] Nicholas T. Wright, "Paul and Caesar: A New Reading of Romans," in *A Royal Priesthood? The Use of the Bible Ethically and Politically: A Dialogue with Oliver O'Donovan* (ed. Craig G. Bartholomew et al.; SHS 3; Grand Rapids: Zondervan, 2002), 179 also explicitly embeds the criticism he assumes in Paul into a larger context: "I suggest that Paul's anti-imperial stance is part of a wider strain in his thinking which has also been marginalized in many systematic treatments of his thought, but which should be acknowledged and rehabilitated: the confrontation between the gospel and the powers of the world, between the gospel and paganism in general."

that are attributed to other persons in the divine drama.[64] This is also different from the proposal of White according to which the Roman Empire belongs to the category of evil because it already was there in advance as the enemy of God. It rather declares itself to be God's enemy where it resists the realities created by him.[65] Salvation around the Messiah is the real thing and everything that is in conflict with it unmasks itself as evil's henchman. Hence, the direction is reversed: Paul's critical attitude is not based on the assumption that God will destroy the Roman Empire, but this attitude surfaces wherever something stands in the way of the kingdom of God.[66] Against this background, the emphasis of Fantin[67] also seems slightly misleading. The definition of "polemic" as "a challenge of one party to another through a claim to a role held by the other" does not leave enough room for the perception of the person using polemical language. From the perspective of this person, it might very well be the case that the criticised party is actively promoting claims concerning specific roles.

Hence, there can be no question of *equating* Rome and evil or integrating the first into the latter. Galinsky rightly sounds a note of caution not to read into Paul our own bias against totalitarian regimes when noting that often connotations of "oppression, injustice, and colonialism" are associated with the concept of 'empire' and then also assumed for Paul.[68] He urges proponents of a counter-imperial interpretation of Paul not to forget that, after all, Paul did not revoke his Roman citizenship.[69] It seems that Barclay himself

---

[64] Wright, *Faithfulness*, 1291 fittingly writes with regard to 2 Thess 2:1–5: "The point where Rome/Caesar takes on divine status is the point where Rome/Caesar is most obviously acting as satan's puppet." Of course, rejecting the claims of the head of the empire automatically implies some scepticism towards other aspects of his kingdom, as David Nystrom, "We Have No King But Caesar: Roman Imperial Ideology and the Imperial Cult," in *Jesus Is Lord, Caesar Is Not: Evaluating Empire in New Testament Studies* (ed. Scot McKnight and Joseph B. Modica; Downers Grove: IVP Academia, 2013), 36 correctly states: "The message of the New Testament conjures a kingdom at variance with the Roman project at many points. The identity of the true King and Lord is the chief among them, as it at once implies the others."

[65] This also means that my proposal *cannot* be classified in the third category suggested by Wright, *Faithfulness*, 1273 (cf. 1282). One could call it a "coincidental significance" view of Rome. That is not the position I am arguing for here. Note that Wright, *Faithfulness*, 1318 can write in a similar way as I do ("Only Rome ... at the time of Paul's writing.").

[66] Cf. the comment by Holtz, *Brief*, 117 on 1 Thess 2:18: "Er ist an vorderer Front einbezogen in den Kampf, den Satan gegen Gott führt. Deshalb sieht er da, wo ihm etwas hinderlich in den Weg tritt, die Spur von Satans Wirken. Die Qualifizierung als Satanswerk ist also nicht von der Art der Hinderung her gewonnen, sondern von ihrer Wirkung auf den Weg des Apostels." This offers a perfect analogy in my opinion.

[67] Fantin, *Lord*, 9.

[68] Galinsky, "Cult," 2–3.

[69] Galinsky, "Cult," 15.

gives good reason for a balanced position that assumes Paul to have seen good and bad aspects in Roman rule:

> Inasmuch as the Roman empire operated by the power and wisdom of 'this world,' opposed Christ and his people, or arrogated to itself false pretensions of significance, it was a manifestation of 'the present evil age' doomed to destruction ... Inasmuch as its authority was subservient to God's and it was capable of preserving and rewarding 'the good,' it could be recognised and honoured accordingly (Rom 13.1–7).[70]

I would only add this: If Paul was capable of locating something Roman in the positive realm (as Barclay assumes with his reference to Rom 13:1–7), we should also expect him to be attentive to concrete negative aspects. In other words: If Rom 13:1–7 fits coherently into "Paul's Political Theology,"[71] negative statements on aspects of the Roman Empire would as well.

We can thus conclude that Wright's recourse to an enemy of God – who looks more at home in the unmodified mindset of Paul than in the transformed worldview Wright convincingly reconstructs – is unnecessary in order to counter Barclay's conclusions. Barclay himself admits that, in a situation in which current political circumstances are in conflict with God's kingdom, the Pauline message did indeed have the *potential* to confront specific circumstances. He thinks that the Confessing Church correctly *applied* Paul's vision to the concrete forms of evil in their day.[72] It seems very appropriate to attribute to Paul the same ability that Barclay acknowledges his followers to have had. There is thus every reason to think that Paul was able to identify specific *manifestations* of evil in Roman imperial rule and ideology.[73]

---

[70] Barclay, "Empire," 385. Cf. similarly Pinter, "Gospel," 110 although I find his examples of a positive role of Rome quite amusing: "Devoid of that [paying attention to the imperial cult], for Luke, the emperors can be vassals of the one true God. They can inadvertently bring about the Bethlehem birth of Jesus and, through their procurators, the fulfilment of the will of God in the death of Jesus. Either Luke is naïve about the imperial cult and the pretensions of the emperor, or he can imagine that relationships with Rome can be developed by working around them." Cf. also Schnelle, *Paulus,* 141–142 for the *pax Romana* as "Voraussetzung der paulinischen Missionsarbeit."

[71] Barclay, "Empire," 383.

[72] Barclay on 19.11.2007 at SBL in San Diego in a debate with N. T. Wright (and Robert Jewett) on the topic of "Paul and Empire." This statement can be found in his response to Jewett and Wright and is available on the internet (John M. G. Barclay, "Response to N. T. Wright and Robert Jewett," n.p. (around minute 27:00) [accessed on 9 January 2015]. Online: http://www.duke.edu/~adr14/Paul%20and%20Empire%20-%20Part%202%20of%202.mp3.

[73] Barclay has pointed out to me in private communication (email from 11.10.2013) that it was not his intention to deny Paul's capacity to challenge specific manifestations of evil in the Roman Empire, but rather that we do not have any specific evidence that he really did so. However, that we do *not* have any critical remarks by Paul – not even on the level of subtext – is a hypothesis that needs to be justified by evidence just as its contrary posi-

Here, an additional aspect from Wright's response to Barclay might indeed come into play: It would be unrealistic to suppose that Paul saw the Roman Empire as on a par with all other nations and therefore was *completely* indifferent to it simply because it was not elevated to the position of cosmic powers.[74] After all, it was the system he was often (though not always; sometimes his opponents were Jews or other non-Roman people) confronted with on a daily basis in his proclamation of the kingdom of God. Does Barclay really want us to expect a completely *neutral* stance even in places where Paul explicitly refers to the Roman realm by means of termini technici (see Chapter 6, Section 2.1)? He seems to be throwing out the baby with the bathwater.

2. From Attitude to Expression: Modifications of the Echo-Hypothesis

2.1 Paul's Personality as Obstacle for the Echo-Hypothesis

In light of the considerations in the last section (and against the backdrop of some of the imperial claims we have already encountered in Chapter 4, Section 1), it seems plausible that Paul did indeed have a critical attitude toward at least some important elements of Roman ideology. We now turn to the potential transition from a critical *attitude* to critical *statements*. Is there any reason to suppose that Paul would have expressed this opinion in the subtext of his letters?

This question immediately evokes the further question whether this does not run counter to what we know about Paul's *personality*. At least at first sight, it seems implausible that Paul would have pulled back and restricted himself to the subtext for *safety reasons*. Barclay's similar question why Paul should have chosen the safe path instead of being confrontational is difficult to answer in light of the clear words Paul finds with regard to idol worship, the biggest provocation of the Empire (cf. Chapter 4, Section 1.2.2.3).[75] The

---

tion. For this evaluation it seems to be an important aspect to clarify whether Paul might have had a critical attitude towards the Empire.

[74] Paul's perception of his pagan environment certainly deserves more attention. The juxtaposition of Ἰουδαῖοι and Ἕλληνες (Rom 1:16; 2:9–10; 3:9; 10:12; 1 Cor 1:24; 10:32; 12:13; Gal 3:28) distinguishes between Jews and non-Jews, that is "Gentiles," which in Paul's day was basically equivalent to the very general category of "Graeco-Romans" (see BDAG, 2514; cf. Col 3:11, where there is an additional distinction between Graeco-Romans and those outside, βάρβαρος, Σκύθης). But in all these cases, the latter category is determined by reference to the Jewish people in the context of the law-free gospel. Hence, one should be careful not to deduce too much with regard to Paul's general perception of his environment.

[75] Barclay. "Empire," 381.

fact that public expression of opinion would have been dangerous (Chapter 4, Sections 1.2.2.5 and 1.3) does not by itself seem to be a sufficient reason for the use of hidden means of communication in light of Paul's character profile. As Barclay writes, the assumption that he considered it necessary to encode his criticism "underrates Paul's courage":[76]

[I]t is hard to imagine Paul, whose preaching frequently landed himself and his converts in trouble, being afraid to speak his mind in his letters; since he expects believers to face 'persecution' (Phil 1.27–30), he is hardly going to shade the gospel to avoid it.[77]

Does Paul suddenly try to please men (Gal 1:10) because he does not want to be persecuted for the sake of the cross of the Messiah (Gal 6:12)? This objection to the subtext-hypothesis is reinforced by Paul's reaction to other pagan cults. The rejection of pagan deities was provocative and not safe due to their important function in the public transcript of the Empire.[78] Roman religion was not simply a private matter of the individual, but had far-reaching implications. Its central concern was the *pax deorum,* the peace with the gods. The foundational idea of this concept assumed that the well-being of society depended on the satisfaction of the deities and thus of the correct execution of their cults.[79] Since Jewish monotheism (and its ban of images) forbade participation in pagan cults,[80] Jewish behaviour was not only interpreted as "atheism" but also – in combination with other separative components of Judaism – as "misanthropy."[81] Accordingly, the rejection of Roman state gods did have *political* conflict potential.[82] However, Paul apparently does not make an effort to deny his Jewish roots. To the contrary, turning away from pagan idols to the true and living god of Israel is *constitutive* of the Christian faith in Paul's view, as, for example, 1 Thess 1:9 demonstrates.[83] Why then should

---

[76] Cf. also Barclay, "Empire," 380.
[77] Barclay, "Empire," 381.
[78] Cf. Price, *Rituals,* 124–125.
[79] David E. Aune, "Religion, Greco-Roman," *DNTB* 921.
[80] Cf., for example, Hardin, *Galatians,* 107. See Chapter 4, Section 1.2.2.3.
[81] Peter Schäfer, *Judenhaß und Judenfurcht: Die Entstehung des Antisemitismus in der Antike* (trans. Peter Schäfer; Berlin: Verlag der Weltreligionen, 2010), 67–100 on the "Gott der Juden." See also Anton Cuffari, *Judenfeindschaft in Antike und Altem Testament* (BBB 153; Hamburg: Philo, 2007), 57–180 for a balanced juxtaposition of anti-Jewish and pro-Jewish statements and acts.
[82] See Price, *Rituals,* 124–125, who concludes his discussion of tension between imperial cult and early Christianity by stating: "The difficulties which the Christians posed for their contemporaries lay firstly with their threat to traditional cults in general and only secondarily with an allegedly subversive attitude to the emperor."
[83] ἐπεστρέψατε πρὸς τὸν θεὸν ἀπὸ τῶν εἰδώλων δουλεύειν θεῷ ζῶντι καὶ ἀληθινῷ;

we assume that Paul would not have handled other kinds of criticism of imperial ideology in a similarly open way, irrespective of potential sanctions?[84]

One could argue of course that Paul was able to be diplomatic in order to avoid trouble, as Acts vividly shows. The dichotomy of confrontational honesty and cowardly reluctance does not do full justice to the multifaceted ministry of Paul. After all, he was able to hold back his personal opinion for pragmatic reasons in order to win people for the faith (cf. 1 Cor 9:19–23). Hence, it seems to be within the range of possibility that he avoided confrontation with imperial authorities for strategic reasons without losing his integrity, especially if his concern was not his own fate but the fate of the church he was writing to.[85] The picture that is painted in Acts 17, therefore, is quite realistic, irrespective of the extent to which it describes a concrete event: Paul can be "upset" in spirit in light of the multitude of idols (Acts 17:16), and nevertheless, he is able to call this behaviour "piety" in direct dialogue (Acts 17:22). All his courage for the sake of the gospel notwithstanding, in principle Paul could also avoid confrontation where he judged this to be helpful.

However, this does not hide the fact that in his letters Paul openly criticises the pagan praxis of idol worship, which was foundational to society. Additionally, I think we *do* have open criticism of Roman authorities in at least one place in his letters, namely in 1 Cor 2:6–10.[86] In light of the sharp criticism in 1 Cor 2:6 (τῶν ἀρχόντων τοῦ αἰῶνος τούτου τῶν καταργουμένων; cf.

---

[84] If the analysis of Gal 6:12 by Hardin, *Galatians* is right, this would reinforce this objection. In that case, we would even have a documented case of persecution because of an imperial cult and of Paul's explicit summons not to turn away from the confession of and faithfulness to the Messiah. In this light, it might also seem promising to revisit Gal 1:10. This verse has often been felt to be rather out of place as an apology. This paradigm could open up the possibility of interpreting this crux, in continuity with the description of the (non)gospel of his opponents mentioned before (Gal 1:6–7), as a positive contrast between Paul's opponents and the apostle, giving the readers a role model: Paul himself does not try to please humans, but his only aim is to be a faithful servant of the Messiah. In this context, there is even some plausibility in reading Gal 5:11 as a direct insight into in the persecution of the apostle because of his loyalty to the Messiah (or, his disloyalty towards the imperial system). In any case, the re-evaluation of Pauline literature against the background of Roman ideology and society certainly is not over yet.

[85] Similarly Wright, *Faithfulness,* 1297 on Phil 3 in response to Barclay's argument, where he agrees that there is some public criticism of the Roman Empire but adds that "Paul, writing to a small congregation already suffering persecution, might not decide to use hints rather than direct statements."

[86] Summed up well by Parrott, "Thought," 220 (emphasis in the original): "In this context, Paul clearly made a deprecatory statement about the rulers. They lacked true wisdom and ruled apart from the Spirit of God. The ultimate evidence of this separation and deficiency was the crucifixion. Interestingly enough, however, this critique also contained the seek [sic] of a positive political affirmation: rulers should seek the wisdom of God and rule according to the Spirit. This is the positive side of Paul's political thought, a side fully in line with Jewish and 'secular' Hellenistic traditions and expressed in Rom 13:1–7."

2:8), it is unclear why Paul would not have formulated *other* criticism clearer[87] – at least if one assumes[88] that earthly rulers are in view here, not demonic powers. It seems unjustified to infer with Barclay that here the rulers are "anonymous, and never specifically identified with Rome."[89] Jesus's death is explicitly described in terms of crucifixion here (1 Cor 2:8: ἐσταύρωσαν).[90] Phil 2:8 demonstrates that reference to the "cross" evoked the concrete historical realities of this terrible death through execution by the Romans – it was not any death but death on a *cross* (μέχρι θανάτου, θανάτου δὲ σταυροῦ).[91] Of course, Paul does not say that the authorities he is talking about were Roman, but this is the case only because *he does not have to* since it is self-evident for his readers. This does not mean that 1 Cor 2:6, 8 only has Roman authorities in view and not Jewish ones also. In fact, the latter is very plausible in light of 1 Thess 1:14–15 (and the historical events). However, this very passage demonstrates that Paul was very aware of and insisted on the fact that the ἄρχοντες were very concrete historical entities. It might well be, that Paul intentionally used the rather ambiguous term ἄρχων, which could be used for human authorities as well as for evil spiritual beings.[92] The possibility that Paul refers to the action of human beings but also sees a spiritual dimension behind their behaviour seems to be confirmed further by their specification as rulers τοῦ αἰῶνος τούτου.[93] But this would not make the real villains anonymous – it would only make their fault graver. In this case, it would be an

---

[87] Similarly Pinter, "Gospel," 109 with regard to Luke-Acts: "Yet even if the Gospel is not written for an insider audience, the sheer brazenness of Luke's assertion that Jesus is Lord and King uncovers the author as a rather poor code writer." (However, cf. p. 110, where Pinter then contradicts himself when he says that such parallels are not subversive.)

[88] E.g., with Fee, *Epistle*, 103–104. For a recent defense of this view, cf. Dale C. Allison, *Constructing Jesus: Memory, Imagination, and History* (Grand Rapids: Baker Academics, 2010), 396–398.

[89] Barclay, "Empire," 375.

[90] Cf. also 1 Cor 1:13.17–18.23; 2:2; 2 Cor 13:4; Gal 3:1; 5:11 and 24; 6:12 and 14; Phil 2:8; 3:18; Col 1:20; 2:14; Eph 2:16; applied to the believer in union with the Messiah: Gal 5:24; 6:14.

[91] Cf. Wright, *Faithfulness*, 1311 for a similar observation with regard to Mark 15:39. See also the more general remark by Strecker, "Taktiken," 156. On this whole issue, cf. Allison, *Jesus*, 392–403. Of course, Allison is driven by his aim as an historian to find traditions about Jesus's death in Paul's letters, but there is also good reason to assume that his findings point to an awareness of the "Romanness" of this event for Paul himself (cf., e.g., the comments of Allison, *Jesus*, 395 on 2 Cor 4:10 and Gal 6:17).

[92] Cf. Rom 13:3 and Eph 2:2.

[93] 2 Cor 4:4: ὁ θεὸς τοῦ αἰῶνος τούτου. Similarly Gal 1:4: ὅπως ἐξέληται ἡμᾶς ἐκ τοῦ αἰῶνος τοῦ ἐνεστῶτος πονηροῦ.

2. From Attitude to Expression: Modifications of the Echo-Hypothesis

excellent example of Paul's multi-layered vision of reality (see Section 1.4.3).[94]

The assumption that Paul's motivation for using the subtext for his counter-imperial remarks was an attempt to avoid persecution thus faces a serious problem. Proponents of the classical echo-hypothesis would at least have to explain why Paul would be so open with his criticism in this case and so careful in other instances.[95] What is the difference between those statements and the sense of 1 Cor 2:6? Why should it be plausible for Paul to expect negative consequences in one case but not in the other? Or, if the potential risks are deemed comparable, why would Paul have exposed himself to this danger in one case but not in the other?

2.2 Two Modification of the Classical Echo-Hypothesis

2.2.1 Criticism and Intention

On the basis of our analysis, we have already concluded (Chapter 4, Section 1.3) that the classical subtext-hypothesis which postulates counter-imperial echoes in Paul on the basis of (a) suppression and (b) avoidance of danger has to be modified with regard to the *object* of criticism in light of the concrete historical nature of the alleged suppression (a). Now it is the second cornerstone of this paradigm – the claim that Paul was motivated by the desire to avoid danger (b) – which leads us to change the framework.

There are some suggestions in the literature or hints, rather, which point away from the idea of external pressure as a sole cause for hidden criticism. First, I would like to mention Whitmarsh's remarks on Greek literature from the Roman period. He points out that avoiding danger is not the only reason for subtle literary resistance (in contrast to open opposition).[96] The fact that many of the authors were themselves *Roman* citizens stipulated the "negotiation of multiple identities." He adds:

For once we broaden the meaning of resistance beyond openly proclaimed hostility, then we see precisely why discursive negotiation was the preferred route for such figures: not only because it is 'safer' (less open, less directly hostile), but also because it can attach to a

---

[94] Allison, *Jesus,* 398 rejects a "double meaning" (Roman authorities *and* demonic powers). However, I think that the position that Paul's phrase at least conveys connotations of the spiritual realm, while nevertheless referring to earthly rulers, should be treated separately and cannot be dismissed that easily.

[95] This conclusion could be strengthened if one were able to demonstrate that Paul's manifold problems with officials were in part a result of his – publicly accessible – counter-imperial message. Of course, here the question arises of what needs to be attributed to a deficient understanding of Paul's gospel, what was rooted in his own intentions, and where conflicts – as unintended as they might have been – were an inevitable consequence of a clash of worldviews. Cf. Strecker, "Taktiken," 131–132 and 153.

[96] Whitmarsh, "Resistance," 62.

safely demarcated area of mental activity that does not (necessarily) conflict with e.g. political duties.

Although this probably is not a good paradigm for understanding the apostle, Pauline scholars can learn an important lesson from this approach: The motive for oblique criticism is transferred from the external to the internal sphere. Some scholars follow this line of thought not focussing on internal tensions in the personality and obligations of Paul himself, but among the people in his congregation. Harrison, for example, writes on Rom 13:[97]

> Paul's use of coded language in Romans 13:1–13 is probably driven not so much by the possible *external* threat of the ruler in the mid fifties ... but by the *internal* social reality that the early church contained slaves from the *familia Caesaris* and from the households of powerful imperial freedmen. ... Moreover, within the Body of Christ at Rome there would also have been believers who were either disenchanted with or antagonistic towards the ruler, or who were generally sympathetic to the anti-imperial propaganda.

Similarly, Wright[98] has recently suggested that Paul might have located his criticism in the subtext in order to avoid that overly enthusiastic members of his congregations would misunderstand his criticism as a summons to revolution:

> Some of his hearers might well take fright at a direct and frank statement of everything Paul believed about Caesar and Rome. Some might waver in their allegiance and find themselves reporting to the authorities that Paul and his communities believed that there was 'another king, namely Jesus.' Better to be oblique; not, perhaps (as I have suggested on other occasions) in case his letters are detected by the authorities, but perhaps because he is anxious, as a pastor writing or speaking to his flock might well be anxious, about people getting the wrong end of the stick, and either seizing too enthusiastically upon, or taking fright at, what to the wrong ears might sound like a literal call to arms.

It should be appreciated that Wright widens the range of possible reasons for choosing the subtext. However, there are reasons to doubt whether this framework is more successful as a hermeneutical key than the proposal of subtext as means of avoiding persecution. After all, it is precisely the act of being oblique that invites misunderstanding. Saying openly that armed resistance is not an option seems unproblematic in all respects. Who should have disliked it? The Roman authorities? Certainly not. Other members of the congregation who were more in favour of violent protests? Maybe. But would Paul have cared to please such people? Wright himself has argued that Rom 13:1–7 is the dialectic counterpart to veiled criticism which aims to prevent Christians from overreaction (cf. Chapter 5, Section 1.2). Hence, it does not seem to be the case that this suggestion can offer us a paradigm for counter-imperial subtext in Paul even though it may have played a role in individual

---

[97] Harrison, *Paul*, 32 with references to Jewett, *Romans*, 780–803.
[98] Wright, *Faithfulness*, 1315.

2. From Attitude to Expression: Modifications of the Echo-Hypothesis 131

cases. Moreover, in other places Wright has continued to emphasise the importance of avoiding persecution.[99]

In what follows, we are going to enquire further into the question of alternative motives for potential counter-imperial statements in the subtext. As we shall see, the obstacle of Paul's personality for the echo-hypothesis can be overcome by modifying or, rather, specifying, it with regard to Paul's *motivation* for using the subtext for his criticism. To do that, we need to rethink what the concepts of 1) 'criticism' and 2) 'subtext' imply. We will discuss these aspects in the next two sections, beginning with the concept of criticism.

It has to be noted that there are varying *kinds of criticism*. One fundamental difference is its direction. "Criticism" can be directed at the criticised party itself and only then is it "confrontation." The second kind wants to inform *others* about the criticism of a third party. Within each of these two classes directed at different addressees, there is a spectrum regarding the varying intensity of criticism. Criticism can be directed at the truth content of a statement (e.g., "The *pax Romana* is not peace!") or only at its exaggerated scope (e.g., "The *pax Romana* is only political peace and not as holistic as it claims!"). It can even merely point to a dimension which the "criticised" concept did not have in view (e.g., "The *pax Romana* might be a good thing for society, but there is more: peace with God!").

With regard to the first broad class ("confrontation" in some sense) Barclay's question would be appropriate: Would a person of Paul's character really have chosen to express the hidden transcript in a veiled form (see Chapter 3, Section 3.1)? Maybe Paul's death itself points to the fact that this was not Paul's strategy before Nero, as is vividly narrated in later tradition in *Mart. Paul*.[100] However, as we have seen above (Chapter 3, Sections 3.1.2

---

[99] E.g., Wright, *Faithfulness,* 1297 on Phil 3: "It may, after all, be safer to make such a hint than to write a letter explaining in detail precisely what he thinks about the blasphemous claims of Caesar."

[100] Twenty years ago, Harry W. Tajra, *The Martyrdom of St. Paul: Historical and Judicial Context, Tradition and Legends* (WUNT II 67; Tübingen: Mohr Siebeck, 1994), 121 wrote: "*The Martyrium Pauli* ... depicts Paul as a dynamic figure, who directly challenges the tyrannical ruler hearing his case and who goes to his death defiantly, warmly embracing martyrdom. The relationship between Paul and Nero is confrontational to the extreme; that between the Church and Roman State overtly hostile and inimical. The *Paul of faith,* the Apostle of the legend, has acquired quite a precise image in the apocryphal tradition: that of a challenger to State authority, an enemy of the Emperor and a seeker after martyrdom. This image bears little resemblance – indeed it is quite alien – to the image of *the historical Paul* as he is understood from his own Epistles and from the canonical Acts." Glenn E. Snyder, *Acts of Paul: The Formation of a Pauline Corpus* (WUNT II 352; Tübingen: Mohr Siebeck, 2013), 64 gets closer to the heart of the matter when he writes that the specifically political front in *Mart. Paul* is "an early, politically engaged form of Pauline faith and practice." Against this background it seems appropriate to reconsider the

and 3.3), potential criticism of the Roman Empire in Paul's letters would belong to the second class, i.e., the one that is directed towards other like-minded people (fellow Christians). Does Barclay's objection apply here, too? If he wanted to deny a Roman claim in the strong sense, i.e., on the one end of the spectrum we have just described, we would indeed expect a more passionate attack from Paul along the lines of 1 Cor 2:6. He certainly would not have wanted his congregations to miss the point if an imperial aspiration was his main concern. In addition to his open remarks on idol worship, we could also add that Paul was not a friend of flattering words for his opponents when he was concerned that they could seriously affect his churches (e.g., Gal 5:12 and Phil 3:2) although this certainly did not contribute to minimising the hostilities he experienced.

On the other side of the spectrum of different kinds of critical remarks directed toward insiders, the reference to an imperial concept would only serve as a point of contact with a known category in order to communicate one's own content.[101] This could take the form of offering a negative foil for the sake of a contrast or enabling the presentation of a "more perfect version of the same concept."[102] As Strecker has pointed out, such "Taktiken der Aneignung" of imperial language[103] do not even necessitate a counter-imperial strategy, but they can nevertheless be effective means of negotiating power.[104] Of course, the assumption of such a usage[105] of imperial language by Paul results in a picture of a relatively unsystematic approach towards the Empire by the apostle.[106] Consequently, it would seem doubtful whether a coherent "code" is what we should expect in Paul.

The most plausible form of counter-imperial statements is probably located between those two extremes. Even where a Roman concept is used just for the purpose of illustration, Paul would have had to be aware of the claims associated with this concept. And he would have known that his usage of it was contrary to the public transcript. Hence, such a clash of concepts would still be "intentional" in some sense and hence relevant for an author-centred exegesis of the text. Let me illustrate this by means of two examples. Firstly, Willitts argues that the Gospel of Matthew with its proclamation of another –

---

suggestion by Willy Rordorf, "Die neronische Christenverfolgung im Spiegel der apokryphen Paulusakten," *NTS* 28 (1982): 365–374, according to whom the military character of *Mart. Paul* is due to the influence of the persecution of the Christians by Nero in 64 CE.

[101] Of course, in this case one would have to evaluate whether such a text still contains enough provocative potential for the use of an echo to be justifiable. (If the criticism is almost not there, is it still necessary to use the subtext for safety reasons?)

[102] Galinsky, "Cult," 23.

[103] Strecker, "Taktiken," 153–161.

[104] Strecker, "Taktiken," 159.

[105] See Strecker, "Taktiken," 155.

[106] Strecker, "Taktiken," 161 is quite clear on this.

God's – empire would have been perceived as subversive by the Romans. On the other hand, he doubts that it was Matthew's *purpose* to "oppose Rome."[107] This is a valid observation, but there is some middle-ground between a neutral stance and deliberate of opposition with regard to the author's intention. The decisive question in determining whether a counter-imperial subtext has any bearing on the exegesis of the text is the question of whether the author would have been *aware* of the (maybe inevitable) critical implications of certain words and expressions in his writing.[108] If an author knows of the effect of his or her words among the recipients of his message and nevertheless keeps them, she or he is willing to accept a certain effect, which hence becomes part of his or her intention,[109] although not necessarily his or her main aim.[110] If this can be established on the basis of the pervasiveness of the corresponding Roman entity, it is noteworthy that the author did not take the effort to use less provocative options.[111] Secondly, Galinsky[112] asks with regard to Paul's use of language in his letter to the Romans: "Again, are we dealing with the rejection of Roman concepts here or their more perfect fashioning in the realm of God?" The designation "supraimperial" instead of "anti-imperial" expresses this nicely: "[T]he emperor and the dispensations of empire go only so far. They are surpassed, in a far more perfect way, by God and the kingdom of heaven." However, a kingdom surpassing the Roman Empire would have been regarded as nothing less than anti-imperial from a

---

[107] Willitts, "Matthew," 97.

[108] To give a contemporary example: Any historian who is a specialist in surveillance techniques during the GDR has to reckon that, in a public lecture on the topic, his or her audience will constantly draw parallels to the current NSA scandal. If he or she does not want to encourage certain associations, the historian needs to address this specifically.

[109] This answers the critique by Denny Burk, "Is Paul's Gospel Counterimperial? Evaluating the Prospects of the 'Fresh Perspective' for Evangelical Theology," *JETS* 51 (2008): 319–322, which is built on the differentiation between "meaning" and "implication."

[110] This corresponds to how Scripture is used in contemporary sermons quite often. Just imagine a pastor preaching on the pericope of the labourers in the vineyard (Matt 20:1–16) or on 1 Thess 3:6–15 during a time of intense political discussion regarding minimum wages. The pastor will have to expect that the congregation will apply Scripture to the current situation automatically. He or she is able to direct the way the connection is drawn to some extent, but he or she will inevitably address the pressing situation. Accordingly, the expression of the preacher's opinion on this topic should not be disassociated from his or her intention simply because it is not the primary issue he or she wanted to address.

[111] Cf. the questions by Strecker, "Taktiken," 129–130: "[Es] stellt sich aber die Frage, ob der paulinische Gebrauch der genannten Begriffe angesichts der Verbreitung der Kaiserideologie und des Kaiserkultes gerade im Missionsgebiet des Apostels, dem Osten des Imperiums, nicht zwangsläufig den Effekt einer subversiven Unterwanderung der römischen Kaiserideologie haben musste? Waren die Termini mit anderen Worten völlig frei von politischen Assoziationen rezipierbar?"

[112] Galinsky, "Shadow," 222.

Roman perspective, of course.¹¹³ And there is no reason to assume that Paul would not have known the clash of claims he provoked by means of such statements.

In sum, it might be helpful to concentrate on Paul's intentions behind the statements that may contain a counter-imperial subtext. Maybe it was not Paul's *primary* intention to say something about Caesar, but to say something about the Messiah and God although he was perfectly aware of the critical *implications* these statements had for other competing worldviews.¹¹⁴ Such a more nuanced understanding of criticism could explain why Paul, although *not* a coward, did not feel any *need* to be more explicit.¹¹⁵ Barclay's objection is directed against the claim that Paul intended to convey the proposition: "Jesus is Lord and Caesar isn't."¹¹⁶ This implies a very specific degree of criticism of the first kind mentioned above. But what if Paul's reference to Jesus's Lordship was not meant to communicate "Since the Messiah is Lord – this means that *Caesar is not!*" but meant, rather, to keep the focus on Jesus himself? If the apostle was aware of the inevitable resonances the term "lord" would evoke, one could construe the underlying semantic structure of such a statement as follows: "You know these claims of Caesar to be 'Lord' – *that is what Jesus is!*" Of course, that Jesus is κύριος in such an all-encompassing sense certainly carries implications for alternative claims, but this is not in the *foreground*. Otherwise, and here Barclay is right, it should be more explicitly challenging. So it seems to be a more plausible model to work with the assumption that potential criticism could have emerged on the basis of *background* knowledge about imperial claims shared by both author and reader. In

---

¹¹³ This is also true for the "Rhetorik der Überbietung" and the "Vergleichgültigung" of Roman citizenship which Krauter, *Studien*, 266 identifies in Phil 3:20 (instead of a "klare Antithese zum römischen Reich"; Krauter, *Studien*, 265).

¹¹⁴ Cf. Fantin, *Lord*, 7: "The goal of this study is to determine whether or not it is probable that Paul intended a polemic against the living Caesar in some of his uses of κύριος for Jesus. If a polemic exists, it does not demand that it be the most important aspect of the usage in any context. It would merely demonstrate that the polemic is part of the message." Cf. also Fantin, *Lord*, 40.

¹¹⁵ I like the conclusions of Peter Oakes, "Re-mapping the Universe: Paul and the Emperor in 1 Thessalonians and Philippians," *JSNT* 27 (2005): 321, according to which Paul is re-mapping the universe in Philippians and 1 Thessalonians: "[H]e is redrawing the map of the universe. The marginalized Christians are brought near to the centre. The centre itself is occupied by Jesus, whose crucifixion had marginalized him as far as it was possible to do. In thus reorganizing space, and consequently the outcome of time, Paul de-centres Rome. He de-centres its earthly power and the security it offers. He de-centres the emperor and the imperial family. In doing this he is inevitably doing away with the imperial cult. However, this does not seem to be a particular emphasis of his."

¹¹⁶ Nicholas T. Wright, "Paul's Gospel and Caesar's Empire," in *Paul and Politics: Ekklesia, Israel, Imperium, Interpretation: Essays in Honor of Krister Stendahl* (ed. Richard A. Horsley; Harrisburg: Trinity Press International, 2000), 173.

2. From Attitude to Expression: Modifications of the Echo-Hypothesis

semantic-communicative terms this means that the relationship of propositions[117] behind such Pauline wording probably would not follow the pattern of *negativum* ("Caesar is not lord ... ") → *positivum* ("... but Christ is!"). Rather, we should expect a semantic relationship of clarification, in which the core ("Jesus is Lord!") gets the main emphasis, and the implicit contrast only supports this assertion and even remains unstated in its subordinate function.[118] Wright's slogan "confrontation not derivation"[119] moves in the right direction but should be developed even further or made more precise[120] as in "contrast not confrontation."[121] The hypothesis of a critical subtext of this kind does not fall prey to Barclay's critique. Interestingly, Kim – who is criticising attempts of interpreting Paul as counter-imperial – demonstrates how such a critical subtext might look like:

> Even if we can see in his reference to 'peace and security' in 1 Thess 5:3 Paul's attack on the Roman propaganda of *pax Romana,* the function of that attack within the overall message of 1 Thess 5:1–11 is not to call Christians to overthrow the imperial order but to exhort them not to fall into the complacency involved in the imperial propaganda.[122]

---

[117] Note the plural. We can speak of two propositions even where we have only one clause on the lexical-grammatical level if the remark presupposes another proposition. See *GGNT* §314 ("Textverstehen – Mitzuverstehendes").

[118] *GGNT* §352b. Andy Crouch, "Foreword," in *Jesus Is Lord, Caesar Is Not: Evaluating Empire in New Testament Studies* (ed. Scot McKnight and Joseph B. Modica; Downers Grove: IVP Academia, 2013), 13 argues that to say "Jesus is Lord" does not entail "*saying* 'Caesar is not [Lord].'" Rather, it entails *not saying* 'Caesar is Lord.'" But on the very same page he writes: "Of course, *saying* 'Jesus is Lord' does require *believing* that Caesar is not Lord – with as we would say today a capital *L*." So in the end, denying lordship to Caesar is judged to be a necessary precondition for the confession of Jesus as Lord, and accordingly, the negative proposition can be read as subtext of such statements with regard to Jesus after all.

[119] Wright, "Paul and Caesar," 178–179: "We must not confuse derivation with confrontation." Cf. Nicholas T. Wright, *What Saint Paul Really Said* (Oxford: Lion, 1997), 79–80. See also his discussion of the term εὐαγγέλιον in Nicholas T. Wright, "Gospel and Theology in Galatians," in *Gospel in Paul: Studies on Corinthians, Galatians and Romans for Richard N. Longenecker* (ed. L. Ann Jervis and Peter Richardson; JSNTSup 108; Sheffield: Sheffield Academic, 1994), 223–229 ("Isaianic Message or Imperial Proclamation?") and the many comments in Wright, *Faithfulness,* 646, 1272, etc.

[120] To be fair, Wright's concept of "confrontation" is not defined narrowly. Wright, *Faithfulness,* 1272 notes that it "can of course cover many things, from friendly engagement to downright rejection, with all stages in between."

[121] Galinsky, "Cult," 11–13 also wants to sensitise his readers to the broad spectrum of possible forms of criticism. He similarly notes that even if we do not have clear "opposition," we can still have "competition."

[122] Kim, *Christ,* 30.

Clearly, Kim does not differentiate enough between different forms of criticism and seems to limit it to *rebellion*. After all, this "attack" (!) would be critical towards the Empire.[123]

2.2.2 Subtext and Effectiveness

We have now taken a closer look at the kind of criticism for which we do not feel compelled to assume that Paul would rather have formulated it quite openly. This also offers us the opportunity to revisit the nature and function of the subtext. How does the category of criticism we have judged to be most plausible fit into this literary category?

The implicit presupposition of Wright and Elliott seems to be: "If Paul had had free hand, he would have formulated his criticism more openly." This assumes that the subtext is not an effective tool for *persuasion*. But is the use of subtext really only explicable in terms of restricting the "actual" opinion? My approach challenges the idea that using the subtext is a kind of second class level of communication necessitated by oppressive circumstances.

This claim is demonstrated – of all things – by the method which the proponents of a subtext-hypothesis adduce: Hays's scriptural "echoes." It is astonishing that Wright and Elliott refer to Hays's *criteria* but do not spend enough time on the question of what this implies for the *character of the literary phenomenon* itself. An echo – be it scriptural or imperial – evokes a scenery in the imagination of the reader by means of only a very short phrase. The echo of Job 13:16^{LXX} in Phil 1:19 (τοῦτό μοι ἀποβήσεται εἰς σωτηρίαν) not only picks up on an isolated, suitable phrase but also tells us something about Paul's opponents by evoking the characterisation of the "friends" of Job. It does so by means of evoking the larger context of the resonating scriptural reference (metalepsis).[124] The effect of an "echo" thus can be much *bigger* than the one of bare juxtaposition. The reason for this effectiveness is that narrative structures are formative for worldviews,[125] and echoes are able to evoke alternative scenarios in the imagination, which can have persuasive power. Stories are able to challenge other stories and the worldviews they represent much more effectively than purely factual criticism.[126]

---

[123] On this, cf. Galinsky "Cult," 12, who thinks that 1 Thess 5:3 uses "certainly ... an Augustan motto," but has some questions concerning its more specific meaning: "[B]ut what is the implication? An outright rejection of Roman Empire? A call to oppose it? Or, in this eschatological context, a juxtaposition with a degree (you determine the percentage) of contestation: peace and security in or of this world will go only so far and will end with the apocalypse?"

[124] Hays, *Echoes*, 21–24.

[125] This fits nicely with what Wright has written in other places about these categories. Cf. Wrjght, *New Testament*, 38–44.

[126] Wright, *New Testament*, 40: "Stories are, actually, peculiarly good at modifying or subverting other stories and their worldviews. Where head-on attack would certainly fail,

This can also be applied to our subject. It is by no means clear that Paul's best option for expressing the Messiah's superiority over against imperatorial claims would have been the blunt assertion "We trust in Jesus not in Caesar!" The claims of Roman imperial ideology were not indifferent statements which could be judged in a detached manner. Nor would this judgement have been something which could have been simply appropriated by decision. These claims, rather, included assertions concerning the structure and nature of reality as it pertained directly to the individual. To question them meant to question a worldview and thus to imply alternative stories. Conversely, alternative narratives implicitly contested the existing paradigm. Contrary to the simple stating of antitheses, stories also offer a *reason* for accepting these dichotomies by offering a superior meta-structure whose acceptance is facilitated by appealing to the imagination.[127] If Rom 1:1–17 really is a "parody of the imperial cult,"[128] this poses the question whether Paul's echo-like, resonance-evoking formulation could not have been the most *appropriate* means to express this powerful contrast (instead of simply being the "safer" way of

---

the parable hides the wisdom of the serpent behind the innocence of the dove, gaining entrance and favour which can then be used to change assumptions which the hearer would otherwise keep hidden away for safety. ... [T]he subversive story comes close enough to the story already believed by the hearer for a spark to jump between them; and nothing will ever be quite the same again."

[127] See the conclusion of Whitmarsh, "Resistance," 76 on "resistance" in Greek literature during the Roman period: "But whereas the realm of the imagination is usually understood as an abnegation of reality, I would see it here rather as a modification of the *perception* of reality. The sites of conflict I have identified are not simply escapist fantasies; they are testing grounds for an alternative 'truth,' whereby ethics and values are assessed as superior to military dominance. This is what I mean by 'discursive' resistance: imaginative literature has the power to shift our perspectives, so that the reach of imperial control no longer seems infinite, but bounded and contained; and the defeated can become victors." Such a "shift in perspective" does not, of course, always need to include a narrative element. I find the example of Sylvia C. Keesmaat, "Reading Romans in the Capital of the Empire," in *Reading Paul's Letter to the Romans* (ed. Jerry L. Sumney; SBLRBS 73; Atlanta: Society of Biblical Literature, 2012), 50–51 quite appealing in this regard. In it she refers "to that old campaign where Christians said 'Jesus is the Real Thing' as a cultural reference to the Coke campaign that proclaimed 'Coke: the Real Thing.' If they had spelled out, 'Jesus, Not Coke, is the Real Thing,' their assertion would have lost some of its power."

[128] Wright, "Paul and Caesar," 176. Similarly already Georgi, "Gott," 195 with more specific focus on the transition from Claudius to Nero. See recently Michael F. Bird, "'One Who Will Arise to Rule Over the Nations': Paul's Letter to the Romans and the Roman Empire," in *Jesus Is Lord, Caesar Is Not: Evaluating Empire in New Testament Studies* (ed. Scot McKnight and Joseph B. Modica; Downers Grove: IVP Academia, 2013), 153–156 for a good summary of a similar interpretation of Rom 1:3–4. Taubes, *Theologie,* 27 even speaks of a "politische[n] Kampfansage."

communication).¹²⁹ Similarly, when Paul tells the story of the exaltation of the Messiah in Phil 2:6–11,¹³⁰ which climaxes in the worship of the κύριος Jesus – a "stilisierte Kurzerzählung darüber, wie ein Hochwohlgeborener sich dafür qualifiziert, die universale Herrschaft zu erhalten"¹³¹ – I am under the impression that it would (a) not have done justice to Paul's *primary aim of discourse* if he had denied the Lordship of Caesar directly (Section 2.2.1) *nor* would it (b) have been more *effective* to choose such a procedure.¹³²

In summary, we have seen in this section that there can be good *literary* reasons for choosing the subtext to communicate criticism. And if the subtext, maybe in the form of an "echo," is not a necessary evil, this implies that the search for necessitating conditions (like Paul's desire to avoid persecution) is no longer needed.

---

[129] For a decisively narrative reading of the beginning of Romans in the context of calender inscription, see also Stanley E. Porter, "Paul Confronts Caesar with the Good News," in *Empire in the New Testament* (ed. Stanley E. Porter and Cynthia L. Westfall; MNTS 10; Eugene: Pickwick, 2011), 175–184. However, the explicit intertextual links he identifies go much further. I am especially cautious with regard to the question of whether this framework really offers an explanatory advantage ('Is Rom 1:1–17 more likely if we presuppose this background than without it?') and has a good background plausibility (that Paul had such a specific alternative narrative in mind; cf. pp. 173–174).

[130] Cf. Wright, *Faithfulness*, 1312.

[131] Popkes, "Thema," 861.

[132] The statements of Wright, *Faithfulness*, 1294 point in this direction: "The passage speaks of universal authority being granted for a specific and narratable reason, by the proper authority. It is this narrative, telling the story of Jesus so that it echoes and upstages the story of Caesar, that lies at the heart of the claim to detect a subversive echo of Caesar in this passage."

Chapter 6

Explanatory Context

1. Introducing Explanatory Potential

The basic question this work wants to help answer is: "In using the wording X, did Paul intend to criticise Roman ideology?" We have analysed the background plausibility of the hypothesis, but there can be no final answer without recourse to these specific statements themselves. Bayes's theorem demands that we investigate whether a concrete wording (the event E) is expected – on the grounds of the hypothetical preupposition that Paul really wanted to formulate criticism. In what follows, I want to focus on those aspects that are most important in determining the explanatory potential of a counter-imperial subtext beneath the surface of a specific Pauline text.

Identifying overlapping vocabulary between a Pauline wording and phrases from Roman ideology is the usual point of departure when searching for critical "echoes" of the Empire.[1] This is the "event" in Bayes's theorem for which we are seeking the best explanation. Adolf Deissman already famously wrote about the New Testament vocabulary in the context of Roman Caesar ideology: "[D]er in die Mittelmeerwelt hinaustretende Christuskult zeigt schon frühe das Bestreben, die dieser Welt geläufigen und jetzt eben auf die vergötterten Kaiser übertragenen (oder im Kaiserkult vielleicht auch neu geschaffenen Kultworte) für Christus zu reservieren."[2] To note an overlap in

---

[1] It is conceivable that there may be a counter-imperial subtext that is founded on a conceptual basis *only*. If there is a clear conflict between a Pauline and a Roman concept, subversive potential exists even if there is no lexical link. But we would also have to ensure that Paul and his readers could make this association in their minds without the lexical help. Often such conceptual dichotomies can secondarily acquire a lexical link since people will naturally start describing competing concepts in terminology that expresses this contrast. In this book we will limit our investigation to cases where a lexical link exists since the data basis is better in such cases. It might be fruitful nevertheless to build on these results and also look for other counter-imperial subtexts in a separate step. For an approach that focuses less on lexical parallels and more on concepts, see Schreiber, "Paulus," 346.

[2] Deissmann, *Licht,* 290. See Strecker, "Taktiken," 114–116 on Deissmann's position forming the basis of more recent contributions to the question of a counter-imperial Paul (cf. pp. 129–130). Cf. Deissmann, *Licht,* 287, fn. 2 for works with a similar orientation preceding him.

terminology is one thing, but the question we have to ask is: Are the concrete parallels we find between the NT writings and their Roman context what we would *expect* based on the assumption of a critical engagement with this cultural background?

On the one hand, from a methodological perspective, this task can be summarised very simply: Would we expect the specific *wording* if we presupposed a *proposition* with counter-imperial content? But on the other hand, since in practical reality we are faced with competing answers to this question, the assessment of individual passages will be more complicated. Therefore, we will now take a closer look at the dynamics of comparing different hypotheses with regard to their explanatory potentials in this chapter. In order to keep the discussion clearer, we will first discuss the comparative assessment of explanatory potentials for intertextual links in general and then focus more specifically on those with critical intent. This also seems a helpful procedure for specific investigations into concrete Pauline phrases since it allows us to begin with a less hotly debated subject and we can then build our assessment of critical intertextual links on some less tendentious preparatory work.

2. Establishing Parallels between Paul and the Empire

2.1 Termini Technici

Estimating the explanatory potential of a hypothesis is only meaningful if compared to the corresponding values of other hypotheses. Even if our expectancy for a specific wording in a given framework is not high, it might still be "likely" if other options give us even less reason to expect the occurrence of the term or phrase we find in Paul. Establishing an intertextual link, i.e., proving a hypothesis of origin or intention for the choice of words in question is easiest if we are confronted with a *terminus technicus* from the realm of Roman propaganda. If the term is used in one context only, we have reason to expect it to occur in statements referring solely to this area. One could only imagine an intellectual lapse, in which the author uses such a word with another context in mind.[3] There are some words – especially Latinisms – in the NT which clearly fall into this category. Here, exemplary reference may be made to the influential work of Helmut Köster on 1 Thess.[4] He argues that

---

[3] I have observed this many times in German political discourse, when words that are typically associated with National Socialism, like "Entartung," are connected with present-day situations without the intent of implying extreme right-wing positions.

[4] Helmut Köster, "Imperial Ideology and Paul's Eschatology," in *Paul and Empire: Religion and Power in Roman Imperial Society* (ed. Richard A. Horsley; Harrisburg: Trinity Press International, 1997), 158–166.

παρουσία – which appears in 2:19, 3:13, 4:15, and 5:23 – is not a term used in apocalyptic literature (and thus cannot simply be regarded as an "eschatological" term) but a technical term for the advent of a ruler.[5] This limitation to the political realm is even more pronounced with regard to the term ἀπάντησις in 4:17, which describes the "festive reception" of the Lord in terminology normally used for "describing the festive and formal meeting of a king or other dignitary who arrives for a visit of a city."[6] The slogan εἰρήνη καὶ ἀσφάλεια in 5:3 is of special importance since a polemical intent is evident here (those who say this slogan are announced to receive "destruction," ὄλεθρος). The only question is who is addressed. Köster argues that there are no parallels for this phrase in apocalyptic literature.[7] He rejects the interpretation that Paul modifies Jer 6:14^{LXX} (λέγοντες εἰρήνη εἰρήνη καὶ ποῦ ἐστιν εἰρήνη), since this presupposes that Paul would have substituted ἀσφάλεια for the second εἰρήνη, a word never used by Paul at all or by the LXX to translate שָׁלוֹם.[8] Moreover, the explanatory poential (to use our own terminology) of Paul using εἰρήνη "for the description of a false illusion of peace" is judged to be low, since this would not correspond to Paul's style.[9] ἀσφάλεια is said to be a typically political term and the phrase εἰρήνη καὶ ἀσφάλεια "is best ascribed to the realm of Roman imperial propaganda," corresponding to *pax et securitas*.

This short illustration might suffice to show how technical vocabulary might play an important role in establishing intertextual links between Pauline writings and the "texts" of Roman propaganda. However, things are not as clear as one might think on the basis of such an argument. Often, the terms and phrases in question are not used in an imperial context alone so that (anti-)Roman connotations are not mandatory per se. Therefore, we will now consider how to handle situations where alternative options come into play.

2.2 Chance?

"Chance" is an important alternative to intertextuality when it comes to the combination of words into phrases. Are the parallels due to an imitation of another text or are any matching words merely the coincidental result of the ordinary flow of the sentence? After all, if we imagine that Paul simply wanted to add a semantically close word after εἰρήνη for rhetorical reasons – is it so improbable that he chose ἀσφάλεια from the available options?

---

[5] Köster, "Ideology," 158.
[6] Cf. Köster, "Ideology," 160 with reference to Erik Peterson, "Die Einholung des Kyrios," *ZST* 7 (1930): 682–702.
[7] Köster, "Ideology," 161.
[8] Köster, "Ideology," 161.
[9] Köster, "Ideology," 161.

Hays is right in claiming that "Volume" is an important factor in determining "Satisfaction" (in his terminology), i.e., the explanatory potential (in our terminology) of the hypothesis of an intertextual link. There are three parameters of the wording in question which determine this value. Firstly, the *degree* of alignment plays a role since, for statistical reasons, a more precise match decreases the number of possible "outcomes" which would still count as "parallels." There are more wordings which fulfil the condition of being of the same semantic field than of a specific form. It is easier to get the event "even number" when casting a dice (2, 4 and 6 fulfil the condition so that the probability is the number 3 divided by all possible outcomes [6], which yields a probability of 0.5) than to get a specific number like 2 (P=1/6=0.167). Also important is the length of the wording in question since longer parallels are less likely to be produced by chance alone.[10] A third factor is the question how *prominent* a specific formulation is in the imperial context.[11] If the phrase in question is a widely known slogan, it is *less* probable that the author would have used it *without* being aware of its original context. If anyone only slightly educated in modern history said the sentence "Ich bin ein Berliner" or "Yes we can," no one would suggest that no intertextual link was intended even though these phrases are quite short.

Generally speaking, the probability that particular phrases in imperial and NT texts correspond to each other simply due to chance gets lower if these parameters get higher. However, for the sake of fairness, we should note that in the classical echo-hypothesis this notion has to be treated with caution. A reference to Roman propaganda which is so clear that it is completely inexplicable without referring to the Roman context should not be expected. If an echo was used as a means to communicate something internally while remaining unsuspicious for outsiders, this would necessarily influence the degree of correspondence we can expect. There still is a correlation between a rising value for the explanatory potential and the explicitness of the imperial echo, but this correlation is limited. If explicitness implied a rising chance of persecution, this would run counter to the interpretative framework of the classical echo-hypothesis. This relativises the criticism of White, who argues that the background for 1 Thess 5:3 that is often assumed – *pax et securitas* as slogan for the *pax Romana* – is not supported by the actual evidence but is later.[12] While it is an important clarification, the question remains whether – in the framework of the classical echo-hypothesis – one should expect such a

---

[10] Cf. Hays, *Echoes,* 30.

[11] Cf. Hays, *Echoes,* 30.

[12] See White, "Subtexts," 313, who also argues that *securitas* itself was not prominent before the time of Nero. See also the more detailed treatment by Joel R. White, "'Peace and Security' (1 Thessalonians 5.3): Is It Really a Roman Slogan?" *NTS* 59 (2013): 382–395.

clear quotation in a definitely negative context or whether it is not more plausible in this context to expect Paul himself to combine two distinct keywords.[13]

2.3 True and False Alternatives

But even if "chance" is not a satisfying explanation for an overlap between NT and Roman vocabulary and phrasing, we have to be cautious since Roman ideology is not the only textual context in which the NT writers act. If the thesis is advocated, for example, that a specific title like "son of god," "saviour," or "lord" is specifically targeted at Caesar, this specific focus needs to be justified in light of other (mainly religious) applications of this terminology.[14] On the other hand, we also have to be careful not simply to refer to other backgrounds as *alternative* explanations, which cancel out any critical engagement with Roman propaganda.

This is especially true with regard to the Septuagint, which is often adduced as an alternative framework for interpreting alleged echoes of the Empire. Now there is some truth in this argument as long as we are talking about *sources*. Much of the "imperial" vocabulary used by Paul already had its firm place in Judaism through the Greek translation of the Hebrew Bible.[15] It is very probable that, for many terms, the early Church – which originated in this Jewish context – drew upon this source.[16] In a certain sense, Paul was

---

[13] It is, of course, possible to postulate other reasons for modifying imperial slogans. Cf., e.g., Schnelle, *Paulus,* 457 on the Christian εὐαγγέλιον in contrast to Roman εὐαγγέλια: The early Christians "nahmen mit dem Evangeliums-Begriff offenbar sehr bewusst Vorstellungen ihres kulturellen Umfelds auf," but by means of the singular, they also made sure to mark themselves off from their environment.

[14] Correctly noted by Galinsky, "Cult," 6. Cf. also Burk, "Gospel," 317, who mentions the possibility that "Paul and the imperial cult were drawing from the common stock of Koine Greek."

[15] Burk, "Gospel, 317; White, "Subtexts," 309. Of course, as Bryan, *Caesar,* 90 remarks, the translators of the Hebrew Scriptures into Greek were also influenced by the politics of their day and used "the language that they found at hand, which is to say the religious language of Hellenism." The way the translators of the Old Greek influenced later Jewish perception of Graeco-Roman culture in general and Roman rule by the early Christians in particular is indeed a question that should be explored further.

[16] White, "Subtexts," 310. Cf. Adela Y. Collins, "The Worship of Jesus and the Imperial Cult," in *The Jewish Roots of Christological Monotheism: Papers from the St. Andrews Conference on the Historical Origins of the Worship of Jesus* (ed. Carey C. Newman, James R. Davila, and Gladys S. Lewis; JSJSup 63. Leiden: Brill, 1999), 234–257 for a synthesis of an *early* (pre-Pauline) high Christology and Roman (and Hellenistic) influence on the earliest stage. However, the adoption of such elements as ontological entities seems doubtful to me as long as they were not *perceived as* Jewish ideas (against Collins, "Worship," 242). I do not see how the rejection of worshipping the emperor should have led to the worship of Jesus – and not, to the contrary, to suspicion towards such praxis in general

presented lexically with a fait accompli.[17] Therefore, it is difficult to imagine how he could have expressed his message *differently* if he had not wanted to criticise the Empire in any way.[18] However, two comments are in order here.

Firstly, although it is true that Paul was presented with a set of established vocabulary, this does not mean that he did not have any stylistic devices for making clear that he was evoking imperial associations, which would go beyond the lexical sense of the words of his source. The assumption of a septuagintal reference *with* imperial association has a higher explanatory potential if there is a difference in usage compared to the normal use of the word or phrase, which emphasises only a specific (e.g., royal) aspect of the concept. One might refer to Rom 1:3–4 as an example. It is, no doubt, noticeable how emphatically the definition of the gospel is centred around the messiahship of Jesus ("son of David," "son of God") and that Paul refers – in an atypical way – to the confirmation by the Spirit in 1:4 in order to describe this status.[19] Also, the flow of the passage sometimes narrows down the focus of a particular component inherent in a concept: 1 Cor 8:5–6 certainly is the most obvious example since the κύριος Ἰησοῦς Χριστός is explicitly contrasted with other lords.[20] Accordingly, the *immediate literary context*[21] can help in

---

(cf. Collins, "Worship," 257). Nevertheless, Collins's interpretation of the "son of God" language in Mark seems valid to me (Collins, "Worship, 257): "[T]he royal and messianic use of the epithet 'son of God' in Jewish traditions is the best analogy and perhaps the source of its application to Jesus in the Gospel of Mark. At least some members of the audience of Mark, however, were aware that the emperor was also honored with equivalent epithets. The phrase 'son of God' would evoke the imperial cult for such individuals and groups. For them the Gospel of Mark was making a case for the worship of Christ as a preferable alternative to the worship of Caesar."

[17] White, "Subtexts," 310. Similarly Bird, "Nations," 149.

[18] White, "Subtexts," 309: "Indeed, it is hard to see how anyone wanting to proclaim in Greek the message that Jesus of Nazareth represented the culmination of OT prophetic expectations could have done so without recourse to that vocabulary." White, "Subtexts," 310: "They [earliest Christian quasi-technical terms] were chosen for him by others, and he could hardly have avoided using them, even if he had wanted to." Galinsky, "Shadow," 222, who urges proponents of a counter-imperial interpretation of Paul not to jump to their conclusions too easily by neglecting important alternatives, himself underestimates the importance of the OT background for Paul's mission when writing: "Unsurprisingly, he and the evangelists use the language of that political environment not in the least because it is understood by their audience." Similarly Carter, *Empire,* 87: "Paul's constant use of language closely associated with imperial power, and his redefinition of these terms with Christian content, indicates a direct challenge to the gospel of Caesar."

[19] Cf. Harrison, *Paul,* 36 who gives ἐν δυνάμει in Rom 1:4 as an example for the fulfilment of his criterion "unusual additions to traditional formulae."

[20] Contra Crouch, "Foreword," 13–14. Even Barclay, "Empire," 377 admits that here we have a clear antithesis, which allows for the safe conclusion of Paul's sensitivity regarding that title. He writes: "Given this evidence it is no surprise that Paul does not refer to political authorities as κύριοι." Sure. Nor does he call them "sons of god" or "saviours"

identifying an intended Roman resonance even if assuming a septuagintal wording with or without Roman connotations might have the same explanatory potential. We may thus conclude that the tradition-historical derivation of a word or phrase sometimes may only be part of the story. It is possible that these literary phenomena acquired additional nuances in conversation with new historical contexts and one may well be able to identify these emphases in certain instances. Limiting the meaning of concepts to their sense components inherent in the original source would mean to ignore from the outset the sensitivity of people for how older traditions enter into conversation with contemporary contexts (by means of lexical links).

Secondly, even if septuagintal conceptuality alone (without later conceptual enrichment) is a satisfying explanation for the lexical choice, this does not mean that the resulting proposition does not evoke implications for the Roman sphere nor that it is neutral with regard to Roman ideology.[22] Many critics jump too easily from establishing a septuagintal background to rejecting a Roman foreground. We always have to keep in mind what the explanandum really is: Is it the *source* of the wording or the *intention* lying behind its use? The interplay of causes for literary phenomena is more complex than it might seem at first sight, and we should not create false dichotomies. As we have already noted above (Chapter 5, Section 2.2.1), this is an important point often made by Wright, who urges his colleagues to differentiate between source and intention or, in his words, *derivation* and *confrontation*. Septuagintal derivation and intended imperial connotation are not exclusive options if – and this has to be analysed in each individual case – the vocabulary in question already possesses semantic elements which would evoke imperial concepts in this new context of Roman claims. Where the pre-existing Jewish concept already possessed a subversive potential, this resonance could take the form of critique, which leads us to the next section of this chapter, where we will not discuss intertextuality as such, but the intention of criticising by such literary means.

(cf. Phil 3:20) by the way. And this is similarly unsurprising given the fact that these designations can only be used in a proper sense for the Messiah Jesus. Where they are used by another party, Paul cannot be comfortable with this usage.

[21] This belongs to the category of "Pauline Context" (see above Chapter 2, Section 3.3.2). Cf. also Hays's "Thematic Coherence" and my integration of this aspect into Bayes's theorem Chapter 2, Section 3.3.1).

[22] As noted correctly, e.g., by Strecker, "Taktiken," 154. See also pp. 156–157: "Grundsätzlich lässt sich aber festhalten, dass die untergründigen Parallelen und assoziativen Querverbindungen der hoheitlichen paulinischen Christologie zur römischen Kaiserverehrung die im Kaiserkult zelebrierte souveräne Macht des Prinzeps notgedrungen aushöhlten."

3. From Intertextuality to Criticism: Neutral Parallel or Antithesis?

3.1 Non-Roman "Echoes" with and without Counter-Imperial "Resonance"

Demonstrating a balance of judgement seldom found after him,[23] Deissmann had already described how this dynamic may have functioned:

> So entsteht ein polemischer Parallelismus zwischen Kaiserkult und Christuskult, der auch da empfunden wird, wo die vom Christuskult bereits mitgebrachten Urworte aus den Schatzkammern der Septuagintabibel und des Evangeliums mit ähnlich- oder gleichklingenden solennen Begriffen des Kaiserkultes zusammentreffen.[24]

To illustrate this by means of an example, it is undoubtedly correct – as emphasised, for example, by White[25] – that the κύριος-title was used by the first Christians to associate the Messiah with Israel's God. But, already as a title for YHWH, this term is inseparably connected to the claim of universal rulership – which evidently is not compatible with the excessive exaltation of human rulers.[26] Accordingly, one does not have to postulate that Paul uses κύριος in discontinuity with pre- and early Christian tradition in order to

---

[23] Other aspects, such as the assumption of purely "religious" motives, are less convincing of course (cf. Strecker, "Taktiken," 115).

[24] Deissmann, *Licht,* 290–291. He is followed recently, e.g., by Meggit, "Clothes," 157–158.

[25] White, "Subtexts," 309.

[26] Hans Bietenhard, "κύριος," *ThBLNT* 1:660: "Als Schöpfer der Welt ist er auch ihr rechtmäßiger Herr, der über sie uneingeschränkte Verfügungsgewalt hat." The questions, which White, "Subtexts," 311 raises point in this direction as well: "Does the use of the terms in question by other Jewish writers (Philo, for example) reveal that they are inherently anti-imperial? Do other Jewish writers who are more amenable to Rome (Josephus comes immediately to mind) avoid them for precisely that reason?" However, one should keep in mind that the designation "lord" could be used with a less significant meaning in the OT^{LXX} itself. Accordingly, it is not surprising to find such usage in Philo and Josephus, too (nor would it be impossible in Paul's letters – although it would have been more difficult for him to use the word without feeling a competition on the level of the concept since his whole theology centred around Jesus as Lord). But Josephus, *B.J.* 7.418–419 also demonstrates that, under the right circumstances, Jews did not feel comfortable calling Caesar "lord" (Καίσαρα δεσπότην ὁμολογήσωσιν and Καίσαρα δεσπότην ἐξονομάσαι) because they thought that this would conflict with their conviction that God was their sole lord (*B.J.* 7.410; cf. also *B.J.* 7.323: God ἐστι καὶ δίκαιος ἀνθρώπων δεσπότης). The word used here is δεσπότης not κύριος so that the designation of these persons as "Kyrios-Märtyrer" (Deissmann, *Licht,* 302) is not correct. But both words overlap significantly (see Josephus, *A.J.* 20.90). In the NT the word is used for God (Rev 6:10) and Jesus (e.g., Jude 1:4). Hence, this incident nicely illustrates the basic point that the Jewish *source* of a christological title does not necessarily count against a counter-imperial *intention*. To the contrary, the connotations necessary for such a usage could even belong to the original repertoire of the term itself.

assume that by using this term he could have formulated criticism of imperial claims. The tradition itself had the *potential* to *inevitably* react critically towards certain elements of imperial ideology.[27] This is illustrated nicely by the fact that White refers to Fee's work on Christology in order to justify the derivation of the κύριος-title from septuagintal usage.[28] At the same time, this position does not keep Fee from seeing a reference to Caesar in individual cases.[29]

Of course, when we are dealing with the counter-imperial potential of traditional terminology, our judgement on how significant the interaction with Roman ideology is will vary from letter to letter, depending on the accessibility of specific motifs. As long as we can assume that the author was aware of the cultural situation of his readers and their sensitivity to certain phrases, this will allow for the assumption that a term will be used without any specific subversive emphasis in many cases but that it can develop much more explosiveness in other contexts.[30] The accumulation of terms that also appear in texts expressing Roman ideology at the beginning of a letter written to the Christians in *Rome* thus deserves more attention than the terms might receive in another letter (or in isolation, cf. Section 2.3 on the literary context). Correspondingly, Wright refers to the factors of *literary and cultural context* as a kind of "booster" for the "Volume" of an imperial echo at the beginning of Romans:

Paul begins [Rom 1:3–4] and ends [Rom 15:12] the theological exposition of the letter with the strong note of Jesus as the Davidic Messiah, risen from the dead ... In fact, the whole introduction to the letter contains so many apparently counter-imperial signals that I find it impossible to doubt that both Paul and his first hearers and readers – in Rome, of all places – would have picked up the message, loud and clear.[31]

---

[27] Hence, I think H. Gregory Snyder, "Response to Karl Galinsky, 'In the Shadow (or Not) of the Imperial Cult: A Cooperative Agenda,'" in *Rome and Religion: A Cross-Disciplinary Dialogue on the Imperial Cult* (ed. Jeffrey Brodd and Jonathan L. Reed; SBLWGRW 5; Atlanta: Scholars Press, 2011), 228 is right in principle when writing: "It would be useful ... when talking about the allegedly anti-imperial nature of Paul's gospel, to make a distinction between a gospel that is anti-imperial by design and one that is incidentally anti-imperial; that is, given its nature and manifestations, it will at various times and places find itself in competition with imperial ideology. However, that is not its sole or chief purpose ... [C]ertain aspects of Paul's message about the God of Israel and his messianic agent Jesus would certainly have found themselves running against the grain of imperial ideology; however, that was not its purpose but rather an incidental result, not a central motivation."

[28] Gordon D. Fee, *Pauline Christology: An Exegetical-Theological Study* (Peabody: Hendrickson, 2007), 41.

[29] Fee, *Christology*, 402–403.

[30] See Chapter 5, Section 2.2.1 on "intention."

[31] Wright, *Perspective*, 76. Cf. Similarly Taubes, *Theologie*, 24: "Also handelt es sich um eine bewußte Betonung derjenigen Attribute, die imperatorisch sind, die königlich sind,

Maybe the term "echo" is not the best description for such a literary phenomenon and evokes inappropriate expectations. The echo describes the relationship between two texts that are connected through the memory of the author. Mediated through this resource, the first text becomes a "source" in the wider sense for the wording of the second. But is this the kind of relationship we find between a "text" of Roman propaganda and a verse in a Pauline letter in those cases where we allow for the Septuagint as a conceptual *and* lexical source? In order to avoid confusion, I think that such a textual phenomenon should better be described – to stay in the realm of acoustic metaphors – as *"resonance"* of another text with the primary text of the letter, thus creating a subtext complementing the information given on the surface.[32] The term "echo" should be reserved for cases in which we have a real linear relationship of dependence.

In this context – and having been led into conversation with Hays again anyway – we can also revisit Hays's criterion of the"History of Interpretation." As we have already noted, it can only play a role in influencing probabilities if we take it to be an indicator for how certain words and phrases could have been understood in the first century and similar contexts. Although we have a similar – sometimes even much more intense – societal situation of persecution and martyrdom in the centuries following Paul and although this should make us expect a heightened sensitivity to counter-imperial subtexts in the Pauline literature, these interpretations do not abound. The *Mart. Paul*[33] remains the exception rather than the rule.[34] How-

---

die kaiserlich sind. Sie werden betont gegenüber der Gemeinde in Rom, wo der Imperator selbst präsent ist, und wo das Zentrum des Cäsar-Kultes, der Cäsarenreligion ist." Cf. already Georgi, "Gott," 194: "Der Exeget muß die Frage beantworten, warum ausgerechnet in einem Brief an den Sitz der römischen Macht ein Text wie dieser als Basistext zitiert wird, um dann in diesem Brief interpretiert zu werden."

[32] Interestingly, this is much closer to Kristeva's original notion of 'intertextuality' than the 'echo.'

[33] Of course, the form of and reason for the counter-imperial stance of *Mart. Paul* is itself the subject of debate. Brandon Walker, "The Forgotten Kingdom: Miracle, the Memory of Jesus, and Counter-Ideology to the Roman Empire," in *Reactions to Empire: Sacred Texts in Their Socio-Political Contexts* (WUNT II 372; ed. John A. Dunne und Dan Batovici; Tübingen: Mohr Siebeck, 2014), 142–143 has recently written with regard to *Mart. Paul* 2.2–2.6 that "the kingdom is not directly related to miracles, rather the references provide the opportunity for explanation of an alternative king who is greater than Caesar and can raise the dead." However, this seems only partially true since the connection between the rescue from death and the kingship of Jesus takes the route of implied messianic-apocalyptic prophecies. (Note that Nero's question begins with οὖν; Zwierlein: "Ist es also jener, der (wie es heißt) herrschen soll über die Äonen und auflösen alle Königreiche unter dem Himmel?").

[34] Cf., for example, Gordon L. Heath, "The Church Fathers and the Roman Empire," in *Empire in the New Testament* (ed. Stanley E. Porter and Cynthia L. Westfall; MNTS 10.

ever, we can also observe an early loss of appreciation for the OT background of many christological concepts.[35] Where designations like "son of David" simply describe the human side of Jesus, and "Christ" becomes something like a second name, these words and phrases naturally lose their explosive force.[36] This means that precisely because the Jewish connotations *no longer* resonate, the counter-imperial potential gets lost.[37] This emphasis runs completely against the role of the LXX in many arguments against a counter-imperial Paul: It is this background *itself* that often yields a critical potential – and it should not automatically be treated as an alternative explanation to intended criticism.

Eugene: Pickwick, 2011), 258–282 for a discussion with reference to the counter-imperial interpretation of the NT. See, however, Wright, *Faithfulness,* 1313 on the *Martyrdom of Polycarp*. He rightly points out that the answer of Polycarp in *Mart. Pol.* 9.3 responds to the demand to confess Caesar as Lord (8.2) and to swear by his fortune (9.2). Cf. Gerd Buschmann, *Das Martyrium des Polykarp* (KAV 6; Göttingen: Vandenhoeck & Ruprecht, 1998), 171. The effective history of potentially "subversive" NT texts and terms, such as "lord," in the early church deserves a detailed investigation.

[35] Some, of course, would argue that this dimension is already absent in Paul himself. For Schnelle, *Paulus,* 498, for example, "Christ" evokes anointing rites "im gesamten Mittelmeerraum" so that it could be understood "als Prädikat für die einzigartige Gottnähe und Heiligkeit Jesu." This naturally removes some politically subversive potential. (Although this does not imply that this removes all conflict since the Roman "political" sphere was still quite "religious." Schnelle hence also correctly notes: "Seine Hoheit relativiert alle anderen Ansprüche, denn nicht der Kaiser oder eine Kultgottheit retten.")

[36] Jesus as the "son of God" occurs quite frequently in Ignatius (Ign. *Smyrn.* 1.1; Ign. *Rom.* 7.3; Ign. *Eph.* 18.2; Ign. *Trall.* 9.1) emphasising Jesus's humanity. Cf., however, Eusebius, *Hist. eccl.* 3.19–3.20.7 and 3.32.1–6. On χριστός as an honorific in Paul, see Mathew V. Novenson, *Christ among the Messiahs: Christ Language in Paul and Messiah Language in Ancient Judaism* (Oxford: Oxford University Press, 2012). Cf. Wolfram Kinzig, "The West and North Africa," in *Redemption and Resistance: The Messianic Hopes of Jews and Christians in Antiquity* (ed. Markus Bockmuehl and James C. Paget; London: T&T Clark, 2007), 204, who notes that the royal dimension of *Christus* was known in the west but also states: "However, not all Christians were as educated as their theological teachers and bishops. ... *Christus* was generally understood as a name rather than a title and, in any case, even if the early Christians, notably those of pagan descent, had Jn 1.41 in mind, this does not mean that they were aware of the Jewish concepts of messianism associated with that title."

[37] This is at least a partial response to the question of Galinsky, "Cult," 15: "Was their resistance to empire so coded that successive generations didn't get it? Or did they mean to juxtapose rather than oppose and once the empire became increasingly Christian, empire, imperial cult, *ecclesiae,* and so forth ceased being an issue because they were appropriated in fact?"

3.2 Imperial References with and without Critical Intention: Neutral Parallel or Antithesis?

Until now, we have examined the critical potential of wordings which are rooted in the Jewish tradition. Now we turn to intertextual links which are produced by the use of terminology from the realm of Roman ideology itself, for example, by use of a technical term or by use of a word which can be used in different contexts but for which it can be shown that it most probably is used in the "Roman" sense.[38] Hence, we have the following options in dealing with overlap in Roman and New Testament vocabulary.[39]

Intention	Source		
	Septuagint	*Roman Empire*	*Other (e.g., traditional cults)*
Criticism	LXX Background/ Counter-Imperial	Roman Background/ Counter-Imperial	→ only possible if Roman dimension is included (e.g., contra *iconic* worship)
Neutral	LXX Background/ Neutral	Roman Background/ Neutral	Other Background/Neutral

After having established this "Roman" background, we still have to decide whether this also implies a critical evaluation of this point of reference. After all, there could be many different reasons for Paul choosing a subtle reference to the imperial realm. In principle, "echoes of the Empire" do not have to be more subversive than "echoes of Scripture." A resonance with Caesar's prop-

---

[38] For example, θριαμβεύω in 2 Cor 2:14 has also been interpreted against alternative backgrounds that are not connected with the Roman sphere, but none of these can be substantiated by an analysis of actual occurrences of the verb in the TLG corpus.

[39] Oakes, "Universe," 303–307 suggests four categories for classifying such overlap: 1) Rome and Christianity follow common models, 2) Christianity follows Rome, 3) Rome conflicts with Christianity, 4) Christianity conflicts with Rome. Basically, they can also be sorted along the axes of "source" and "intention": 1) Non-Roman source; undetermined intention; 2) Roman Source; no critical intention; 3) and 4) Roman source; critical intention. I am not so sure whether the differentiation between 3) and 4) is very helpful since any "attack" from the Christian side (→ 4) would be based on the perception of some conflict initiated from the Roman side (e.g., Caesar claiming an inappropriate role). Also, I think that it is a pity that Oakes does not pay more attention to the potential of the *first* category. Surprisingly to me, he refers to Deissmann's polemical parallels but also writes (Oakes, "Universe," 303): "However, our interest is in the origin of parallel terminology. If a parallel stems from the use of a common model, then it does not give us direct evidence about the relationship between Christianity and Rome." Cf. also the critique of Carter, "Paul," 22 who responds: "But investigating the origin of various concepts ... contributes little to discerning Christian-empire relations."

aganda, therefore, does not automatically imply resistance to his rule or a clash of ideologies. This is also the counter-argument of Barclay, who admits that there "is much common 'political' vocabulary" between the two textual worlds.[40] Nevertheless, he questions that this implies a polemical intention, that a *parallel* should be understood in terms of an *antithesis*.[41] He argues that, after all, the designation of the Corinthians as the temple of God (collectively in 1 Cor 3:16 and individually in 6:19) also presupposes the *legitimacy* of the temple in Jerusalem instead of questioning its authority.[42] Only with regard to the κύριος-title is Barclay willing to speak of such an exclusivity on the basis that Paul in 1 Cor 8:6 creates the dichotomy himself.[43] But the pseudepigraphical 1 Tim is said to attribute the title "king" to human rulers (1 Tim 2:2) although it is also used as a designation for Christ (6:15): "In other words, the relationship between two holders of the same title need not be antithetical; it might be that one is the *supreme* holder of a title that others share, at a subordinate rank."[44] Miller[45] has made a similar point when noting that the existence of "slaves of Artemis" in Ephesus demonstrates that the Emperor did not demand "complete loyalty." From this he deduces that Paul's self-designation as a "slave of Christ" would not have been especially subversive.

However, if we take into account the modifications of the subtext hypothesis from the last chapter, Barclay's criticism becomes less persuasive. This variant of the hypothesis of a critical subtext in Paul does not require an "antithesis" but only 1) a lexical proximity that makes a resonance of imperial connotations plausible and 2) a conceptual proximity that allows for a transferral and application of some isolated aspects to the new context. If we then 3) do not have a completely successful integration of the two concepts with each other, this already allows for a subversive function.[46] Contrary to Bar-

---

[40] Barclay, "Empire," 376.
[41] Barclay, "Empire," 376: "The question is whether this overlap of vocabulary implies an *antithetical* relationship between the two domains, and, conversely, whether Paul's antithetical constructs place Christ or the church in opposition to the Roman empire in the way suggested by Wright and others." Cf. Pinter, "Gospel," 110 who agrees almost verbatim: "[O]verlap in terminology – even between divine and human possessors of the same title – need not signal a competitive relationship."
[42] Barclay, "Empire," 376. (Nota bene: this is a true "echo" from Barclay's perspective although not a subversive one.)
[43] Barclay, "Empire," 377.
[44] Barclay, "Empire," 378.
[45] Miller, "Cult," 328.
[46] Kim, *Christ,* 29 correctly notes that parallels do not only have to exhibit formal correspondence but also a certain conceptual closeness. However, I doubt that he is right that there is no provocative overlap with regard to "son of god" language (so also Bryan, *Caesar,* 91). See the contrary assessment of Michael Peppard, *The Son of God in the Roman World: Divine Sonship in its Social and Political Context* (Oxford: Oxford University

clay's assertion, a thoroughgoing dichotomy is not required. Although nothing depends on it, I think that one could even claim that the arguments Barclay adduces are not only not convincing but even demonstrate the opposite of his conclusion: The temple language of Paul is not "founded on the continuing" validity of the present temple system but rather questions its status as the only valid mediation of YHWH's presence. After all, the Christian movement is described as Ezekiel's temple and thus as the true fulfilment of the Jewish hope.[47] The *believers* are the sanctuary (ναός) where God dwells (cf. also 2 Cor 6:16 and Eph 2:21–22). The argument is certainly not *directed* at the cult in Jerusalem, but it *presupposes* ideas that would have been absolutely unacceptable to the priesthood in Jerusalem.[48] Hence, the application of this concept to the church by all means has a provocative potential. The Qumran community offers at least a partial parallel.[49] Of course, the parallel is not thoroughgoing. While Paul had *heilsgeschichtliche* reasons for his view, the people at Qumran still assumed Jerusalem to be the appropriate place for

---

Press, 2011). On the other hand, the principal concern is justified. For example, the following difference that Carter, *Empire*, 21 adduces for Paul's collection and Rome's taxing practice, seems contrived: "[T]he intent is to relieve suffering rather than cause it." But for the *beneficiaries* of taxation (analogous to those benefiting from the collection), the intended result, likewise, was not to suffer!

[47] Fee, *Epistle*, 147.

[48] From my perspective, this does not run counter to the convincing argument by Friedrich W. Horn, "Paulus und der Herodianische Tempel,"*NTS* 53 (2007): 184–203, according to which the institution in Jerusalem could still be used by Paul. The question, rather, is to what *extent* Paul would have accepted its claims to mediate God's presence. Here, I think, Horn underestimates the relevance of the modification of Paul's theology of the people of God in light of the Spirit (Wright, *Faithfulness*, 1074–1078). Accordingly, I do not understand, for example, how Wolfgang Schrage, *Der erste Brief an die Korinther: 1Kor 1,1–6,11* (EKK 7,1; Zürich: Benziger 1991), 305 can say that, on the one hand, "die Gemeinde als endzeitliche Gemeinschaft an Stelle des (damals noch nicht zerstörten!) alten Tempels im Prozeß der Erneuerung der gesamten Schöpfung [steht]" but that, on the other hand, he does not think that this implies that "Gottes Shekinah nicht länger auf dem alten Tempel ruht."

[49] Most scholars assume that the movement originated in conflict with the Jerusalem priesthood (cf. CD I, 3 etc.; see Johann Maier, "Temple, Second Temple," *EDSS* 2:923–924). The "wicked" priest, the opponent of the Teacher of Righteousness, probably is a wordplay on the "high" priest (cf. הכוהן הרשע and הכהן הראש; he appears in 4Q171 1–10 IV, 7–10; 1QpHab [reconstructed I, 13]; VIII, 8; IX, 9; XI, 4; XII, 2.8. Cf. also 1QpHab VIII, 16; IX, 16; maybe also the "liar" in X, 9. 4QMMT probably discusses this conflict in some detail. See on this Lawrence H. Schiffman, "Miqtsat Ma'asei Ha-Torah," *EDSS* 1:448–560. On the Wicked Priest in general, cf. Timothy H. Lim, "Wicked Priest," *EDSS* 2:973–967). Accordingly, since the present temple is defiled, the *Temple Scroll* depicts God's eschatological temple (1Q19 XXIX, 8–10). In the meantime, the Qumran community itself is described as the real temple of God (1QS VIII, 5–9; IX, 6; maybe 4Q174, but there is much discussion whether 4Q174 I, 6 (מקדש אדם) refers to an eschatological or a spiritual temple).

sacrifice. Their withdrawal from the temple was only temporary, and their reason for it, disagreement about the right execution of the cult.⁵⁰ With regard to Paul's temple language, we have observed that a concept is taken up and modified in a way that questions the status that it typically assumes. We can observe the very same dynamic in Barclay's example from 1 Timothy. First, we should note that it is God, not the Messiah, who is described as "eternal king" and "king of kings" (1 Tim 1:17 and 6:15; if there is a reference to Christ it is in the former case, not the latter). But be this as it may, Barclay is right, that earthly rulers (1 Tim 2:2) can also be called βασιλεῖς. It is also true that this demonstrates that titles can be attributed on different levels to different parties. However, this does not at all mean that, from a Roman perspective, there is no subversive potential. After all, it is very doubtful that the Roman understanding of the term "king" really did allow for an expansion of the concept so that a Jewish rebel could be integrated.⁵¹ This is all the more doubtful since Jesus is explicitly described as the *superior* bearer of this title ("king of kings"!), which implies that the other rulers – including Caesar – are *subordinate* to him.⁵² This is not an "antithesis" but a clear curtailment of

---

⁵⁰ Cf. on this Lawrence H. Schiffman, "The Qumran Community's Withdrawal from the Jerusalem Temple," in *Gemeinde ohne Tempel/Community without Temple: Zur Substituierung und Transformation des Jerusalemer Tempels und seines Kults im Alten Testament, antiken Judentum und frühen Christentum* (ed. Beate Ego, Armin Lange, and Peter Pilhofer; WUNT 118; Tübingen: Mohr Siebeck, 1999), 267–284. For comparative assessments of the Christian and Qumran community as temple, see Georg Klinzing, *Die Umdeutung des Kultus in der Qumrangemeinde und im Neuen Testament* (SUNT 7; Göttingen: Vandenhoeck & Ruprecht, 1971), and Bertil Gärtner, *The Temple and the Community in Qumran and the New Testament: A Comparative Study in the Temple Symbolism of the Qumran Texts and the New Testament* (SNTSMS 1; Cambridge: Cambridge University Press, 1965). For an up-to-date discussion of the different temples described in the sectarian texts of Qumran, see Johann Maier, "Temple," 921–926.

⁵¹ See also Wright, *Faithfulness,* 1312, who rightly remarks: "The word 'president' is used in the United States of America not only for the elected head of state but for the senior official in thousands of businesses, colleges, golf clubs and other organizations. This causes neither confusion nor confrontation. But if a new group were to arise, claiming that they were the rightful heirs of the whole country and that their leader was its true ruler, and referring to that leader as 'President,' the word would spring to life in a rather different way." I would respond analogously to Harrill, *Paul,* 88, who argues that calling Jesus "lord" did not have any subversive potential "because the term specified not the emperor alone but was a commonplace epithet of respect for both noble society and deities." While it is true that one has to be careful not to create a dichotomy between Christ and Caesar alone (traditional deities were not often called "lord," but it was quite common in mystery religions indeed; cf. Fee, *Corinthians,* 373), the reference to "lord" as an address of "social betters" seems inappropriate since, with regard to Jesus, the term clearly denotes a different concept.

⁵² Cf., e. g., Josephus, *B.J.* 3.351; 5.563. After Julius Caesar, Roman emperors were naturally cautious not to call themselves *rex,* but in the Greek part of the Empire they were

current claims from a Roman perspective. Hence, Nero's reaction in *Mart. Paul* 4.4–6 to the "echo" of 1 Tim 1:17 in *Mart. Paul* 4.2 is quite understandable. Even where such a subordination under the titular Jesus is not expressed as explicitly as in the juxtaposition of "king" and "king of kings," a subversive potential of this kind can usually be assumed since it is precisely the characteristic feature of New Testament Christology that the designations for the Messiah go hand in hand with absolute claims.[53] This is especially the case since these terms are almost always integrated into the larger Christian story, and it is within this context that their true potential can be seen.[54] These observations confirm the procedure of Fantin, who counter's the argument of James Dunn according to whom "different lordships could be acknowledged in different spheres without implying conflict of loyalties"[55] by focussing on the concept of 'supreme lord.'[56]

That the thesis of a compatibility is often not justifiable is even more obvious in the rather strange argument of Miller.[57] On the one hand, the analogy which is adduced – Greek cults – was nothing less than the religio-historical context for the *acceptance and integration* of Roman power. On the other hand, we are dealing with the Jewish messianic expectancy, which was a characteristic expression of a tradition known for opposing foreign rule. The two situations could not be more different from a Roman perspective. Greek gods were no competitors for Caesar but collaborators. But other individuals with political significance were not treated as graciously. Accordingly, it is not very surprising – although it is fatal for Miller's picture of a thoroughgo-

---

called βασιλεύς nevertheless – a designation that also demonstrates the realistic perception of the population (Evangelos K. Chrysos, "The Title ΒΑΣΙΛΕΥΣ in Early Byzantine International Relations," *DOP* 32 [1978]: 66; also correctly noted by Meggitt, "Clothes," 157). In the NT, see John 19:15 (οὐκ ἔχομεν βασιλέα εἰ μὴ Καίσαρα) and 1 Pet 2:13, 17. Cf. also Acts 17:7 (although the reference is not completely clear there), Rev 17:9, etc. It is telling that the reluctance to accept the title "king" from Augustus onwards was connected to the fact that "he was above all kings, and in many cases he was the actual king-maker, since it was in his power to recognize and invest the client kings" (Chrysos, "Title," 69). (For the later designation of the Sasanian monarch as "king of kings" see Chrysos, "Title," 70).

[53] Jesus is *the* Messiah, he is *the* Saviour, he is *the* Lord, he is *the* Son of God. It is only through the connection – by means of faith and baptism, by being "in Christ" (Gal 3:26b) – with the one true son of God (Gal 2:20) that believers can also be called "sons of God" (3:26a) in a wider sense.

[54] Jesus is not any "lord," but he is the Lord every human being will have to acknowledge (Phil 2:10–11). Similarly Bird, "Nations," 161: "It is not simply the 'parallel' terminology that Paul uses like *Kyrios* or *euangelion,* but the apocalyptic and messianic narrative that such language is couched in that makes it tacitly counterimperial."

[55] James D. G. Dunn, *The Theology of the Apostle* (Grand Rapids: Eerdmans, 1998), 247.

[56] Fantin, *Lord,* 217.

[57] Similarly put forward by Bryan, *Caesar,* 91–92.

ing tolerance[58] – that the rule of Augustus meant the end for all public cults for *other individuals* (who did not belong to Caesar's family).[59] Suddenly, they were "politically undesirable."[60] And already in the time of Tiberius, we hear of the accusation that the Pompey-follower Theophanes was approached with divine honours.[61]

In the end, we have to determine for each individual case whether the wording we find in the biblical text would 1) evoke a comparison with current concepts described in a similar way and 2) whether there is a subversive potential the author probably was aware of. For the moment, we can note, quite generally, that the denial of a critical potential of lexical parallels cannot be proved easily by noting that an "antithesis" is not apparent – at least not if we opt for a more modest hypothesis of critical engagement with imperial propaganda, such as described in the last chapter.

---

[58] The concrete case of Paul being the "slave" of Christ would demand more detailed analysis. What Hays has said with regard to the *centrality* of a term as an important parameter for determining the probability of an echo (see Chapter 2, Section 3.1) may come into play here. Barclay's example of the title "king" seems to me to be of much greater significance. The aspect of religious pluralism and tolerance is also emphasised by Galinsky, "Cult," 8. However, I think the very example he gives shows that one should be careful in assuming that this attitude extends to potentially subversive groups like the early Christians: The reaction to Paul and Jason in Acts 17 is described as "simply to take a security bond and let them go" although the incident probably rather indicates that they were regarded as forming an illegal association, see Chapter 4, Section 1.2.2.3.

[59] Price, *Rituals,* 49–50.

[60] Price, *Rituals,* 50.

[61] Price, *Rituals,* 50. Tacitus, *Ann.* 6.18.2: "The crime laid to their account was that Theophanes of Mytilene (great-grandfather of Pompeia and her brother) had been numbered with the intimates of Pompey, and that, after his death, Greek sycophancy had paid him the honour of deification."

Chapter 7

Conclusions

1. Summary

We are now in the position to summarise our results on the subtext-hypothesis of Wright and Elliott, which rests on the assumption of (a) suppression by Roman authorities and (b) Paul's wish to avoid persecution. How is the background plausibility to be evaluated in light of the nested necessary conditions we have discussed in this book?

If one wants to accept Wright's and Elliott's suggestion of suppression (→ a) as reason for Paul's choice of the subtext for his criticism one has to modify – or rather specify – the *object* of criticism insofar as challenging it openly would have been dangerous (Chapter 4, Section 1.3). However, even in this modified form, the hypothesis seems to run into a serious problem if we consider Paul's personality: Would Paul really have refrained from open criticism in order to avoid persecution (→ b)? This does not seem to be the best suggestion for Paul's potential motivation for placing his criticism in the subtext (Chapter 5, Section 2.1). These observations fit nicely into what we have already seen with regard to Philo (Chapter 1, Section 3), where we already concluded that hermeneutical and literary reasons (and not avoidance of persecution alone) are important factors in explaining his use of the subtext for "counter-imperial" remarks.

Hence, a further modification of the classical subtext-hypothesis seems prudent. Paul's use of the subtext for expressing counter-imperial criticism could be explained in two ways. First, one could postulate that it was not Paul's *primary intention* to criticise the Empire so that more overt criticism would have detracted from his main focus (Chapter 5, Section 2.2.1). Second, one could maintain that Paul was explicitly engaging Roman ideas but that more open criticism would not have been *more effective* (Chapter 5, Section 2.2.2). So the first specification of the subtext-hypothesis modifies the notion of *criticism,* whereas the second attempt to make the subtext-hypothesis plausible focuses on Paul's rationale for choosing the *subtext* for his criticism. It is important to note that, in this framework of a modified subtext-hypothesis, the qualifications that emerged in the discussion of what would not have been offensive in the public transcript of the Empire (→ object of criticism) no longer present a criterion for excluding subtextual criticism. Even if Paul could have formulated his criticism outspokenly, this does not mean that he *had* to do so. Again, expressing his critical attitude more openly either might have distracted from what he wanted to say primarily or – if criticising was his main emphasis – might have been communicatively less persuasive. Therefore, while such a modified subtext-hypothesis may be more cautious in assuming extremely sharp criticism, such a paradigm would also widen the focus of the exegete to take into account engagement with aspects of Paul's Roman environment that were not central cornerstones of imperial ideology. So in some sense, we might expect even more, though maybe less spectacular, subtext.

Of course, both considerations – the kind of criticism that is intended and the motive for using the subtext as an effective means of communication – can be combined to a certain extent, and there is no reason to suspect that only one of these two aspects influenced Paul's writings. In general, it seems reasonable to expect the former aspect to be of importance especially regarding the use of expressions that were already predetermined by the Jewish heritage of early Christianity (Chapter 6, Section 2.3 and 3.1). Much of Paul's christological discourse, such as Phil 2:6–11, comes to mind in this regard. This is where Strecker's paradigm of "Aneignung" seems to have its greatest explanatory potential as a paradigm that helps us understand how Paul used and transformed imperial language[1] in order to subvert the idea of Roman superiority. Here, we are dealing with a *resonance* of Roman concepts that are in conflict with Christian ideas. Nevertheless, even in this category we might find passages where Paul's extensive use of, for example, messianic terminology is so striking that it is plausible to assume a sharper focus on the Roman front (Chapter 6, Section 3.1). Rom 1:3–4 comes to mind as an example. Also, in 1 Cor 8:5 the explicit dichotomy makes it plausible that Paul is not only aware but consciously thinking about cases of illegitimate "lordship."

The second aspect, i.e., the effectiveness of using the subtext, may play a role in those cases where reference to the imperial realm is more obvious, where we really have an *echo* (or more generally, an intertextual allusion). The slogan εἰρήνη καὶ ἀσφάλεια in 1 Thess 5:3 is the most prominent example that might belong to this category. The explanatory potential of this option is greatest when we are dealing with *technical terms* from Roman ideology. In this case, unlike cases of "resonance," Paul does not open up a kind of "dritten Raum zwischen dem jüdischen und dem römischen Diskursuniversum."[2] He is rather *infiltrating* the Roman sphere itself. Of course, this does not automatically imply an anti-thesis but we should be open to look for conceptual clashes (Chapter 6, Section 3.2). The frequently discussed citizenship

---

[1] See Strecker, "Taktiken," 153–161.
[2] Strecker, "Taktiken," 154.

in Phil 3:20 and the almost completely ignored Roman triumph in 2 Cor 2:14 come to mind as possible cases where Paul may consciously be subverting Roman ideals. Of course, even in these cases of conscious engagement with Roman concepts, we must be careful not to assume that an abstract discussion of Roman ideology is Paul's *sole* intention. Monolithic explanations of passages as pamphlets against the Empire are in danger of neglecting other factors that shape Paul's discourse, such as the concrete parenetic function of the proposition. Even if one concludes, for example, that Phil 3:20 is somehow critical towards any kind of loyalty that goes hand in hand with Roman citizenship, the important exegetical question remains how this relates specifically to the situation in the Philippian church.[3] Similarly, even if 2 Cor 2:14 in some sense runs counter to Roman claims of power, the question remains how exactly this helps Paul in his broader aim of defending his apostolic ministry.

2. Outlook

In the end, what has been demonstrated in this book is that it is not possible to falsify the subtext-hypothesis (in some of its forms) by reference to general objections that are said to affect its background plausibility in a very fundamental way. Our considerations were not meant to prove that the background plausibility of a counter-imperial subtext beneath a specific Pauline wording is especially high. But on the other hand, we can say that Barclay's assessment certainly is too pessimistic with regard to the value of the background plausibility of counter-imperial statements in Paul and too optimistic with regard to the validity of his objections. This conclusion might be a modest contribution to the discussion on counter-imperial "echoes" in the letters of Paul, but nevertheless, it is a necessary preparatory step for more detailed inquiries. Accordingly, what this study encourages is the re-evaluation of specific Pauline statements as being potentially subversive of Roman imperial ideology. I will close with some comments on how such analyses should build on this work from a methodological perspective. It should be remembered that this book does not offer a new "methodology" for evaluating such phrases. Rather, it offers an evaluation of the general plausibility of the hypothesis that there is a counter-imperial subtext in Paul. On this basis, individual passages need to be analysed. In taking into account specific Pauline passages, we move beyond the scope of this book in a twofold way.

---

[3] Paul is not interested in abstract discussions of political theory. Rather, Phil 3:20–21 offers the basis for the appeal in 3:17–19 to follow Paul's example. See Gordon D. Fee, *Paul's Letters to the Philippians* (NICNT; Grand Rapids: Eerdmans, 1995), 377–378.

2. Outlook

First, the spectrum of data that is relevant for the background plausibility itself grows. When we considered the "Pauline context" (Chapter 5) in this book, we only considered Paul's worldview and theology in general. If we turn to specific passages, contextual factors become much more specific due to concrete indications in the *literary context* (we have touched on this also in Chapter 6, Section 2.3). Are we to expect the specific propositional content that is suggested for a certain verse on the basis of the larger Pauline corpus or not? What does the immediate context of the pericope imply? These considerations have to be taken into account in the exegesis of Pauline texts which are proposed as counter-imperial texts before any final judgement on background plausibilities is possible. Similarly, there might be other factors that could influence the background probability of a counter-imperial statement in a specific Pauline passage, such as *historical circumstances* that could have triggered Paul's interaction with prevalent imperial motifs and ideas. To give one example, let us look shortly at 2 Cor 2:14. When Paul speaks of God as the one πάντοτε θριαμβεύοντι ἡμᾶς ἐν τῷ Χριστῷ, the verb θριαμβεύω is understood by most exegetes as referring to the rite of the Roman triumphal procession after military victories. Does this mean that Paul is attacking the Roman Empire here in some form? Answering such a question demands a detailed analysis that has to take into consideration a multitude of factors. With regard to the background plausibility, it is of interest whether Paul even knew of the Roman rite of the triumphal procession at all, and if so, how well. After all, it could be that Paul is referring to a completely different background, which would, in consequence, nullify any suggestion of a counter-*imperial* statement. Apart from these historical considerations, we have to take the immediate literary context into consideration, e.g., the preceding verses 2:12–13. Why does Paul interrupt his travel narrative – which seems to be continued in 7:5 – for such a thanksgiving? Is a reference to the "Roman triumph" in general and a criticism of this institution in particular anything that would be expected from the flow of the passage? Also, what does it contribute to the question of the meaning of the participle phrase that it is juxtaposed with καὶ τὴν ὀσμὴν τῆς γνώσεως αὐτοῦ φανεροῦντι δι' ἡμῶν ἐν παντὶ τόπῳ? Does this talk about "scent" strengthen the assumption that θριαμβεύοντι refers to the Roman realm or does it rather indicate a (pagan or Jewish) cultic context?

Second, the kind of analysis this book wants to stimulate moves beyond the scope of this book in another way, namely by considering explanatory potentials, which could not be evaluated within the confines of this book since it did not focus on concrete Pauline passages. One will have to decide whether a Pauline phrase is best predicted on the basis of the assumption of a counter-imperial statement or whether there might be other reasons that would explain Paul's choice of words better. Would we, for example, expect the use of the word θριαμβεύω to express the idea of celebrating a *triumphus*?

Are there perhaps other, more common ways of referring to the celebration of a Roman triumphal procession?[4] And could it, therefore, be more likely to assume that Paul used the verb to express another thought, without any relation to the Roman world?

Assessing Paul's engagement with the thought-world of his day is probably the most intruiging but also the most controversial task in Pauline studies. It is mandatory for understanding the apostle's writings and it offers opportunities to contextualise his ideas in our own day. With regard to Paul's Jewish heritage, reconstructing the opinion of his dialogue partners is difficult, but at least we can be certain that Paul is actively negotiating this front. Regarding Paul's interaction with various aspects of Graeco-Roman society, we possess a vast amount of background knowledge, but it is difficult to ascertain whether and how Paul picked up on it, especially where his interaction does not take place explicitly. There is a risk of overinterpreting parallels. But the risk of overlooking important elements of Pauline thought by rejecting such a research project altogether is equally real. Despite the associated problems, we should not, therefore, avoid this complex of questions but tackle it in the most methodologically sound way possible. If this book is judged to have contributed to this endeavour, it has fulfilled its purpose.

---

[4] This means that every inquiry into potential subversive statements by the apostle will be comparative in a twofold way. On the one hand, explanatory potentials and background plausibilities of alternative interpretations for the Pauline wording have to be taken into account. On the other hand – and this factor is usually neglected in evaluating explanatory potentials – the actual choice of words has to be contrasted with potential phrases that would seem not far to seek if the suggested hypotheses for the meaning of the passage in question were true. Hence, the question is not simply whether the assumption of counter-imperial criticism would explain the textual phenomenon well, not even solely whether it would explain it better than other interpretations, but whether it really takes the form we would expect on the basis of the assumed proposition.

Bibliography

1. Sources

Aland, Barbara, Kurt Aland, Johannes Karavidopoulos, Carlo M. Martini, Bruce M. Metzger, eds. *Novum Testamentum Graece*. 9th printing of the 27th ed. Stuttgart: German Bible Society, 2006.

Augustus. *Res Gestae Divi Augusti*. Translated and annotated by Alison E. Cooley. Cambridge: Cambridge University Press, 2009.

Burnett, Andrew, Michel Amandry, and Pere P. Ripollès, eds. *From the Death of Caesar to the Death of Vitellius (44BC–AD 69)*. Vol. 1 of *Roman Provincial Coinage*. London: British Museum Press, 1992.

Burrows, Millar, with the assistance of John C. Trevor and William H. Brownlee, eds. *The Dead Sea Scrolls of St. Mark's Monastery. Volume II: Plates and Transcription of the Manual of Discipline*. New Haven: American Schools of Oriental Research, 1951.

Cassius Dio. *Roman History*. Translated by Earnest Cary. 9 vols. Loeb Classical Library. Cambridge: Harvard University Press, 1914–1927.

Cicero. *Orations: In Catilinam 1–4, Pro Murena, Pro Sulla, Pro Flacco*. Translated by Coll MacDonald. Loeb Classical Library. Cambridge: Harvard University Press, 1917.

Cohn, Leopoldus, Paul Wendland, and Siegfried Reiter. *Philonis operae quae supersunt*. 7 vols. Berlin: Georg Reimer, 1896–1930.

Cornell, Tim J., ed. *The Fragments of the Roman Historians*. 3 vols. Oxford: Oxford University Press, 2013.

Die Apostolischen Väter: Erster Teil (Didache, Barnabas, Klemens I und II, Ignatius, Polykarp, Papias, Quadratus, Diognetbrief. Edited by Karl Bihlmeyer. Sammlung ausgewählter Kirchen- und Dogmengeschichtlicher Quellenschriften: Zweite Reihe 1,1. 2nd ed. Tübingen: Mohr Siebeck, 1956.

Discoveries in the Judean Desert. 40 vols. Oxford: Clarendon: 1955–2009.

Dittenberger, Wilhelm, ed. *Orientis Graeci Inscriptiones Selectae: Supplementum Sylloges Inscriptionum Graecarum*. 2 vols. Leipzig: Hirzel, 1903–1905.

Edson, Charles, ed. *Inscriptiones Graecae, X: Inscriptiones Epiri, Macedoniae, Thraciae, Scythiae. Pars II, fasc. 1: Inscriptiones Thessalonicae et viciniae*. Berlin: de Gruyter, 1972.

Elliger, Karl and Wilhelm Rudolph, eds. *Biblia Hebraica Stuttgartensia / quae antea cooperantibus A. Alt, O. Eissfeldt, P. Kahle ediderat R. Kittel; editio funditus renovata, adjuvantibus H. Bardtke ... [et al.] cooperantibus H.P. Rüger et J. Ziegler ediderunt K. Elliger et W. Rudolph; textum Masoreticum curavit H. P. Rüger, Masoram elaboravit G. E. Weil*. 5th ed. Stuttgart: German Bible Society, 1997.

Euripides. Translated by Arthur S. Way. 4 vols. Loeb Classical Library. London: Heinemann, 1912.

Eusebius. *Ecclesiastical History.* Translated by Kirsopp Lake and John E. L. Oulton. 2 vols. Loeb Classical Library. London: Heinemann, 1926–1932.
Flavius Josephus. *Against Apion.* Translated and annotated by John M. G. Barclay. Flavius Josephus: Translation and Commentary 10. Leiden: Brill, 2007.
Grenfell, Bernard P., and Arthur S. Hunt, eds. *The Oxyrhynchus Papyri: Vol. XII.* London: Egypt Exploration Society, 1916.
Holmes, Michael W., ed. *The Apostolic Fathers: Greek Texts and English Translations.* 3rd ed. Grand Rapids: Baker Academic, 2007.
Josephus. Translated by Henry St. J. Thackeray, Ralph Marcus, Allen Wikgren, and Louis H. Feldman 9 vols. Loeb Classical Library. Cambridge: Harvard University Press, 1926–1965.
Ovid. *Trista, Ex Ponto.* Translated by Arthur L. Wheeler. Loeb Classical Library. Cambridge: Harvard University Press, 1924.
Pausanias. *Description of Greece.* Translated by William H. S. Jones, Henry A. Ormerod, and Richard W. Wycherley. 5 vols. Loeb Classical Library. Cambridge: Harvard University Press, 1918–1935.
Philo. Edited by Leopold Cohn, Isaak Heinemann, Maximilian Adler, and Willy Theiler. Berlin: de Gruyter, 1909–1964.
Philo. Translated by F. H. Colson, G. H. Whitaker, and R. Marcus. 10 vols. (and 2 supplementary vols.) Loeb Classical Library. Cambridge: Harvard University Press, 1929–1962.
Philo. Translated by Charles D. Yonge. Updated edition. Peabody: Hendrickson, 1993.
Philo. *Legatio ad Gaium.* Translated and annotated by E. Mary Smallwood. 2nd ed. Leiden: Brill, 1961.
Plutarch. *Moralia.* Translated by Frank C. Babbitt, William C. Helmbold, Paul A. Clement, Herbert B. Hoffleit, Edwin L. Minar Jr., Francis H. Sandbach, Harold N. Fowler, Lionel Pearson, Harold Cherniss, Benedict Einarson, Phillip H. De Lacy, Edward N. O'Neil (index). 16 vols. Loeb Classical Library. Cambridge: Harvard University Press, 1927–2004.
Rahlfs, Alfred and Robert Hanhart, eds., *Septuaginta: Editio altera.* Stuttgart: German Bible Society, 2006.
Sallust. Translated by John C. Rolfe. 2nd ed. Loeb Classical Library. Cambridge: Harvard University Press, 1931.
Scheid, John. *Res Gestae Divi Augusi: Hauts faits du divin Auguste.* Collection des universités de France, publiée sous le patronage de l'Association Guillaume Budé. Paris: Les Belles Lettres, 2007.
Seneca. *Apokolokyntosis.* Translated and annotated by Gerhard Binder. Sammlung Tusculum. Düsseldorf: Artemis & Winkler, 1999.
Seneca. *Moral Essays.* Translated by John W. Basore. 3 vols. Loeb Classical Library: Cambridge: Harvard University Press, 1928–1935.
Suetonius. Translated by John C. Rolfe. 2 vols. Loeb Classical Library. Cambridge: Harvard University Press, 1913–1914.
Tacitus. *Dialogus, Agricola, Germania.* Translated by Sir William Peterson, Maurice Hutton. Loeb Classical Library. Cambridge: Harvard University Press, 1914.
Tacitus. *The Histories and The Annals.* Translated by Cliffard H. Moore and John Jackson. 4 vols. Loeb Classical Library. Cambridge: Harvard University Press, 1937.
Virgil. Translated by H. Rushton Fairclough. 2 vols. 2nd ed. Loeb Classical Library. Cambridge: Harvard University Press, 1934–1935.

Zwierlein, Otto. *Petrus in Rom: Die literarischen Zeugnisse: Mit einer kritischen Edition der Martyrien des Petrus und Paulus auf neuer handschriftlicher Grundlage*. Untersuchungen zur antiken Literatur und Geschichte 96. Berlin: de Gruyter, 2009.

2. Tools

Alexander, Patrick H., John F. Kutsko, James D. Ernest, Shirley Decker-Lucke, and David L. Petersen. *The SBL Handbook of Style: For Ancient Near Eastern, Biblical, and Early Christian Studies*. Peabody: Hendrickson, 1999.
Coenen, Lothar, and Klaus Haacker, eds. *Theologisches Begriffslexikon zum Neuen Testament: Neubearbeitete Ausgabe*. 2 Vols. Wuppertal: Brockhaus, 1997–2002.
Danker, Frederick W., ed. *A Greek-English Lexicon of the New Testament and Other Early Christian Literature*. 3rd ed. Chicago: University of Chicago Press, 1999. Earlier editions by W. F. Arndt, F. W. Gingrich, and F. W. Danker. Based on *Griechisch-deutsches Wörterbuch zu den Schriften des Neuen Testaments und der frühchristlichen Literatur*. Edited by W. Bauer. 6th ed. Berlin: de Gruyter, 1988.
Evans, Craig A., and Stanley E. Porter, eds. *Dictionary of New Testament Background: A Compendium of Contemporary Biblical Scholarship*. Downers Grove: InterVarsity, 2000.
Hawthorne, Gerald F., Martin, Ralph P., and Daniel G. Reid, eds. *Dictionary of Paul and his Letters: A Compendium of Contemporary Biblical Scholarship*. Downers Grove: InterVarsity, 1993.
Hornblower, Simon, Antony Spawforth, and Esther Eidinow, eds. *The Oxford Classical Dictionary*. 4th ed. Oxford: Oxford University Press, 2012.
Liddell, Henry G. and Robert Scott. *A Greek–English Lexicon*. Revised and Augmented by H. S. Jones with the assistance of R. McKenzie. 9th ed. with revised supplement. Oxford: Clarendon, 1996.
Schiffman, Lawrence H., and James C. VanderKam, eds. *Encyclopedia of the Dead Sea Scrolls*. 2 vols. Oxford: Oxford University Press, 2000.
Schmidt, Heinrich and Martin Gessmann, eds. *Philosophisches Wörterbuch*. 23rd ed. Stuttgart: Kröner, 2009.
Schwertner, Siegfried. *Internationales Abkürzungsverzeichnis für Theologie und Grenzgebiete*. 2nd ed. Berlin: de Gruyter, 1992.
Siebenthal, Heinrich von. *Griechische Grammatik zum Neuen Testament: Neubearbeitung und Erweiterung der Grammatik Hoffmann/von Siebenthal*. Gießen: Brunnen, 2011.
Thesaurus Linguae Graecae. University of California. Online: http://www.tlg.uci.edu.

3. Secondary Literature

Achtemeier, Paul J. "Rome and the Early Church: Background of the Persecution of Christians in the First and Early Second Century." Pages 235–250 in *Foster Biblical Scholarship: Essays in Honor of Kent Harold Richards*. Edited by Frank R. Ames and Charles W. Miller. Society of Biblical Literature Biblical Scholarship in North America 24. Atlanta: Society of Biblical Literature, 2010.
Adams, Edward. "First-Century Models for Paul's Churches: Selected Scholarly Developments Since Meeks." Pages 60–78 in *After the First Urban Christians: The Social-*

Scientific Study of Pauline Christianity Twenty-Five Years Later. Edited by Todd D. Still and David G. Horrell. London: Continuum, 2009.

Adams, Sean A. "Paul's Letter Openings and Greek Epistolography: A Matter of Relationship." Pages 33–56 in *Paul and the Ancient Letter Form.* Edited by Stanley E. Porter and Sean A. Adams. Pauline Studies 6. Leiden: Brill 2010.

Allison, Dale C. *Constructing Jesus: Memory, Imagination, and History.* Grand Rapids: Baker Academics, 2010.

Altman, Marion. "Ruler Cult in Seneca." *Classical Philology* 33 (1938): 198–204.

Ando, Clifford. *Imperial Ideology and Provincial Loyalty in the Roman Empire.* Classics and Contemporary Thought 6. Berkeley: University of California Press, 2000.

Arnaoutoglou, Ilias N. "Roman Law and *collegia* in Asia Minor." *Revue Internationale des droits de l'Antiquité* 49 (2002): 27–44.

Ascough, Richard S. "Comparative Perspectives: Early Christianity and the Roman Empire." *Archiv für Religionsgeschichte* 14 (2013): 328–335.

Baldick, Chris. "Subtext." Online version of *The Oxford Dictionary of Literary Terms.* Edited by Chris Baldick. 3rd ed. Oxford: Oxford University Press, 2008.

Barclay, John M. G. *Flavius Josephus: Against Apion.* Flavius Josephus: Translation and Commentary 10. Leiden: Brill, 2007.

Barclay, John M. G. *Jews in the Mediterranean Diaspora from Alexander to Trajan (323 BCE–117 CE).* Edinburgh: T&T Clark, 1996.

Barclay, John M. G. "Mirror-Reading a Polemical Letter: Galatians as a Test Case." *Journal for the Study of the New Testament* 10 (1987): 73–93.

Barclay, John M. G. "Paul, Roman Religion and the Emperor: Mapping the Point of Conflict." Pages 345–362 in *Pauline Churches and Diaspora Jews.* Edited by John M. G. Barclay. Wissenschaftliche Untersuchungen zum Neuen Testament 275. Tübingen: Mohr Siebeck, 2011.

Barclay, John M. G. "Response to N. T. Wright and Robert Jewett." No pages (around minute 27:00). Accessed on 9 January 2015. Online: http://www.duke.edu/~adr14/Paul%20and%20Empire%20-%20Part%202%20of%202.mp3.

Barclay, John M. G. "Snarling Sweetly: A Study of Josephus on Idolatry." Pages 332–344 in *Pauline Churches and Diaspora Jews.* Edited by John M. G. Barclay. Wissenschaftliche Untersuchungen zum Neuen Testament 275. Tübingen: Mohr Siebeck, 2011.

Barclay, John M. G. "Why the Roman Empire was Insignificant to Paul." Pages 363–387 in *Pauline Churches and Diaspora Jews.* Edited by John M. G. Barclay. Wissenschaftliche Untersuchungen zum Neuen Testament 275. Tübingen: Mohr Siebeck, 2011.

Barraclough, Ray. "Philos' Politics, Roman Rule and Hellenistic Judaism." *ANRW* 21.1:417–553. Part 2, *Principat,* 21.1. Edited by W. Haase. Berlin: de Gruyter, 1984.

Bassler, Jouette M. "Philo on Joseph: The Basic Coherence of *De Iosepho* and *De Somniis* II." *Journal for the Study of Judaism in the Persian, Hellenistic, and Roman Period* 16 (1985): 240–55.

Beard, Mary, John A. North and Simon R. F. Price. *A History.* Vol. 1 of *Religions of Rome.* Cambridge: Cambridge University Press, 1998.

Berthelot, Katell. "Philo's Perception of the Roman Empire." *Journal for the Study of Judaism in the Persian, Hellenistic, and Roman Period* 42 (2011): 166–187.

Bird, Michael F., ed. *Four Views on the Apostle Paul.* Counterpoints: Bible & Theology. Grand Rapids: Zondervan, 2012.

Bird, Michael F. "'One Who Will Arise to Rule Over the Nations': Paul's Letter to the Romans and the Roman Empire." Pages 146–165 in *Jesus Is Lord, Caesar Is Not:*

Evaluating Empire in New Testament Studies. Edited by Scot McKnight and Joseph B. Modica. Downers Grove: IVP Academia, 2013.

Böhm, Martina. *Rezeption und Funktion der Vätererzählungen bei Philo von Alexandria: Zum Zusammenhang von Kontext, Hermeneutik und Exegese im frühen Judentum*. Beihefte zur Zeitschrift für die neutestamentliche Wissenschaft 128. Berlin: de Gruyter, 2005.

Bormann, Lukas. *Philippi: Stadt und Christengemeinde zur Zeit des Paulus*. Studien zum Neuen Testament 78. Leiden: Brill, 1995.

Box, Herbert. *Philonis Alexandrini: In Flaccum*. London: Oxford University Press, 1939.

Bruce, Frederick F. *1 & 2 Thessalonians*. Word Biblical Commentary 45. Waco: Word Books, 1982.

Bryan, Christopher. *Render to Caesar: Jesus, The Early Church, and the Roman Superpower*. Oxford: Oxford University Press, 2005.

Burge, Gary M., Lynn H. Cohick, and Gene L. Green. *The New Testament in Antiquity: A Survey of the New Testament within Its Cultural Contexts*. Grand Rapids: Zondervan, 2009.

Burk, Denny. "Is Paul's Gospel Counterimperial? Evaluating the Prospects of the 'Fresh Perspective' for Evangelical Theology." *Journal of the Evangelical Theological Society* 51 (2008): 309–337.

Burnett, Andrew. "The Augustan Revolution Seen from the Mints of the Provinces." *Journal of Roman Studies* 101 (2011): 1–30.

Burrell, Barbara. *Neokoroi: Greek Cities and Roman Emperors*. Cincinnati Classical Studies. New Series 9. Leiden: Brill, 2004.

Buschmann, Gerd. *Das Martyrium des Polykarp*. Kommentar zu den Apostolischen Vätern 6. Göttingen: Vandenhoeck & Ruprecht, 1998.

Canavan, Rosemary. *Clothing the Body of Christ at Colossae*. Wissenschaftliche Untersuchungen zum Neuen Testament II 334. Tübingen: Mohr Siebeck, 2012.

Cancik, Hubert. *Römische Religion im Kontext: Kulturelle Bedingungen religiöser Diskurse*. Vol. 1 of *Gesammelte Aufsätze*. Edited by Hildegard Cancik-Lindemaier. Tübingen: Mohr Siebeck, 2008.

Carrier, Richard. *On the Historicity of Jesus: Why We Might Have Reason for Doubt*. Sheffield: Sheffield Phoenix, 2014.

Carter, Warren. "Paul and the Roman Empire: Recent Perspectives." Pages 7–26 in *Paul Unbound: Other Perspectives on the Apostle*. Edited by Mark D. Given. Peabody: Hendrickson, 2009.

Carter, Warren. *Roman Empire and the New Testament: An Essential Guide*. Nashville: Abingdon, 2006.

Carter, Warren. "Roman Imperial Power: A New Testament Perspective." Pages 137–151 in *Rome and Religion: A Cross-Disciplinary Dialogue on the Imperial Cult*. Edited by Jeffrey Brodd and Jonathan L. Reed. Society of Biblical Literature Writings from the Greco-Roman World 5. Atlanta: Scholars Press, 2011.

Cazeaux, Jacques. "'Nul n'est prophète en son pays': Contribution à l'étude de Joseph d'après Philon." Pages 41–81 in *The School of Moses: Studies in Philo and Hellenistic Religion in Memory of Horst R. Moehring*. Brown Judaic Studies 304 = Studia Philonica Monographs 1. Edited by John P. Kenney. Atlanta: Scholars Press, 1995.

Champlin, Edward. *Nero*. Cambridge: Belknap, 2003.

Champlin, Edward. "Nero, Apollo, and the Poets." *Phoenix* 57 (2003): 273–283.

Chaniotis, Angelos. "Der Kaiserkult im Osten des Römischen Reiches im Kontext der zeitgenössischen Ritualpraxis." Pages 3–28 in *Die Praxis der Herrscherverehrung in*

Rom und seinen Provinzen. Edited by Hubert Cancik and Konrad Hitzl. Tübingen: Mohr Siebeck, 2003.

Christ, Karl. *Geschichte der römischen Kaiserzeit*. 6th ed. München: C. H. Beck, 2009.

Chrysos, Evangelos K. "The Title ΒΑΣΙΛΕΥΣ in Early Byzantine International Relations." *Dumbarton Oaks Papers* 32 (1978): 29–75.

Clauss, Manfred. *Kaiser und Gott: Herrscherkult im römischen Reich*. Stuttgart: Teubner, 1999.

Cohick, Lynn H. "Philippians and Empire: Paul's Engagement with Imperialism and the Imperial Cult." Pages 165–182 in *Jesus Is Lord, Caesar Is Not: Evaluating Empire in New Testament Studies*. Edited by Scot McKnight and Joseph B. Modica. Downers Grove: IVP Academia, 2013.

Collins, Adela Y. "The Worship of Jesus and the Imperial Cult." Pages 234–257 in *The Jewish Roots of Christological Monotheism: Papers from the St. Andrews Conference on the Historical Origins of the Worship of Jesus*. Edited by Carey C. Newman, James R. Davila, and Gladys S. Lewis. Journal for the Study of Judaism: Supplement Series 63. Leiden: Brill, 1999.

Collins, John J. *Between Athens and Jerusalem: Jewish Identity in the Hellenistic Diaspora*. New York, Crossroad: 1983.

Cotter, Wendy. "The Collegia and Roman Law: State Restrictions on Voluntary Associations 64 BCE–200 CE." Pages 74–89 in *Voluntary Associations in the Graeco-Roman World*. Edited by John S. Kloppenborg and Stephen G. Wilson. London: Routledge, 1996.

Cramer, Frederick H. "Bookburning and Censorship in Ancient Rome: A Chapter from the History of Freedom of Speech." *Journal of the History of Ideas* 6 (1945): 157–196.

Crossan, John D., and Jonathan L. Reed. *In Search of Paul: How Jesus' Apostle Opposed Rome's Empire with God's Kingdom: A New Vision of Paul's Words and World*. San Francisco: HarperSanFrancisco, 2004.

Crouch, Andy. "Foreword." Pages 7–14 in *Jesus Is Lord, Caesar Is Not: Evaluating Empire in New Testament Studies*. Edited by Scot McKnight and Joseph B. Modica. Downers Grove: IVP Academia, 2013.

Cuffari, Anton. *Judenfeindschaft in Antike und Altem Testament*. Bonner Biblische Beiträge 153. Hamburg: Philo, 2007.

Cullmann, Oscar. *Der Staat im Neuen Testament*. 2nd ed. Tübingen: Mohr Siebeck, 1961.

Dawid, Philip. "Bayes's Theorem and Weighing Evidence by Juries." Pages 71–90 in *Bayes's Theorem*. Edited by Richard Swinburne. Proceedings of the British Academy 113. Oxford: Oxford University Press, 2002.

Day, Mark. *The Philosophy of History: An Introduction*. London: Continuum, 2008.

Day, Mark and Gregory Radick. "Historiographic Evidence and Confirmation." Pages 87–97 in *A Companion to the Philosophy of History and Historiography*. Edited by Aviezer Tucker. Blackwell Companions to Philosophy. Oxford: Blackwell, 2009.

Deines, Roland. "Historische Analyse I: Die jüdische Mitwelt." Pages 101–104 in *Das Studium des Neuen Testaments*. Edited by Heinz-Werner Neudorfer and Eckhard J. Schnabel. 2nd ed. Wuppertal: R. Brockhaus/Gießen: Brunnen, 2006.

Deissmann, G. Adolf. *Licht vom Osten: Das Neue Testament und die neuentdeckten Texte der hellenistisch-römischen Welt*. 4th ed. Tübingen: Mohr, 1923.

DeMaris, Richard E. "Cults and the Imperial Cult in Early Roman Corinth." Pages 73–91 in *Zwischen den Reichen: Neues Testament und Römische Herrschaft*. Edited by Michael Labahn and Jürgen Zangenberg. Texte und Arbeiten zum neutestamentlichen Zeitalter 36. Tübingen: A. Francke, 2002.

Diehl, Judith A. "Anti-Imperial Rhetoric in the New Testament." Pages 38–81 in *Jesus Is Lord, Caesar Is Not: Evaluating Empire in New Testament Studies*. Edited by Scot McKnight and Joseph B. Modica. Downers Grove: IVP Academia, 2013.
Diehl, Judith A. "Empire and Epistles: Anti-Roman Rhetoric in the New Testament Epistles." *Currents in Biblical Research* 10 (2012): 217–263.
Dormeyer, Detlev. "The Hellenistic Letter-Formula and the Pauline Letter-Scheme." Pages 59–95 in *The Pauline Canon*. Edited by Stanley E. Porter. Pauline Studies 1. Leiden: Brill, 2004.
Douven, Igor. "Abduction (The Stanford Encyclopedia of Philosophy; Spring 2011 Edition; ed. Edward N. Zalta)." No pages. Accessed on 25 September 2013. Online: http://plato.stanford.edu/archives/spr2011/entries/abduction/.
Dunn, James D. G. *Romans 1–8*. Word Biblical Commentary 38A. Dallas: Word Books, 1988.
Dunn, James D. G. *The Theology of the Apostle*. Grand Rapids: Eerdmans, 1998.
Dunne, John A. "The Regal Status of Christ in the Colossian 'Christ-Hymn': A Re-Evaluation of the Influence of Wisdom Traditions." *Trinity Journal* 32 (2011): 3–18.
Eckert, Jost. "Das Imperium Romanum im Neuen Testament: Ein Beitrag zum Thema 'Kirche und Gesellschaft.'" *Trierer Theologische Zeitschrift* 96 (1987): 253–271.
Elliott, Neil. "'Blasphemed among the Nations': Pursuing an Anti-Imperial 'Intertextuality' in Romans." Pages 213–233 in *As it is Written: Studying Paul's Use of Scripture*. Edited by Stanley E. Porter and Christopher D. Stanley. Society of Biblical Literature Symposium Series 50. Atlanta: Scholars Press, 2008.
Elliott, Neil. *The Arrogance of Nations: Reading Romans in the Shadow of Empire*. Minneapolis: Fortress, 2008.
Elliott, Neil. "The 'Patience of the Jews': Strategies of Resistance and Accommodation to Imperial Cultures." Pages 32–41 in *Pauline Conversations in Context: Essays in Honor of Calvin J. Roetzel*. Edited by Janice C. Anderson, Philip Sellew, and Claudia Setzer. Journal for the Study of the New Testament Supplement Series 221. Sheffield: Sheffield Academic, 2002.
Elliott, Neil. "Romans 13:1–7 in the Context of Imperial Propaganda." Pages 184–204 in *Paul and Empire: Religion and Power in Roman Imperial Society*. Edited by Richard A. Horsley. Harrisburg: Trinity Press International, 1997.
Elliott, Neil. "Strategies of Resistance and Hidden Transcripts in the Pauline Communities." Pages 97–122 in *Hidden Transcripts and the Arts of Resistance: Applying the Work of James C. Scott to Jesus and Paul*. Edited by Richard A. Horsley. Semeia Studies 48. Atlanta: Scholars Press, 2004.
Evans, Craig A., and James A. Sanders, eds. *Paul and the Scriptures of Israel*. Journal for the Study of the New Testament: Supplement Series 83. Sheffield: Sheffield Academic, 1993.
Fantin, Joseph D. *The Lord of the Entire World: Lord Jesus, a Challenge to Lord Caesar?* New Testament Monographs 31. Sheffield: Sheffield Phoenix, 2011.
Fantin, Joseph D. Review of Colin Miller, "The Imperial Cult in the Pauline Cities of Asia Minor and Greece." *Bibliotheca sacra* 168 (2011): 98–99.
Fee, Gordon D. *Paul's Letters to the Philippians*. New International Commentary on the New Testament. Grand Rapids: Eerdmans, 1995.
Fee, Gordon D. *Pauline Christology: An Exegetical-Theological Study*. Peabody: Hendrickson, 2007.
Fee, Gordon D. *The First Epistle to the Corinthians*. New International Commentary on the New Testament. Grand Rapids: Eerdmans, 1987.

Feldman, Louis H. *Philo's Portrayal of Moses in the Context of Ancient Judaism*. Christianity and Judaism in Antiquity Series 15. Notre Dame, Indiana: University of Notre Dame Press, 2007.
Feldman, Louis H. *Scholarship on Philo and Josephus, 1937–1962*. New York: Yeshiva University, 1963.
Frazier, Françoise. "Les visages de Joseph dans le *De Josepho*." *The Studia Philonica Annual* 14 (2002): 1–30.
Frey, Jörg. "Paul's Jewish Identity." Pages 285–321 in *Jewish Identity in the Greco-Roman World/Jüdische Identität in der griechisch-römischen Welt*. Edited by Jörg Frey, Daniel R. Schwartz, and Stephanie Gripentrog. Ancient Judaism and Early Christianity 71. Leiden: Brill, 2007.
Friesen, Steven J. "Normal Religion, or, Words Fail Us: A Response to Karl Galinsky's 'The Cult of the Roman Emperor: Uniter or Divider?.'" Pages 23–26 in *Rome and Religion: A Cross-Disciplinary Dialogue on the Imperial Cult*. Edited by Jeffrey Brodd and Jonathan L. Reed. Society of Biblical Literature Writings from the Greco-Roman World 5. Atlanta: Society of Biblical Literature, 2011.
Gäckle, Volker. "Historische Analyse II: Die griechisch-römische Umwelt." Pages 141–180 in *Das Studium des Neuen Testaments*. Edited by Heinz-Werner Neudorfer and Eckhard J. Schnabel. 2nd ed. Wuppertal: R. Brockhaus/Gießen: Brunnen, 2006.
Gärtner, Bertil. *The Temple and the Community in Qumran and the New Testament: A Comparative Study in the Temple Symbolism of the Qumran Texts and the New Testament*. Society for New Testament Studies Monograph Series 1. Cambridge: Cambridge University Press, 1965.
Gal, Susan. "Language and the 'Arts of Resistance.'" *Cultural Anthropology* 10 (1995): 407–424.
Galinsky, Karl. "Continuity and Change: Religion in the Augustan Semi-Century." Pages 71–82 in *A Companion to Roman Religion*. Edited by Jörg Rüpke. Blackwell Companions to the Ancient World. Blackwell: Chichester, 2007.
Galinsky, Karl. "In the Shadow (or Not) of the Imperial Cult: A Cooperative Agenda." Pages 215–225 in *Rome and Religion: A Cross-Disciplinary Dialogue on the Imperial Cult*. Edited by Jeffrey Brodd and Jonathan L. Reed; Society of Biblical Literature Writings from the Greco-Roman World 5. Atlanta: Scholars Press, 2011.
Galinsky, Karl. "The Cult of the Roman Emperor: Uniter or Divider?" Pages 1–21 in *Rome and Religion: A Cross-Disciplinary Dialogue on the Imperial Cult*. Edited by Jeffrey Brodd and Jonathan L. Reed; Society of Biblical Literature Writings from the Greco-Roman World 5. Atlanta: Scholars Press, 2011.
Gehring, Roger W. *House Church and Mission: The Importance of Household Structures in Early Christianity*. Translated from Roger W. Gehring. Peabody: Hendrickson Publishers, 2004.
Georgi, Dieter. "Gott auf den Kopf stellen: Überlegungen zu Tendenz und Kontext des Theokratiegedankens in paulinischer Praxis und Theologie." Pages 148–205 in *Theokratie*. Edited by Jacob Taubes. Vol. 3 of *Religionstheorie und Politische Theologie*. Edited by Jacob Taubes. München: Ferdinand Schöningh/Wilhelm Funk, 1987.
Georgi, Dieter. "Who is the True Prophet?" Pages 36–46 in *Paul and Empire: Religion and Power in Roman Imperial Society*. Edited by Richard A. Horsley. Harrisburg: Trinity Press International, 1997.
Goodenough, Erwin R. *An Introduction to Philo Judaeus*. 2nd ed. Oxford: Blackwell, 1962.

Goodenough, Erwin R. *The Politics of Philo Judaeus: Practice and Theory.* New Haven: Yale University Press, 1938.
Gradel, Ittai. *Emperor Worship and Roman Religion.* Oxford Classical Monographs. Oxford. Oxford University Press, 2002.
Gruen, Erich S. "Augustus and the Making of the Principate." Pages 33–51 in *The Cambridge Companion to the Age of Augustus.* Edited by Karl Galinsky. Cambridge Companion to the Classics. Cambridge: Cambridge University Press, 2005.
Gruen, Erich S. *Heritage and Hellenism: The Reinvention of Jewish Tradition.* Hellenistic Society and Culture 30. Berkeley: University of California Press, 1998.
Gupta, Nijay. "Mirror-Reading Moral Issues in Paul." *Journal for the Study of the New Testament* 34 (2011): 361–381.
Habicht, Christian. *Gottmenschentum und griechische Städte.* 2nd ed. München: C. H. Beck, 1970.
Hafemann, Scott J. *Suffering and the Spirit: An Exegetical Study of 2 Cor 2:14–3:3 within the Context of the Corinthian Correspondence.* Wissenschaftliche Untersuchungen zum Neuen Testament II 19. Tübingen: Mohr Siebeck 1986.
Hall, Jon. *Politeness and Politics in Cicero's Letters.* Oxford: Oxford University Press, 2009.
Hardin, Justin K. "Decrees and Drachmas at Thessalonica: An Illegal Assembly in Jason's House (Acts 17.1–10a)." *New Testament Studies* 52 (2006): 29–49.
Hardin, Justin K. *Galatians and the Imperial Cult.* Wissenschaftliche Untersuchungen zum Neuen Testament II, 237. Tübingen: Mohr Siebeck, 2008.
Harrill, J. Albert. *Paul the Apostle: His Life and Legacy in Their Roman Context.* Cambridge: Cambridge University Press, 2012.
Harrison, James R. *Paul and the Imperial Authorities at Thessalonica and Rome.* Wissenschaftliche Untersuchungen zum Neuen Testament 273. Tübingen: Mohr Siebeck, 2011.
Harter-Uibopuu, Kaja. "Kaiserkult und Kaiserverehrung in den Koina des griechischen Mutterlandes." Pages 209–231 in *Die Praxis der Herrscherverehrung in Rom und seinen Provinzen.* Edited by Hubert Cancik and Konrad Hitzl. Tübingen: Mohr Siebeck, 2003.
Hay, David M. "Politics and Exegesis in Philo's Treatise on Dreams." Pages 429–438 in *SBL Seminar Papers, 1987.* Society of Biblical Literature Seminar Papers 26. Atlanta: Scholars Press, 1987.
Hays, Richard B. *Echoes of Scripture in the Letters of Paul.* New Haven: Yale University Press: 1989.
Hays, Richard B. *The Conversion of the Imagination. Paul as Interpreter of Israel's Scripture.* Grand Rapids: Eerdmans, 2005.
Heath, Gordon L. "The Church Fathers and the Roman Empire." Pages 258–282 in *Empire in the New Testament.* Edited by Stanley E. Porter and Cynthia L. Westfall. McMaster Divinity College Press New Testament Studies Series 10. Eugene: Pickwick, 2011.
Heilig, Christoph. "Anonymes oder Spezifisches Design? Vergleich zweier methodischer Ansätze für Forschung im Rahmen der teleologischen Perspektive." Pages 73–125 in *Die Ursprungsfrage: Beiträge zum Status teleologischer Antwortversuche.* Edited by Christoph Heilig and Jens Kany. Edition Forschung 1. Münster: Lit, 2011.
Heilig, Christoph. "Methodological Considerations for the Search of Counter-Imperial 'Echoes' in Pauline Literature." Pages 73–92 in *Reactions to Empire: Proceedings of Sacred Texts in Their Socio-Political Contexts.* Edited by John A. Dunne and Dan Batovici. Wissenschaftliche Untersuchungen zum Neuen Testament II 372. Tübingen: Mohr Siebeck, 2014.

Hekster, Olivier. "The Roman Army and Propaganda." Pages 339–358 in *A Companion to the Roman Army*. Edited by Paul Erdkamp. Blackwell Companions to the Ancient World. Malden: Blackwell, 2007.
Herz, Peter. "Emperors: Caring for the Empire and Their Successors." Pages 304–316 in *A Companion to Roman Religion*. Edited by Jörg Rüpke. Blackwell Companions to the Ancient World. Blackwell: Chichester, 2011.
Hilgert, Earle. "A Survey of Previous Scholarship on Philo's *De Somniis* 1–2." Pages 394–402 in *SBL Seminar Papers, 1987*. Society of Biblical Literature Seminar Papers 26. Atlanta: Scholars Press, 1987.
Holtz, Traugott. *Der erste Brief an die Thessalonicher*. Evangelisch-Katholischer Kommentar zum Neuen Testament. Zürich: Benziger, 1986.
Hon, Giora and Sam S. Rakover, eds. *Explanation: Theoretical Approaches and Applications*. Dordrecht: Kluwer, 2001.
Horn, Friedrich W., ed. *Paulus Handbuch*. Tübingen: Mohr Siebeck, 2013.
Horn, Friedrich W. "Paulus und der Herodianische Tempel." *New Testament Studies* 53 (2007): 184–203.
Horsley, Greg H. R. "The Politarchs." Pages 419–431 in *The Book of Acts in Its Graeco-Roman Setting*. Edited by David W. J. Gill and Conrad Gempf. Vol. 2 of *The Book of Acts in Its First Century Setting*. Edited by Bruce W. Winter. Grand Rapids: Eerdmans/Carlisle: Paternoster, 1994.
Horsley, Richard A., ed. *Hidden Transcripts and the Arts of Resistance: Applying the Work of James C. Scott to Jesus and Paul*. Semeia Studies 48. Atlanta: Scholars Press, 2004.
Horsley, Richard A., ed. *In the Shadow of Empire: Reclaiming the Bible as a History of Faithful Resistance*. Louisville: Westminster John Knox, 2008.
Horsley, Richard A. "Introduction: Jesus, Paul, and the 'Arts of Resistance': Leaves from the Notebook of James C. Scott." Pages 1–26 in *Hidden Transcripts and the Arts of Resistance: Applying the Work of James C. Scott to Jesus and Paul*. Edited by Richard A. Horsley. Semeia Studies 48; Atlanta: Scholars Press, 2004.
Horsley, Richard A., ed. *Paul and Empire: Religion and Power in Roman Imperial Society*. Harrisburg: Trinity Press International, 1997.
Horsley, Richard A., ed. *Paul and Politics: Ekklesia, Israel, Imperium, Interpretation: Essays in Honor of Krister Stendahl*. Harrisburg: Trinity Press International, 2000.
Horsley, Richard A., ed. *Paul and the Roman Imperial Order*. Harrisburg: Trinity Press International, 2004.
Horsley, Richard A. "General Introduction." Pages 1–8 in *Paul and Empire: Religion and Power in Roman Imperial Society*. Edited by Richard A. Horsley. Harrisburg: Trinity Press International, 1997.
Horst, Willem van der. *Philo's Flaccus: The First Pogrom: Introduction, Translation and Commentary*. Philo of Alexandria Commentary Series 2. Leiden: Brill, 2003.
Howson, Colin. "Bayesianism in Statistics." Pages 39–71 in *Bayes's Theorem*. Edited by Richard Swinburne; Proceedings of the British Academy 113. Oxford: Oxford University Press, 2002.
Howson, Colin and Peter Urbach. *Scientific Reasoning: The Bayesian Approach*. Chicago: Open Court, 1993.
Hurtado, Larry. *One God, One Lord: Early Christian Devotion and Ancient Jewish Monotheism*. 2nd ed. Repr. London: T&T Clark, 2005.
Jay, Jeff. "The Problem of the Theater in Early Judaism." *Journal for the Study of Judaism* 44 (2013): 218–253.
Jewett, Robert. *Romans: A Commentary*. Hermeneia. Minneapolis: Fortress, 2007.

Jewett, Robert. *The Thessalonian Correspondence: Pauline Rhetoric and Millenarian Piety*. Foundations and Facets. Philadelphia: Fortress, 1986.
Johns, Richard. "Inference to the Best Explanation." Accessed on 14 August 2012. Online: http://faculty.arts.ubc.ca/rjohns/ibe.pdf.
Jones, Christopher P. *Plutarch and Rome*. Oxford: Clarendon, 1971.
Jones, Darryl L. "The Sermon as 'Art' of Resistance: A Comparative Analysis of the Rhetorics of the African-American Slave Preacher and the Preacher to the Hebrews." *Semeia* 79 (=*Rhetorics of Resistance: A Colloquy on Early Christianity as Rhetorical Formation*. Edited by Vincent L. Wimbush) (1997): 11–26.
Judge, Edwin A. "The Decrees of Caesar at Thessalonica." *Reformed Theological Review* 30 (1971): 71–78.
Judge, Edwin A. *The First Christians in the Roman World: Augustan and New Testament Essays*. Wissenschaftliche Untersuchungen zum Neuen Testament 229. Tübingen: Mohr Siebeck, 2008.
Junker, Reinhard. *Spuren Gottes in der Schöpfung? Eine kritische Analyse von Design-Argumenten in der Biologie*. Studium Integrale. Holzgerlingen: SCM Hänssler, 2009.
Kahn, Jean-Georges. "La Valeur et la Légitimité des Activités politiques d'après Philon d'Alexandrie." *Méditerranées* 16 (1998): 117–127.
Kahneman, Daniel, Paul Slovic, and Amos Tversky, eds. *Judgement under Uncertainty: Heuristics and Biases*. Cambridge: Cambridge University Press, 1982.
Kahl, Brigitte. "Acts of the Apostles: Pro(to)-Imperial Script and Hidden Transcript." Pages 137–156 in *In the Shadow of Empire: Reclaiming the Bible as a History of Faithful Resistance*. Edited by Richard A. Horsley. Louisville: Westminster John Knox, 2008.
Keesmaat, Sylvia C. "Reading Romans in the Capital of the Empire." Pages 47–64 in *Reading Paul's Letter to the Romans*. Edited by Jerry L. Sumney. Society of Biblical Literature Resources for Biblical Studies 73. Atlanta: Society of Biblical Literature, 2012.
Keith, Chris and Anthony Le Donne, eds. *Criteria, and the Demise of Authenticity*. London: T&T Clark, 2012.
Kim, Seyoon. *Christ and Caesar: The Gospel and the Roman Empire in the Writings of Paul and Luke*. Grand Rapids: Eerdmans, 2008.
Kinzig, Wolfram. "The West and North Africa." Pages 198–214 in *Redemption and Resistance: The Messianic Hopes of Jews and Christians in Antiquity*. Edited by Markus Bockmuehl and James C. Paget. London: T&T Clark, 2007.
Klauck, Hans-Josef. *Herrscher- und Kaiserkult, Philosophie, Gnosis*. Vol. 2 of *Die religiöse Umwelt des Urchristentums*. Kohlhammer Studienbücher Theologie 9,2. Stuttgart: Kohlhammer, 1996.
Klauck, Hans-Josef. "Des Kaisers schöne Stimme: Herrscherkritik in Apg 12,20–23." Pages 251–267 in *Religion und Gesellschaft im frühen Christentum: Neutestamentliche Studien*. Wissenschaftliche Untersuchungen zum Neuen Testament 152. Tübingen: Mohr Siebeck, 2003.
Klinzing, Georg. *Die Umdeutung des Kultus in der Qumrangemeinde und im Neuen Testament*. Studien zur Umwelt des Neuen Testaments 7. Göttingen: Vandenhoeck & Ruprecht, 1971.
Klötzer, Sylvia. *Satire und Macht: Film, Zeitung, Kabarett in der DDR*. Zeithistorische Studien 30. Köln: Böhlau, 2006.

Köster, Helmut. "Imperial Ideology and Paul's Eschatology." Pages 158–166 in *Paul and Empire: Religion and Power in Roman Imperial Society*. Edited by Richard A. Horsley. Harrisburg: Trinity Press International, 1997.

Kraft, Robert A. "Philo and the Sabbath Crisis: Alexandrian Jewish Politics and the Dating of Philo's Works." Pages 131–141 in *The Future of Early Christianity: Essays in Honour of Helmut Koester*. Edited by Birger A. Pearson. Minneapolis: Fortress, 1991.

Krauter, Stefan. *Studien zu Röm 13,1–7: Paulus und der politische Diskurs der neronischen Zeit*. Wissenschaftliche Untersuchungen zum Neuen Testament 243. Tübingen: Mohr Siebeck, 2009.

Kreitzer, Larry J. *Striking New Images: Roman Imperial Coinage and the New Testament World*. Journal for the Study of the New Testament: Supplement Series 134. Sheffield: Sheffield Academic, 1996.

Kristeva, Julia. "Bakhtine, le mot, le dialogue et le roman," *Critique* 33 (1967): 438–465.

Leisegang, Hans. "Philons Schrift über die Gesandtschaft der alexandrinischen Juden an den Kaiser Gaius Caligula." *Journal of Biblical Literature* 57 (1938): 377–405.

Lietzmann, Hans. *Die Anfänge*. Vol. 1 of *Geschichte der Alten Kirche*. 3rd ed. Berlin: de Gruyter, 1953.

Lightstone, Jack N. "Roman Diaspora Judaism." Pages 345–377 in *A Companion to Roman Religion*. Edited by Jörg Rüpke. Blackwell Companions to the Ancient World. Blackwell: Chichester, 2011.

Lipton, Peter. *Inference to the Best Explanation*. 2nd ed. London: Routledge, 2004.

Markschies, Christoph. *Kaiserzeitliche christliche Theologie und ihre Institutionen: Prolegomena zu einer Geschichte der antiken christlichen Theologie*. Tübingen: Mohr Siebeck, 2007.

Markschies, Christoph. *Christian Theology and its Institutions in the Early Roman Empire: Prolegomena to a History of Early Christian Theology*. Translated by Wayne Coppins. Baylor-Mohr Siebeck Studies in Early Christianity 3. Waco: Baylor University Press, 2015.

McHugh, Mary R. "Historiography and Freedom of Speech: The Case of Cremutius Cordus." Pages 391–408 in *Free Speech in Classical Antiquity*. Edited by Ineke Sluiter and Ralph M. Rosen. Mnemosyne, Supplements 254. Leiden: Brill, 2004.

McLaren, James S. "Jews and the Imperial Cult: From Augustus to Domitian." *Journal for the Study of the New Testament* 27 (2005), 257–278.

McKnight, Scot and Joseph B. Modica, "Conclusion," Pages 211–214 in *Jesus Is Lord, Caesar Is Not: Evaluating Empire in New Testament Studies*. Edited by Scot McKnight and Joseph B. Modica. Downers Grove: IVP Academia, 2013.

McKnight, Scot and Joseph B. Modica, "Introduction," Pages 15–21 in *Jesus Is Lord, Caesar Is Not: Evaluating Empire in New Testament Studies*. Edited by Scot McKnight and Joseph B. Modica. Downers Grove: IVP Academia, 2013.

McKnight, Scot, and Joseph B. Modica, eds. *Jesus Is Lord, Caesar Is Not: Evaluating Empire in New Testament Studies*. Downers Grove: IVP Academic, 2013.

Meeks, Wayne A. *The First Urban Christians: The Social World of the Apostle Paul*. New Haven: Yale University Press, 1983.

Meggitt, Justin. "Taking the Emperor's Clothes Seriously: The New Testament and the Roman Empire." Pages 143–168 in *The Quest for Wisdom: Essays in Honour of Philip Budd*. Edited by Christine E. Joynes. Cambridge: Orchard Academic, 2002.

Mellor, Ronald. *Tacitus' Annals*. Oxford Approaches to Classical Literature. New York: Oxford University Press, 2011.

Millar, Fergus. "State and Subject: The Impact of Monarchy." Pages 37–60 in *Caesar Augustus: Seven Aspects*. Edited by Fergus Millar and Erich Segal. Oxford: Clarendon, 1984.
Miller, Colin. "The Imperial Cult in the Pauline Cities of Asia Minor and Greece." *Catholic Biblical Quarterly* 72 (2010): 314–332.
Mitchell, Stephen. *The Rise of the Church.* Vol. 2 of *Anatolia: Land, Men and Gods in Asia Minor*. Oxford: Clarendon, 1993.
Momigliano, Arnaldo. Review of Erwin R. Goodenough, *An Introduction to Philo Judaeus*. *Journal of Roman Studies* 34 (1944): 163–165.
Moo, Douglas. "Review of N. T. Wright, *Paul and the Faithfulness of God*." No pages. Accessed on 5 December 2013. Online: http://thegospelcoalition.org/bookreviews/review/ paul_and_the_faithfulness_of_god.
Murphy-O'Connor, Jerome. *Paul the Letter-Writer: His World, His Options, His Skills*. Good News Studies 41. Collegeville: Liturgical Press, 1995.
Niehoff, Maren R. "New Garments for Biblical Joseph." Pages 33–56 in *Biblical Interpretation: History, Context, and Reality*. Edited by Christine Helmer and Taylor G. Petrey. Society of Biblical Literature Symposium Series 26. Atlanta: Society of Biblical Literature, 2005.
Niehoff, Maren R. *Philo on Jewish Identity and Culture*. Texte und Studien zum Antiken Judentum 86. Mohr Siebeck: Tübingen, 2011.
Niehoff, Maren R. *The Figure of Joseph in Post–Biblical Jewish Literature*. Arbeiten zur Geschichte des antiken Judentums und des Urchristentums 16. Leiden: Brill, 1992.
Noethlichs, Karl L. "Die äußere Entwicklung (Historische Kontexte. Das Imperium Romanum von der Republik zum Prinzipat)." Pages 143–149 in *Prolegomena, Quellen, Geschichte, Recht*. Vol. 1 of *Neues Testament und Antike Kultur*. Edited by Kurt Erlemann, Karl L. Noethlichs, Klaus Scherberich, and Jürgen Zangenberg. Neukirchen-Vluyn: Neukirchener, 2004.
Novenson, Matthew V. *Christ among the Messiahs: Christ Language in Paul and Messiah Language in Ancient Judaism*. Oxford: Oxford University Press, 2012.
Novenson, Matthew V. "What the Apostles Did not See." Pages 55–72 in *Reactions to Empire: Proceedings of Sacred Texts in Their Socio-Political Contexts*. Edited by John A. Dunne and Dan Batovici. Wissenschaftliche Untersuchungen zum Neuen Testament II 372. Tübingen: Mohr Siebeck, 2014.
Nystrom, David. "We Have No King But Caesar: Roman Imperial Ideology and the Imperial Cult." Pages 23–37 in *Jesus Is Lord, Caesar Is Not: Evaluating Empire in New Testament Studies*. Edited by Scot McKnight and Joseph B. Modica. Downers Grove: IVP Academia, 2013.
Oakes, Peter. "Re-mapping the Universe: Paul and the Emperor in 1 Thessalonians and Philippians." *Journal for the Study of the New Testament* 27 (2005): 301–322.
Öhler, Markus. "Römisches Vereinsrecht und christliche Gemeinden." Pages 51–71 in *Zwischen den Reichen: Neues Testament und Römische Herrschaft*. Edited by Michael Labahn and Jürgen Zangenberg. Texte und Arbeiten zum neutestamentlichen Zeitalter 36. Tübingen: A. Francke, 2002.
Oertelt, Friederike. *Herrscherideal und Herrschaftskritik bei Philo von Alexandria: Eine Untersuchung am Beispiel seiner Josephsdarstellung in De Josepho und De somniis I*. Studies in Philo of Alexandria 8. Leiden: Brill, 2015.
Omerzu, Heike. "Paulus als Politiker? Das paulinische Evangelium zwischen Ekklesia und Imperium Romanum." Pages 267–287 in *Logos – Logik – Lyrik: Engagierte exegetische Studien zum biblischen Reden Gottes: Festschrift für Klaus Haacker*. Edited by Volker

A. Lehnert and Ulrich Rüsen-Weinhold. Arbeiten zur Bibel und ihrer Geschichte 27. Leipzig: Evangelische Verlagsanstalt, 2007.
Paget, James C. "Egypt." Pages 183–197 in *Redemption and Resistance: The Messianic Hopes of Jews and Christians in Antiquity*. Edited by Markus Bockmuehl and James C. Paget. London: T&T Clark, 2007.
Parrott, Rodney L. "Paul's Political Thought: Rom 13:1–7 in the Light of Hellenistic Political Thought." Ph.D. diss., The Claremont Graduate School, 1980, 143–162.
Peachin, Michael. Review of C. Ando, *Imperial Ideology and Provincial Loyalty in the Roman Empire*. *American Historical Review* 107 (2002): 921–922.
Peppard, Michael. *The Son of God in the Roman World: Divine Sonship in its Social and Political Context*. Oxford: Oxford University Press, 2011.
Peterson, Erik. "Die Einholung des Kyrios." *Zeitschrift für Systematische Theologie* 7 (1930): 682–702.
Pilhofer, Peter. *Katalog der Inschriften von Philippi*. Vol. 2 of *Philippi*. 2nd ed. Tübingen: Mohr Siebeck, 2009.
Pinter, Dean L. "Divine and Imperial Power: A comparative analysis of Paul and Josephus." PhD diss., Durham University, 2009.
Pinter, Dean L. "The Gospel of Luke and the Roman Empire." Pages 101–115 in *Jesus Is Lord, Caesar Is Not: Evaluating Empire in New Testament Studies*. Edited by Scot McKnight and Joseph B. Modica. Downers Grove: IVP Academia, 2013.
Popkes, Wiard. "Zum Thema 'Anti-imperiale Deutung neutestamentlicher Schriften.'" *Theologische Literaturzeitung* 127 (2002): 850–862.
Porter, Stanley E. "Paul Confronts Caesar with the Good News." Pages 164–196 in *Empire in the New Testament*. Edited by Stanley E. Porter and Cynthia L. Westfall. McMaster Divinity College Press New Testament Studies Series 10. Eugene: Pickwick, 2011.
Porter, Stanley E. "When and How Was the Pauline Canon Compiled? An Assessment of Theories." Pages 95–127 in *The Pauline Canon*. Edited by Stanley E. Porter. Pauline Studies 1. Leiden: Brill, 2004.
Price, Simon R. F. "Gods and Emperors: The Greek Language of the Roman Imperial Cult." *Journal of Hellenic Studies* 104 (1984): 79–95.
Price, Simon R. F. *Rituals and Power: The Roman Imperial Cult in Asia Minor*. Cambridge: Cambridge University Press, 1984. Repr., Cambridge: Cambridge University Press, 2002.
Revell, Louise. *Roman Imperialism and Local Identities*. Cambridge: Cambridge University Press, 2009.
Riedo-Emmenegger, Christoph. *Prophetisch-messianische Provokateure der Pax Romana: Jesus von Nazaret und andere Störenfriede im Konflikt mit dem Römischen Reich*. Novum Testamentum et Orbis Antiquus/Studien zur Umwelt des Neuen Testaments 56. Göttingen: Vandenhoeck & Ruprecht, 2005.
Riesner, Rainer. "Geographie, Archäologie, Epigraphik und Numismatik." Pages 181–214 in *Das Studium des Neuen Testaments*. Edited by Heinz-Werner Neudorfer and Eckhard J. Schnabel. 2nd ed. Wuppertal: R. Brockhaus/Gießen: Brunnen, 2006.
Robb, Graham. *Strangers: Homosexual Love in the Nineteenth Century*. New York: W. W. Norton & Company, 2003.
Rordorf, Willy. "Die neronische Christenverfolgung im Spiegel der apokryphen Paulusakten." *New Testament Studies* 28 (1982): 365–374.
Rudich, Vasily. *Dissidence and Literature under Nero: The Price of Rhetoricization*. London: Routledge, 1997.

Rudich, Vasily. "Navigating the Uncertain: Literature and Censorship in the Early Roman Empire." *Arion* 14 (2006): 7–28.
Rudich, Vasily. *Political Dissidence under Nero: The Price of Dissimulation.* London: Routledge, 1993.
Rüpke, Jörg. *Religion of the Romans.* Translated by Richard Gordon. Cambridge: Polity, 2007.
Sailor, Dylan. "The *Agricola.*" Pages 23–44 in *A Companion to Tacitus.* Edited by Victoria E. Pagán. Blackwell Companions to the Ancient World. Chichester: Wiley-Blackwell, 2012.
Sanders, Ed P. *Paul and Palestinian Judaism: A Comparison of Patterns of Religion.* London: SCM, 1977.
Sandmel, Samuel. *Philo of Alexandria: An Introduction.* New York: Oxford University Press, 1979.
Schäfer, Peter. *Judenhaß und Judenfurcht: Die Entstehung des Antisemitismus in der Antike.* Translated by Peter Schäfer. Berlin: Verlag der Weltreligionen, 2010.
Schenck, Kenneth. *A Brief Guide to Philo.* Louisville: Westminster John Knox, 2005.
Schiffman, Lawrence H. "The Qumran Community's Withdrawal from the Jerusalem Temple." Pages 267–284 in *Gemeinde ohne Tempel/Community without Temple: Zur Substituierung und Transformation des Jerusalemer Tempels und seines Kults im Alten Testament, antiken Judentum und frühen Christentum.* Edited by Beate Ego, Armin Lange, and Peter Pilhofer. Wissenschaftliche Untersuchungen zum Neuen Testament 118. Tübingen: Mohr Siebeck, 1999.
Schnabel, Eckhard J. *Paul and the Early Church.* Vol. 2 of *Early Christian Mission.* Downers Grove: InterVarsity, 2004.
Schneider, Wolfgang C. "Herrscherverehrung und Kaiserkult." Pages 210–217 in *Weltauffassung, Kult, Ethos.* Vol. 3 of *Neues Testament und Antike Kultur.* Edited by Kurt Erlemann, Karl L. Noethlichs, Klaus Scherberich, and Jürgen Zangenberg. Neukirchen-Vluyn: Neukirchener, 2005.
Schneider, Wolfgang C. "Politik und Religion." Pages 22–31 in *Prolegomena, Quellen, Geschichte, Recht.* Vol. 1 of *Neues Testament und Antike Kultur.* Edited by Kurt Erlemann, Karl L. Noethlichs, Klaus Scherberich, and Jürgen Zangenberg. Neukirchen-Vluyn: Neukirchener, 2004.
Schnelle, Udo. *Einleitung in das Neue Testament.* 8th ed. Uni-Taschenbücher 1830. Göttingen: Vandenhoeck & Ruprecht, 2013.
Schnelle, Udo. *Paulus: Leben und Denken.* de Gruyter Lehrbuch. Berlin: de Gruyter, 2003.
Schönberger, Otto. *Apocolocyntosis divi Claudii: Einführung, Text und Kommentar.* Würzburg: Königshausen und Neumann, 1990.
Schrage, Wolfgang, *Der erste Brief an die Korinther: 1Kor 1,1–6,11.* Evangelisch-Katholischer Kommentar 7,1. Zürich: Benziger 1991.
Schrage, Wolfgang. *Der erste Brief an die Korinther: 1Kor 6,12–11,16.* Evangelisch-Katholischer Kommentar 7,2. Solothurn: Benziger, 1995.
Schreiber, Stefan. "Caesar oder Gott (Mk 12,17)? Zur Theoriebildung im Umgang mit politischen Texten des Neuen Testaments." *Biblische Zeitschrift* 48 (2004): 65–85.
Schreiber, Stefan. "Paulus als Kritiker Roms? Politische Herrschaftsdiskurse in den Paulusbriefen." *Theologie und Glaube* 101 (2011): 338–359.
Schüssler Fiorenza, Elisabeth. "Paul and the Politics of Interpretation." Pages 40–57 in *Paul and Politics: Ekklesia, Israel, Imperium, Interpretation: Essays in Honor of Krister Stendahl.* Edited by Richard A. Horsley. Harrisburg: Trinity Press International, 2000.

Schuol, Monika. *Augustus und die Juden. Rechtsstellung und Interessenpolitik der kleinasiatischen Diaspora.* Studien zur Alten Geschichte 6. Frankfurt: Verlag Antike, 2007
Schwartz, Daniel R. "Philonic Anonyms of the Roman and Nazi Periods: Two Suggestions." *The Studia Philonica Annual* 1 (1989): 241–268.
Scott, James C. *Domination and the Arts of Resistance: Hidden Transcripts.* New Haven: Yale University Press, 1990.
Scott, Kenneth. "Humor at the Expense of the Ruler Cult." *Classical Philology* 27 (1932): 317–328.
Scott, Kenneth. "Plutarch and the Ruler Cult." *Transactions and Proceedings of the American Philological Association* 60 (1929): 117–135.
Seland, Torrey. "'Colony' and 'metropolis' in Philo: Examples of Mimicry and Hybridity in Philo's Writing Back from the Empire?." *Études Platoniciennes* 7 (2010): 13–36.
Seland, Torrey. "Philo as a Citizen: *Homo Politicus.*" Pages 47–74 in *Reading Philo: A Handbook to Philo of Alexandria.* Edited by Torrey Seland. Grand Rapids: Eerdmans, 2014.
Sills, Deborah. "Strange Bedfellows: Politics and Narrative in Philo." Pages 171–190 in *The Seductiveness of Jewish Myth: Challenge or Response?* Edited by S. Daniel Breslauer. SUNY Series in Judaica. Albany: State University of New York Press, 1997.
Smallwood, E. Mary. *Philonis Alexandrini: Legatio ad Gaium.* 2nd ed. Leiden: Brill, 1961.
Snyder, Glenn E. *Acts of Paul: The Formation of a Pauline Corpus.* Wissenschaftliche Untersuchungen zum Neuen Testament II 352. Tübingen: Mohr Siebeck, 2013.
Snyder, H. Gregory. "Response to Karl Galinsky, 'In the Shadow (or Not) of the Imperial Cult: A Cooperative Agenda.'" Pages 227–234 in *Rome and Religion: A Cross-Disciplinary Dialogue on the Imperial Cult.* Edited by Jeffrey Brodd and Jonathan L. Reed. Society of Biblical Literature Writings from the Greco-Roman World 5. Atlanta: Scholars Press, 2011.
Sober, Elliott. "Bayesianism: Its Scope and Limits." Pages 21–38 in *Bayes's Theorem.* Edited by Richard Swinburne. Proceedings of the British Academy 113. Oxford: Oxford University Press, 2002.
Spaeth, Barbette S. "Imperial Cult in Roman Corinth: A Response to Karl Galinsky's 'The Cult of the Roman Emperor: Uniter or Divider?.'" Pages 61–82 in *Rome and Religion: A Cross-Disciplinary Dialogue on the Imperial Cult.* Edited by Jeffrey Brodd and Jonathan L. Reed; Society of Biblical Literature Writings from the Greco-Roman World 5. Atlanta: Scholars Press, 2011.
Städele, Alfons. "Tacitus und die Barbaren." Pages 123–143 in *Reflexionen antiker Kulturen.* Edited by Peter Neukam. Klassische Sprachen und Literaturen 20. München: Bayerischer Schulbuch-Verlag, 1986.
Standhartinger, Angela. "Die paulinische Theologie im Spannungsfeld römisch-imperialer Machtpolitik: Eine neue Perspektive auf Paulus, kritisch geprüft anhand des Philipperbriefs." Pages 364–382 in *Religion, Politik und Gewalt.* Edited by Friedrich Schweitzer; Veröffentlichungen der Wissenschaftlichen Gesellschaft für Theologie 29. Gütersloh: Gütersloher Verlagshaus, 2006.
Stanley, Christopher D. *Arguing with Scripture: The Rhetoric of Quotations in the Letters of Paul.* New York: T&T Clark, 2004.
Starr, Chester G. Jr. "The Perfect Democracy of the Roman Empire." *American Historical Review* 58 (1952): 1–16.
Stirewalt, M. Luther Jr. *Paul: The Letter Writer.* Grand Rapids: Eerdmans, 2003.
Strecker, Christian. "Taktiken der Aneignung: Politische Implikationen der paulinischen Botschaft im Kontext der römischen imperialen Wirklichkeit." Pages 114–161 in *Das*

Neue Testament und politische Theorie: Interdisziplinäre Beiträge zur Zukunft des Politischen. Edited by Eckart Reinmuth. ReligionsKulturen 9. Stuttgart: Kohlhammer, 2011.

Süss, Jürgen. "Kaiserkult und Urbanistik: Kultbezirke für römische Kaiser in kleinasiatischen Städten." Pages 249–281 in *Die Praxis der Herrscherverehrung in Rom und seinen Provinzen*. Edited by Hubert Cancik and Konrad Hitzl. Tübingen: Mohr Siebeck, 2003.

Swinburne, Richard, ed. *Bayes's Theorem*. Proceedings of the British Academy 113. Oxford: Oxford University Press, 2002.

Swinburne, Richard. "Introduction." Pages 1–20 in *Bayes's Theorem*. Edited by Richard Swinburne. Proceedings of the British Academy 113. Oxford: Oxford University Press, 2002.

Tajra, Harry W. *The Martyrdom of St. Paul: Historical and Judicial Context, Tradition and Legends*. Wissenschaftliche Untersuchungen zum Neuen Testament II 67. Tübingen: Mohr Siebeck, 1994.

Taubes, Jacob. *Die Politische Theologie des Paulus*. 2nd ed. München: Wilhelm Fink, 1995.

Touratsoglou, Ioannis. *Die Münzstätte von Thessaloniki in der römischen Kaiserzeit: 32/31 v. Chr. bis 268 n. Chr*. Antike Münzen und Geschnittene Steine 12. Berlin: de Gruyter, 1988.

Tucker, Aviezer. *Our Knowledge of the Past: A Philosophy of Historiography*. Cambridge: Cambridge University Press, 2008.

Van Belle, Gilbert and Joseph Verheyden, eds. *Christ and the Emperor: The Gospel Evidence*. Biblical Tools and Studies 20. Leuven: Peeters, 2014.

Vollenweider, Samuel. "Politische Theologie im Philipperbrief?" Pages 457–469 in *Paulus und Johannes: Exegetische Studien zur paulinischen und johanneischen Theologie und Literatur*. Edited by Dieter Sänger and Ulrich Mell. Wissenschaftliche Untersuchungen zum Neuen Testament 198. Tübingen: Mohr Siebeck, 2006.

Walker, Brandon. "The Forgotten Kingdom: Miracle, the Memory of Jesus, and Counter-Ideology to the Roman Empire." Pages 129–146 in *Reactions to Empire: Sacred Texts in Their Socio-Political Contexts*. Wissenschaftliche Untersuchungen zum Neuen Testament II 372. Edited by John A. Dunne und Dan Batovici. Tübingen: Mohr Siebeck, 2014.

Wanamaker, Charles A. *The Epistles to the Thessalonians: A Commentary on the Greek Text*. New International Greek Testament Commentary. Grand Rapids: Eerdmans, 1990.

Weima, Jeffrey A. D. "Sincerely, Paul: The Significance of the Pauline Letter Closing." Pages 307–345 in *Paul and the Ancient Letter Form*. Edited by Stanley E. Porter and Sean A. Adams. Pauline Studies 6. Leiden: Brill 2010.

Wengst, Klaus. *Pax Romana: Anspruch und Wirklichkeit: Erfahrungen und Wahrnehmungen des Friedens bei Jesus und im Urchristentum*. München: Kaiser, 1986.

White, Joel R. "Anti-Imperial Subtexts in Paul: An Attempt at Building a Firmer Foundation." *Biblica* 90 (2009): 305–307.

White, Joel R. "'Peace and Security' (1 Thessalonians 5.3): Is It Really a Roman Slogan?" *New Testament Studies* 59 (2013): 382–395.

Whitmarsh, Tim. "Resistance is Futile? Greek Literary Tactics in the Face of Rome." Pages 57–78 in *Les Grecs héritiers des Romains*. Edited by Paul Schubert. Entretiens sur l'Antiquité classique 59. Geneva: Hardt Foundation, 2013.

Williams, Jonathan. "Religion and Roman Coins." Pages 143–163 in *A Companion to Roman Religion*. Edited by Jörg Rüpke. Blackwell Companions to the Ancient World. Blackwell: Chichester, 2011.

Williams, Travis B. "The Divinity and Humanity of Caesar in 1Peter 2,13." *Zeitschrift für die neutestemantliche Wissenschaft* 105 (2014): 131–147.

Willitts, Joel. "Matthew." Pages 82–100 in *Jesus Is Lord, Caesar Is Not: Evaluating Empire in New Testament Studies*. Edited by Scot McKnight and Joseph B. Modica. Downers Grove: IVP Academia, 2013.

Winter, Bruce W. *After Paul Left Corinth: The Influence of Secular Ethics and Social Change*. Grand Rapids: Eerdmans, 2001.

Winter, Bruce W. *Philo and Paul among the Sophists*. Society for New Testament Studies Monograph Series 96. Cambridge: Cambridge University Press, 1997.

Winter, Bruce W. "The Enigma of the Imperial Cultic Activities and Paul in Corinth." Pages 49–72 in *Greco-Roman Culture and the New Testament: Studies Commemorating the Centennial of the Pontifical Biblical Institute*. Edited by David E. Aune and Frederick E. Brenk. Supplements to Novum Testamentum 143. Leiden: Brill, 2012.

Witulski, Thomas. *Die Adressaten des Galaterbriefes: Untersuchungen zur Gemeinde von Antiochia ad Pisidiam*. Forschungen zur Religion und Literatur des Alten und Neuen Testaments 193. Göttingen: Vandenhoeck & Ruprecht, 2000.

Wolter, Michael. *Paulus: Ein Grundriss seiner Theologie*. Neukirchen-Vluyn: Neukirchener Theologie, 2011.

Woolf, Greg. "Inventing Empire in Ancient Rome." Pages 311–322 in *Empires: Perspectives from Archaeology and History*. Edited by Susan E. Alcock, Terrence N. D'Altroy, Kathleen D. Morrison, and Carla M. Sinopoli. Cambridge: Cambridge University Press, 2001.

Woyke, Johannes. *Götter, 'Götzen,' Götterbilder: Aspekte einer paulinischen 'Theologie der Religionen.'* Beihefte zur Zeitschrift für die neutestamentliche Wissenschaft und die Kunde der älteren Kirche 132. Berlin: de Gruyter, 2005

Wright, Nicholas T. "Gospel and Theology in Galatians." Pages 222–239 in *Gospel in Paul: Studies on Corinthians, Galatians and Romans for Richard N. Longenecker*. Edited by L. Ann Jervis and Peter Richardson. Journal for the Study of the New Testament: Supplement Series 108. Sheffield: Sheffield Academic, 1994.

Wright, Nicholas T. "Paul and Caesar: A New Reading of Romans." Pages 173–193 in *A Royal Priesthood? The Use of the Bible Ethically and Politically: A Dialogue with Oliver O'Donovan*. Edited by Craig G. Bartholomew, Jonathan Chaplin, Robert Song, and Al Wolters. Scripture and Hermeneutics Series 3; Grand Rapids: Zondervan, 2002.

Wright, Nicholas T. *Paul and the Faithfulness of God*. Christian Origins and the Question of God 4. London: SPCK, 2013.

Wright, Nicholas T. "Paul in Current Anglophone Scholarship." *Expository Times* 128 (2012): 367–381.

Wright, Nicholas T. *Paul: In Fresh Perspective*. Minneapolis: Fortress, 2005.

Wright, Nicholas T. "Paul's Gospel and Caesar's Empire." Pages 160–183 in *Paul and Politics: Ekklesia, Israel, Imperium, Interpretation: Essays in Honor of Krister Stendahl*. Edited by Richard A. Horsley. Harrisburg: Trinity Press International, 2000.

Wright, Nicholas T. "The Letter to the Romans." Pages 393–770 in *The Acts of the Apostles, Introduction to Epistolary Literature, The Letter to the Romans, The First Letter to the Corinthians*. Vol. 10 of *New Interpreter's Bible*. Edited by Leander E. Keck. Nashville: Abingdon, 2002.

Wright, Nicholas T. *The New Testament and the People of God.* Christian Origins and the Question of God 1. Minneapolis: Fortress, 1992.
Wright, Nicholas T. *What Saint Paul Really Said.* Oxford: Lion, 1997.
Yoder, Joshua. "Sympathy for the Devil? Philo on Flaccus and Rome." *The Studia Philonica Annual* 24 (2012): 167–182.
Zangenberg, Jürgen. "'*Pax Romana*' im NT." Pages 165–168 in *Prolegomena, Quellen, Geschichte, Recht.* Vol. 1 of *Neues Testament und Antike Kultur.* Edited by Kurt Erlemann, Karl L. Noethlichs, Klaus Scherberich, and Jürgen Zangenberg. Neukirchen-Vluyn: Neukirchener, 2004.
Zanker, Paul. *Augustus und die Macht der Bilder.* 5th ed. München: C. H. Beck, 2008.

Index of Ancient Sources

1 Old Testament

Genesis
1:27^{LXX} 40
23:3 11
37:3 8
37:31 8
37:7 10
37:9 9

Exodus
20:3–6 101

Deuteronomy
5:7–10 101

Jeremiah
6:14^{LXX} 141

Daniel
(the book) 32, 114, 115
2 121
2:44 120
7 121
7:22 120

2 Apocrypha

2 Maccabees
9:12 102

3 Dead Sea Scroll

4Q174
(the document) 152
I, 6 152

4QMMT
(the document) 152

Damascus Document
I, 3 152

Pesher Habakkuk
I, 13 152
VIII, 8 152
VIII, 16 152
IX, 9 152
IX, 16 152
X, 9 152
XI, 4 152
XII, 2 152
XII, 8 152

Rule of the Community
IX, 6   152

VIII, 5–9   152

4 New Testament

Q
(the source)   16, 59

Matthew
(the gospel)   93, 132, 133
3:10   16
20:1–16   133
23:23   24
24:15   103

Mark
(the gospel)   59, 144
12:13–17   106
13:14   103
14:53–65   58
15:1–5   58
15:39   128

Luke
(the author)   22, 124, 128
(the gospel)   59, 60
3:9   16

John
1:41   149
10:33   103
15   16
19:15   154

Acts
(the book)   19, 38, 58, 59, 122, 127, 131
12:21–23   103
12:22   103
12:23   103
16:20–39   19
16:37–39   71
17   127, 155
17:1–9   63, 81, 122
17:5   63
17:7   63, 88, 154
17:13–15   122
17:16   127
17:21   71
17:22   127
19:40   62
21:39   71
22:25–29   71
23–26   58
23:27   71
24:10   71
25:7–8   88
25:11   71
25:16   71

Romans
(the letter)   39, 118, 133
1:1–17   137, 138, 147
1:3–4   85, 137, 138, 144, 147, *157*
1:4   144
1:13   122
1:16   125
1:23   100
2:9–10   125
2:26   118
2:29   118
3:9   125
3:22   118
5:2   33, 34
10:12   125
13   22, 23, 37, 130
13:1–7   19, 22, 24, 31, 32, 38, 55, 89, 110, 112, 113, 124, 127, 130
13:1–13   130
13:3   128
13:4   20, 55
13:6–7   71
13:11–12a   115
15:12   147
15:22   122
16:20a   115

Index of Ancient Sources

1 Corinthians
1:13	128
1:17–18	128
1:23	128
1:24	125
2:2	128
2:6	127, 128, 129, 132
2:6–10	127
2:8	128
3:16	151
6:2	115
6:2–3	120
6:19	151
7:29–31	115
8:4	103
8:5	100, 101, *157*
8:5–6	144
8:5a	100
8:5b	100
8:6	100, 151
9:19–23	127
10:19	103
10:20	103
10:32	125
11:10	64
12:13	125
14:23	63
15:22	120
15:24	120
15:24–26	120
15:24–28	115
15:25–26	120
15:26	115, 120
15:56	120
16:21	63

2 Corinthians
1:1	64
2:12–13	159
2:14	107, 109, 150, *158*, 159
4:4	128
4:10	128
6:16	152
7:5	159
11:23–28	122
12:7	122
13:4	128

Galatians
1:2	64
1:4	128
1:6–7	127
1:10	126, 127
2:20	154
2:21	117
3:1	128
3:26a	154
3:26b	154
3:28	40, 125
4:8–9	100
4:9	100
5:7–8	122
5:11	127, 128
5:12	132
5:17	122
5:19–26	122
5:24	128
6:11	63
6:12	126, 127, 128
6:14	128
6:16	118
6:17	128

Ephesians
2:2	128
2:16	128
2:21–22	152
6:12	120
6:14–17	120

Philippians
(the letter)	65, 134
1:19	35, 136
1:27–30	126
2:6–11	138, *157*
2:8	128
2:10–11	154
3	127, 131
3:2	132
3:3	118
3:4–6	116
3:17–19	158
3:18	128
3:20	30, 103, 114, 134, 145, *158*
3:20–21	158

Colossians
1:20   128
2:14   128
3:11   125
4:16   64
4:18   63

1 Thessalonians
(the letter)   134, 140
1:9   126
1:14–15   128
2:18   122, 123
2:19   141
3:1   122
3:6–15   133
3:13   141
4:10–12   20
4:13–17   30, 114
4:15   141
4:17   141
5:1–11   135
5:3   30, 39, 114, 135, 136, 141, 142, *157*
5:8   120
5:23   141
5:27   63, 64

2 Thessalonians
2:4   103
2:1–5   123

2:3–5   115
3:17   63

1 Timothy
(the letter)   151, 153
1:17   153, 154
2:2   151, 153
6:15   151, 153

Titus
3:1   20

Hebrews
(the letter)   58
4:16   33

1 Peter
(the letter)   32–33
2:13   32, 103, 154
2:13–17   32
2:17   154

Jude
1:4   146

Revelation
6:10   146
17:9   154

5 Josephus

Antiquitates judaicae
18.256   102
18.256–309   103
19.343–350   103
20.90   146

Bellum judaicum
2.184–203   103
2.197   79
3.351   153
5.563   153
7.323   146
7.410   146
7.418–419   146

Contra Apionem
(the work)   89
2.73–78   60
2.73–78   89
2.74   60
2.75   69
2.75–76   102

Vita
(the book)   59

6 Philo

De Abrahamo		2.48	16
228	13	2.49	16
229	13	2.61–64	16
		2.62	16, 17
De Iosepho		2.63	17
(the book)	3, 5, 6, 7, 14, 18, 19	2.63–64	17
72–73	5	2.64	16
		2.78	10
De opificio mundi		2.78–79	12, 14
105	9	2.79	10
129	9	2.80	11
		2.80–82	11
De somniis		2.81–92	3
1	6, 7, 8, 15	2.83	11
1.1	6	2.83–92	12, 13
1.2	6	2.84	11
1.122	7	2.85–86	11
1.122–124	14	2.86	11, 14
1.124	7	2.87–88	11
1.124–126	7	2.88	12
1.126	7	2.89	11, 12, 13
1.155	7	2.90–92	13
1.219	8	2.91	11, 12, 13, 14, 19
1.219–223	8	2.91–92	13
1.220	8	2.92	14
1.221	8	2.93	13, 14
1.222	9	2.98	14
1.224	18	2.99	15
1.224–225	9	2.101–104	14
1.243	15	2.105–109	15
1.244	15	2.115	9
2	2, 3, 4, 5, 6, 7, 8, 9, 10, 15, 17, 18, 43, 69	2.115–133	10
		2.117–120	9
		2.121–122	9
2.1	6	2.123	9, 11, 14
2.2–3	6	2.133	10
2.4	6	2.136	9
2.5	6	2.155	7
2.5–16	15	2.182–184	18
2.16	7	2.203	7
2.25	7	2.219	18
2.26	11	2.283–302	18
2.42–64	16		
2.43	16	*In Flaccum*	
2.44	17	(the book)	2, 4, 13, 18, 69
2.47	17	188	14

53	14	144	80
		149	4, 80
Legatio ad Gaium		149–151	102
(the book)	2, 4, 13, 15, 69, 79, 81, 82	150–151	80
		152	80
1	9	153	80
75	79	154	80
78–92	80	155–158	80
93	80	182	9
94–114	80	189	103
115	80	206	81
116	80	357	69, 82
118	80, 101, 102		
134–140	80	*Quod Deus sit immutabilis*	
143–158	4	173–176	4
143–159	80		

7 Early Church

Eusebius

Historia ecclesiastica
2.18.4	6
3.19–3.20.7	149
3.32.1–6	149

Ignatius
To the Ephesians
18.2	149

To the Romans
7.3	149

To the Smyrnaeans
1.1	149

To the Trallians
9.1	149

Martyrdom of Paul
(the work)	131, 132, 148
2.2–2.6	148
4.2	154
4.4–6	154

Martyrdom of Polycarp
(the work)	149
8.2	149
9.2	149
9.3	149

8 Greek and Roman Authors

Augustus

Res gestae divi Augusti
(the work)	15, 107
4.1	107

Cassius Dio

Historia Romana
56.25.5–6	81
56.27.1	86
57.20.3	88
57.23.1–3	87
57.24.3–4	87

Index of Ancient Sources

57.24.4	86
58.24.4	87
59.26.8–9	63

Cicero

In Catalinam
3.6–13	65

Cremutius Cordus
FRHist 71	87

Euripides

Phoenissae
393	87

Ovid

Tristia
2	86

Pausanias

Graeciae description
1.18.6–9	101
2	97

Plutarch

Moralia
170E	83

Sallust

Bellum catalinae
46–47	65

Scaurus

Atreus
(the play)	87

Seneca

De clementia
(the work)	81
1.10.3	84

Apocolocyntosis
(the work)	82, 83

1.1	82
1.2	82
3.1–2	82
4	83
5.2	82
5.2–3	82
5.3	82
6.2	82
7.1–2	82
7.4	82
10.3–11.5	82
11.4	83
12.3	82
13.4–14.2	82
14.4–15.1	82

Suetonius

Gaius Caligula
22	76

Nero
16.2	89

Vespasianus
23.4	83

Tacitus

Agricola
(the book)	72
21	72
28	72
28.2	72
28.3	72
30–32	71
30.4	69, 71
32.3	71, 72

Annales
(the work)	72
3.49–51	88
4.30	86
4.35	86
6.18.2	155
6.29	87
13.3	83
15.44	89

Historiae
5.9   103

Vergil

Aeneid
(the work)   70, 107

9 Non-Literary Sources

P.Oxyrhynchus
1453.10–11   75

IG X
2.1, no. 31   96

OGIS
458   106
655.1–2   75

RPC 1
nos. 1554–1555 96

Index of Modern Authors

Achtemeier, P. J. 62
Adams, E. 66
Adams, S. A. 63, 64
Alcock, S. E. 91
Alexander, P. H. XVII
Allison, D. C. 128, 129
Altman, M. 83, 84
Ames, F. R. 62
Anderson, J. C. 12
Ando, C. 91, 99
Arnaoutoglou, I. N. 62
Ascough, R. S. 95
Aune, D. E. 97, 126

Baldick, C. XVIII, 22
Barclay, J. M. G. XVI, 1, 2, 23, 25, 37, 42, 54, 60, 61, 63, 66, 68, 69, 70, 72, 73, 78, 80, 81, 82, 84, 89, 90, 100, 101, 102, 103, 104, 110, 112, 113, 114, 119, 121, 122, 123, 124, 125, 126, 127, 128, 131, 132, 134, 135, 144, 151, 152, 153, 155, 158
Barraclough, R. 4, 5, 7, 10, 12, 13, 15, 16, 18
Bartholomä, P. XV
Bartholomew, C. G. 122
Bassler, J. M. 6, 7, 8, 10, 13, 18
Batovici, D. XVI, 66, 90, 148
Bayes, T. XV, 27, 29
Beard, M. 76
Berthelot, K. 2, 4
Bietenhard, H. 146
Bird, M. F. 23, 137, 144, 154
Bockmuehl, M. 5, 149
Böhm, M. 5
Bormann, L. 96
Box, H. 4
Brenk, F. E. 97
Brodd, J. 32, 75, 90, 95, 106, 147

Bruce, F. F. 122
Bryan, C. 65, 143, 151, 154
Burge, G. M. 92
Burk, D. 133, 143
Burnett, A. 106
Burrell, B. XVI, 96
Buschmann, G. 149

Canavan, R. 95
Cancik, H. 75, 82, 96, 105
Cancik-Lindemaier, H. 82
Carrier, R. 27
Carter, W. 21, 61, 65, 93, 95, 119, 144, 150, 152
Cazeaux, J. 6
Champlin, E. 37, 39, 56, 83
Chaniotis, A. 75
Chaplin, J. 122
Christ, K. 86
Chrysos, E. K. 154
Clark, E. Jr. VIII
Clauss, M. 74, 75, 76, 77, 78, 83
Cohick, L. H. 64, 69, 85, 92
Collins, A. Y. 143, 144
Collins, J. J. 5, 13, 17
Coppins, W. XVI, 64
Cornell, T. J. XVII
Cotter, W. 62
Cramer, F. H. 56, 85, 86, 87
Crossan, J. D. 22, 94, 105
Crouch, A. 135, 144
Cuffari, A. 126
Cullmann, O. 21

D'Altroy, T. N. 91
Davila, J. R. XVI, 143
Dawid, P. 28, 35, 49
Day, M. 28, 33, 48
De Troyer, K. XV

Decker-Lucke, S. XVII
Deines, R. 92
Deissmann, G. A. 21, 139, 146, 150
DeMaris, R. E. 97
Diehl, J. A. 21, 63, 69, 94
Dormeyer, D. 63
Douven, I. 48
Dunn, J. D. G. 33, 34, 154
Dunne, J. A. XVI, 66, 90, 95, 148

Eckert, J. 22
Ego, B. 153
Eidinow, E. XVII
Eliot, G. 52
Elliott, M. W. XV
Elliott, N. 1, 12, 20, 24, 25, 35, 38, 39, 40, 55, 57, 58, 60, 61, 66, 136, 156
Erdkamp, P. 91
Erlemann, K. 70, 73, 74
Ernest, J. D. XVII
Evans, C. A. XVII, 35

Fantin, J. D. 24, 94, 95, 123, 134, 154
Fee, G. D. 64, 100, 120, 128, 147, 152, 153, 158
Feldman, L. H. 16, 101
Fisher, A. XVI
Frazier, F. 6
Frey, J. XVI, 117
Friesen, S. J. 75

Gäckle, V. 22
Gal, S. 51
Galinsky, K. 32, 74, 75, 82, 90, 98, 99, 106, 108, 123, 132, 133, 135, 136, 143, 144, 147, 149, 155
Gärtner, B. 153
Gehring, R. W. 64, 66
Gempf, C. 63
Georgi, D. 21, 70, 107, 137, 148
Gessmann, M. 25
Gill, D. W. J. 63
Goodenough, E. R. 2, 3, 4, 5, 6, 7, 8, 9, 10, 12, 13, 14, 16, 17, 18, 37, 69, 81, 101
Gradel, I. 75
Green, G. L. 92
Gripentrog, S. 117

Gruen, E. S. 7, 10, 19, 74
Gupta, N. 25

Habicht, C. 73
Hafemann, S. J. XV, 108, 109
Hall, J. 65
Hardin, J. K. 63, 70, 77, 78, 79, 81, 89, 99, 105, 106, 107, 126, 127
Harrill, J. A. 23, 63, 84, 89, 90, 91, 113, 153
Harrison, J. R. 1, 12, 26, 91, 96, 99, 107, 108, 130, 144
Harter-Uibopuu, K. 96
Hay, D. M. 6, 7, 8, 9, 10, 13, 14, 15, 18
Hays, R. B. VII, 24, 25, 26, 29, 35, 36, 37, 38, 39, 40, 41, 42, 55, 108, 110, 114, 136, 142, 145, 148, 155
Heath, G. L. 148
Heilig, C. 26, 48, 49, 66
Heilig, T. XV
Hekster, O. 91
Helmer, C. 15
Herz, P. 105
Hilgert, E. 3
Hitzl, K. 75, 96, 105
Holtz, T. 64, 123
Hon, G. 48
Horn, F. W. 22, 152
Hornblower, S. XVII
Horrell, D. G. 66
Horsley, G. H. R. 63
Horsley, R. A. 1, 21, 55, 58, 59, 60, 61, 66, 70, 93, 134, 140
Horst, W. v. d. 4
Howson, C. 27, 49
Hurtado, L. 101

Jay, J. 105
Jervis, L. A. 135
Jewett, R. 63, 100, 122, 124, 130
Johns, R. 46
Jones, C. P. 83
Jones, D. L. 58
Joynes, C. E. 81
Judge, E. A. 81
Junker, R. 49

Kahl, B. 58

Kahn, J.-G. 2
Kahneman, D. 34
Kany, J. 26
Keck, L. E. 71
Keesmaat, S. C. 137
Keith, C. 25
Kenney, J. P. 6
Kim, S. 41, 135, 136, 151
Kinzig, W. 149
Klauck, H.-J. 69, 74, 75, 76, 77, 78, 89, 103
Klinzing, G. 153
Kloppenborg, J. S. 62
Klötzer, S. 40
Köster, H. 140, 141
Kraft, R. A. 3, 5, 9, 10
Krauter, S. 2, 17, 20, 24, 71, 81, 99, 104, 111, 115, 134
Kreitzer, L. J. 106, 109
Kristeva, J. 25, 148
Kutsko, J. F. XVII

Labahn, M. 62, 97
Lange, A. 153
Le Donne, A. 25
Lehnert, V. A. 84
Leisegang, H. 79, 80, 81
Lewis, G. S. 143
Lietzmann, H. 98
Lightstone, J. N. 78, 79
Lipton, P. 31, 34, 46, 47, 48
Luther, M. 116, 117, 121

Maier, J. 152
Markschies, C. 64
McHugh, M. R. 87
McKnight, S. 19, 23, 60, 63, 64, 93, 113, 123, 135, 137
McLaren, J. S. 79
Meeks, W. A. 66
Meggitt, J. 81, 98, 99, 105, 154
Mell, U. 93
Mellor, R. 72, 87
Millar, F. 106
Miller, C. 93, 94, 95, 96, 97, 98, 99, 102, 104, 105, 107, 151, 154
Miller, C. W. 62
Mitchell, S. 79

Modica, J. B. 19, 23, 60, 63, 64, 93, 113, 123, 135, 137
Momigliano, A. 14
Moo, D. 116
Morrison, K. D. 91
Murphy-O'Connor, J. 64

Neudorfer, H. W. 22, 92, 106
Newman, C. C. 143
Niehoff, M. R. XVI, 4, 5, 14
Noethlichs, K. L. 70, 73, 74
North, J. A. 76
Novenson, M. V. 90, 93, 100, 149
Nystrom, D. 123

O'Brien, P. T. 63
Oakes, P. 134, 150
Oertelt, F. 2, 5, 6, 7, 13, 14, 15, 16, 17, 18, 19
Öhler, M. 62, 89
Omerzu, H. 84, 115, 116

Pagán, V. E. 71
Paget, J. C. 5, 149
Parrott, R. L. 22, 83, 114, 127
Peachin, M. 91
Peppard, M. 151
Petersen, D. L. XVII
Peterson, E. 141
Petrey, T. G. 15
Pilhofer, P. 96, 153
Pinter, D. L. 60, 61, 124, 128, 151
Popkes, W. 21
Porter, S. E. XVII, 38, 63, 64, 138, 148
Price, S. R. F. 73, 75, 76, 79, 83, 84, 94, 95, 97, 98, 99, 104, 106, 107, 126, 155
Pucci Ben Zeev, M. 77

Radick, G. 28, 33
Rajak, T. 77
Rakover, S. S. 48
Reed, J. L. 22, 32, 75, 90, 94, 95, 105, 106, 147
Reinmuth, E. 21
Revell, L. 90, 91
Richardson, P. 135
Riedo-Emmenegger, C. 84

Riesner, R. 106
Robb, G. 37
Rordorf, W. 132
Rosen, R. M. 87
Rudich, V. XVI, 65, 85, 86, 87, 88
Rüpke, J. 62, 74, 77, 78, 105, 106
Rüsen-Weinhold, U. 84

Sailor, D. 71, 72
Sanders, E. P. 116, 117
Sanders, J. A. 35
Sandmel, S. 3, 6, 17
Sänger, D. 93
Schäfer, P. 126
Schenck, K. 3
Scherberich, K. 70, 73, 74
Schiffman, L. H. 152, 153
Schiffman, L. W. XVII
Schmidt, H. 25
Schnabel, E. J. 22, 92, 106
Schneider, W. C. 73, 74, 75, 76
Schnelle, U. 32, 33, 64, 89, 95, 99, 118, 119, 124, 143, 149
Schönberger, O. 82, 83, 84
Schrage, W. 100, 152
Schreiber, S. 1, 45, 65, 70, 71, 87, 90, 110, 139
Schubert, P. 19
Schuol, M. 62
Schüssler Fiorenza, E. 66
Schwartz, D. R. 9, 10, 117
Schwertner, S. XVII
Scott, J. C. 50, 51, 52, 53, 54, 55, 56, 57, 58, 59, 60, 61, 65, 66, 68
Scott, K. 83, 84
Segal, E. 106
Sellew, P. 12
Setzer, C. 12
Siebenthal, H. v. XVII
Sills, D. 5, 18
Sinopoli, C. M. 91
Slovic, P. 34
Sluiter, I. 87
Smallwood, E. M. 4
Snyder, G. E. 131
Snyder, H. G. 147
Sober, E. 31, 33, 48
Song, R. 122
Spaeth, B. S. 106

Spawforth, A. XVII
Städele, A. 72
Standhartinger, A. 65
Stanley, C. D. 38, 108
Starr, C. G. Jr. 72, 74
Still, T. D. 66
Stirewalt, M. L. Jr. 63
Strecker, C. 21, 22, 23, 62, 68, 91, 93, 99, 105, 107, 128, 129, 132, 133, 139, 145, 146, 157
Sumney, J. L. 137
Süss, J. 105
Swinburne, R. 27, 28, 31, 33, 49

Tajra, H. W. 131
Taubes, J. 21, 85, 137, 147
Touratsoglou, I. 96
Tucker, A. 28
Tversky, A. 34

Urbach, P. 27

Van Belle, G. 23
VanderKam, J. C. XVII
Verheyden, J. 23
Vollenweider, S. 93

Walker, B. 148
Wanamaker, C. A. 122
Weima, J. A. D. 63
Wengst, K. 21
Westfall, C. L. 138, 148
White, J. R. V, 22, 24, 29, 30, 31, 32, 114, 115, 116, 123, 142, 143, 144, 146, 147
Whitmarsh, T. 19, 88, 101, 129, 137
Williams, J. 105
Williams, T. B. 103
Willitts, J. 93, 132, 133
Wilson, S. G. 62
Wimbush, V. L. 58
Winter, B. W. 8, 62, 63, 64, 97, 100
Witulski, T. 100, 101, 104
Wolter, M. 89, 121
Wolters, A. 122
Woolf, G. 91
Woyke, J. 101

Wright, N. T. VII, 1, 24, 25, 26, 29, 35, 36, 37, 38, 39, 40, 42, 54, 70, 71, 76, 95, 100, 101, 104, 107, 110, 111, 112, 113, 114, 116, 117, 118, 119, 120, 121, 122, 123, 124, 125, 127, 128, 130, 131, 134, 135, 136, 137, 138, 145, 147, 149, 151, 152, 153, 156

Yoder, J. 4

Zalta, E. N. 48
Zangenberg, J. 62, 70, 71, 72, 73, 74, 97
Zanker, P. 99, 105

Index of Subjects

Abraham 11, 118, 119
Achaia 98
Administration 37, 58, 93
– and *pax Romana* 70–72
– and violence 55
– Josephus 69
– Municipal magistrates 86
– Paul 19, 70–71, 112–13, 121, 127
– – Open criticism *127–29*
– Philo *18*, 69
– Politarchs 63
aediles 86
Alexander the Great 73
Alexandria 1, 4, 12, 13, 18, 69, 80, 102
Allegory *See* Philo
Anarchy 111
Ancyra 94
Anonymity 56, 128
Apocalyptic *See* Worldview
Apotheosis 74, 75, 76, 77, 83, 82–84, 84, 101, 102, 105, 106, 111, 155
Asia Minor 43, 73, 75, 92, 93, 94, 98, 105
Assyria 119
Athens 94, 101
Audience 2, 3, 6, 38, 144
– and discourse level 57, 132
– Implied and actual reader 108
– Rome 33, 39, 40, 61, 89, *147*, *148*
Awareness *See* Intentionality

Babylon 119
Bayes's theorem *27–28*
– and method 28
– Background knowledge 30–33, 34
– Background plausibility 29, 158, 159
– – Historical circumstances 159
– Comparisons 33–34

– Explanatory potential 28, 139–40, 159
– Likelihood *See* Explanatory potential
– Prior-Probability *See* Background plausibility
Berea 122

Calgacus 69
Cenchreae 94
Censorship 65, *85–88*
– Book burning 86, *87*
– Executions 87, 88
– Exile 82, 86
– Prison 85
Character *See* Personality
Christological titles *See individual titles*
– and narrative 154
Christus See Messiah (honorific)
Cicero 64
Circumcision 118, 121
Citizenship 103, 123, 129, 134, 157
City 93, 99
– Affairs of 8
– *polis* 73, 93
Clients 64
Clutorius Priscus 88
Code 2, 5, *23*, 37, 53, 56, 57, 60, 68, 69, 87, 113, 128, 130, *132*, 149
Coinage 96, 105–6, 109
– Propaganda 106
collegia 61, 62, 81
Colony 93, 95, 97
Confessing Church 124
Corinth 59, 64, 94, 95, 96–97
Covenant 111, 118
Creation 111, 119
– Subordinate to the creator 102
Criteria
– and praxis 26

- Function 24–26
- Hays *See* Echoes
- Life-of-Jesus-research 25
- mirror-reading 25

Criticism
- *Aneignung* 132, 157
- Antithesis 151, 153
- Attack 135, 136
- Confrontation 131, 135, 145
- Contrast 132, 135
- Definition *129–36*
- Derivation 145
- Object 68–91, 129, 156
- – in the framework of the modified subtext-hypothesis *156*
- Opposition 135
- Parody 82, 137
- Polemic 134
- *Polemischer Parallelismus* 146
- Rebellion 136
- Resistance 13, 14, 19, *56*, 57, 58, 59, 85, 101, 129, 130, 137, 151
- Surpassing 132–134

Cross *See* Crucifixion
Crucifixion 61, 112, 117, 118, 120, 126, 127, 128, 134
Cultic background 33
Cultural Revolution 37

Damascus 115, 116, 117
Danger
- as reason for subtext 19, 39, 125, 129, *See* Persecution, *See* Subtext

Death 112, 118, 119, 120
Deification *See* Apotheosis
delatores 86
Demons 113, 128
deus 75
divi filius 75
Divinity
- of the emperor *See* Ideology, *See* Imperial cults

divus 75
divus Iulius 75
Drusus the Younger 88
ecclesiae 149

Echoes *35–43*
- as not necessarily subversive 150

- Criteria 43
- Narrative 136
- of Scripture 35–36
- of the Empire 36–40
- Resonance 148, 157

Election *See* People of God
Elite 57, 61, 65, 83, 107, 110
Emperor 1, 33, 60, 69, 75, 76, 77, 78, 79, 80, 81, 82, 83, 84, 85, 87, 88, 89, 90, 93, 94, 96, 97, 98, 99, 100, 103, 104, 105, 106, 108, 111, 126, 133, 134, 143, 144, 153
- Augustus 4, 15, 62, 74, 75, 74–75, 76, 79, 80, 82, 84, 86, 87, 96, 98, 99, 102, 104, 105, 106, 107, 154, 155
- Julius Caesar 73, 74, 75, 76, 87, 153
- Caligula 3, 4, 9, 19, 63, 69, 76, 77, 79, 80, 81, 87, 102, 103
- Claudius 77, 81, 82, 83, 84, 87, 89, 137
- Domitian 33, 72, 77, 78, 79, 89
- Hadrian 101
- Nero 37, 39, 56, 77, 81, 82, 83, 87, 89, 94, 103, 131, 132, 137, 142, 148, 154
- Tiberius 9, 62, 76, 87, 88, 155
- Titus 77
- Trajan 78
- Vespasian 77, 83, 87

Emperor worship *See* Imperial cults
Empire 1, 2, 3, 4, 6, 10, 13, 19, 21, 22, 23, 24, 25, 35, 36, 37, 38, 39, 40, 41, 42, 43, 44, 45, 50, 55, 56, 57, 58, 59, 60, 61, 62, 63, 64, 65, 66, 68, 69, 70, 71, 72, 73, 74, 79, 80, 81, 82, 83, 84, 85, 89, 90, 92, 93, 94, 95, 99, 100, 105, 110, 111, 112, 113, 114, 115, 118, 119, 120, 121, 122, 123, 124, 125, 126, 127, 128, 132, 133, 134, 135, 136, 137, 138, 139, 140, 143, 144, 148, 150, 151, 152, 153, 156, 158, 159

Ephesus 94
Euphemism 56, 57
Explanations *See* Inference to the Best Explanation, *See* Bayes's theorem: Explanatory potential

Faith 118

- Content 126
- Mission strategy 127
- *familia Caesaris* 130
- Figured speech 87
- Flaccus 3, 4, 7, 9, 14, 19, 69
- Folk tales 54, 56
- Fourth (Danielic) kingdom 114, 115, 120, 121

genius 76
Gentiles 3, 37, 43, 63, 114, 118, 121, 125
Germanicus 88
Gestures 54
Gnaeus Naevius 85
Gospel 84, 104, 111, 127, 129, 144, *See* Greek terms and phrases: εὐαγγέλιον
- Misunderstanding 129
Gossip 54
Graffiti 56
Greece 43, 60, 78, 81, 83, 92, 93, 94, 97, 98, 101, 116, 153, 154
Greek terms and phrases
- ἀπάντησις 30, 141
- ἄρχων 12, 127, 128
- ἀσφάλεια *See* εἰρήνη καὶ ἀσφάλεια
- βασιλεύς 11, 153–54
- βία 13, 14
- δεσπότης 146
- δικαιοσύνη 38
- εἴδωλον 103, 126
- εἰρήνη καὶ ἀσφάλεια 141, 142, 157
- Ἕλληνες 125
- ἐπίτροπος 16
- εὐαγγέλιον 38, 143, 154
- εὐεργέτης 4, 73
- εὐλάβεια 11
- ἡγεμονικός 9
- ἡγεμών 16
- θριαμβεύω 107, 108, 150, 159
- ἰσόθεος 102
- κύριος 22, 32, 38, 100, 114, 134, 138, 144, 146, 147, 151, 154
- λεγόμενοι θεοί 100
- παρουσία 30, 38, 141
- πολιτεία 8
- πολίτευμα 103
- προσαγωγή 33, 34
- στοιχεῖα 100, 101
- σωτήρ 38, 73
- τιμή 12
- φόβος 12
- χάρις 34
- χριστός 32, 149
Grumbling 56, 57

Hebrew Bible 1, 29, 35, 111
- Greek translation 35, 108, 141, 146
- – Pauline vocabulary *143–45*
- – Politics 143
Hidden transcripts *51–54*
- and churches 59, *See* House churches
- and courts 58
- Paul *54–67*
- Philo *1–20*
- Pure form 53, 58–65
- Veiled form 53, 54–58, 80
Hierapolis 94
Historical Plausibility 38, *See* Echoes
History of Interpretation 39, 91, 148, *See* Echoes
Homosexuality 37
Horace 70, 107
House churches 64, 66
Hypotheses *See* Bayes's theorem, *See* Inferences

Ideology 19, 20, 22, 24, 37, 39, 42, 45, 53, 70, 71, 73, 79, 81, 82, 84, 85, 90, 91, 93, 105, 106, 107, 108, 109, 110, 111, 113, 114, 120, 124, 125, 127, 137, 139, 143, 145, 147, 150, 157, 158
- and public space 105
- Coinage *105–6*, *See* Coinage
- Defintion 90
- Emperor
- – Exclusiveness 84
- Narrative 106–7, 120
- Pluriformity and Unity 90–91
- Statues 105
- Temporal dimension 99, 106–7, 107
- Theatre 105
Idols *See* Pagan gods
Imperial cults *93–98*
- and imperatorial ideology 84, 97–98
- and Jews 78–84
- and other expressions of loyalty 79

- and other pagan cults 75, 78, *98–104*
- Expectations 76, 78–79, 79, *89*
- History *73–78*
- Imperial festivals 79, 93, 111
- Neocorate 95, 96
- Perceptibility *98–104*
- Pluriformity 76
- Priesthoods 74, 75
- Sacrifices 69, 74, 77, 79, 104
- Statues 74, 77, 100, 102, 103, 105, 111
- Temples 73, 74, 95, 96, 97, 102, 104

imperium 74
Inference to the Best Explanation *46–49*
Inferences
- Comparisons 33–34
- Inference to the Best Explanation *See* Inference to the Best Explanation
- Structure 26–27

Inscriptions 95, 96, 105
Intentionality 39, *132–34*, 129–36, 142, 145
- Aims 134–35, 138, 156, 157

Intertextuality
- and Bayes 29
- and Intentionality *See* Intentionality
- and subversive potential *146–55*
- and *termini technici* 140–41
- Derivation 145
- Lexical parallels 139, *140–45*
- – and the LXX *143–45*
- – Chance 141–43
- – Degree of alignment 142
- – Neutral and antithetical 150–55
- – Prominence 142
- Original definition 25, 148
- Resonance 148, 157

Isaiah 119
Israel *See* People of God
Jesus 58, 59, 118

Jews *See* Judaism, *See* Worldview
- and 'atheism' 126
- and Christian conflicts with Roman administration 62
- and covenant *See* Covenant
- and creation *See* Creation
- and imperial cults 78–84
- and misanthropy 126

- and monotheism 78, 101, 103, 117, 126

Jokes 54, 83
Judaism 3, 4, 43, 78, 81, 89, 101, 105, 111, 115, 116, 121, 126, 143, 149
- *religio licita* 77

King(ship) 5, 33, 34, 63, 81, 83, 84, 112, 123, 128, 130, 141, 148, 151, 153, 154, *153–54*, 154, *153–54*
Kingdom of God 4, 32, 113, 114, 123, 124, 125, 133
- Miracles 148

laesa maiestas 86
Latinisms 140
laudatio funebris 83
Law 116, 117, 121
Leadership 1
Legend
- and Paul 131

Letters
- and levels of discourse 63–65

Literacy 108
Literary context 110, 144, 147, 159
Lord(ship) 16, 24, 37, 77, 81, 82, 84, 100, 101, 103, 112, 113, 119, 123, 128, 134, 135, 138, 141, 143, 146, 149, 153, 154, 157

Messiah (honorific) 149, 154
Messianism 84, 103, 104, 112, 154
Miracles *See* Kingdom of God
Mission *See* Faith, *See* Gospel
Monarchy 73, 74
Monotheism *See* Jews
Moses 101

Necessary conditions *43–46*
numen 76

Ochlocracy 18
Octavian *See* Augustus

Pagan gods *See* Society
- and Christian faith 126
- and piety 127

- Criticism 68, 103, 125, *126–27*, 127, 132
- Olympian gods 96, 97, 99, 102, 104
Parody *See* Criticism
Parting of the ways 89
Pastorals 59
Pausanias 97
pax deorum 126, *See* Pagan gods
pax et securitas See Greek terms and phrases: εἰρήνη καὶ ἀσφάλεια
pax Romana 70, 71, 70–72, 74, 84, 131, 135, 142
- as precondition for mission 124
People of God 115, 118, 119, 121
Persecution
- and Galatians 127
- and the cross 126
- Avoidance 39, 57, 68, 88, 125, 129, 130, 131, 138, 156
- in Philippi 127
- Intensity 148
- Martyrdom 131, 148
- of believers 126
- of the Apostle 127
- Risk 142
- under Nero 87, 132
Personality *125–29*
- and confrontation 131
- Cautiousness 127
- Courage 126
- Integrity 127
- Pastorality 130
Pessinus 94
Philippi 61, 94, 95, 96, 158
Philo
- Allegory of the soul 6–7
- Political allegory 15
- Political subtext 15–17, 37
- Political theory 3–5
- Writings 2–3
- - *Allegorigcal Commentary* 3
- - *Exposition of the Law* 3
- - *Questions and Answers on Genesis and Exodus* 3
Philosophy 8, 73
Pilate 58
Pisidian Antioch 94
Platonism 103
Poems 88

Polemic *123*
Pompey 73, 155
Power 20, 93, 100, 105, 112
- and discourse 51, *See* Public transcripts
- and economy 65
- Symbolic reversal 56
princeps 74, 86
Propaganda 25, 37, 38, 39, 45, 55, 71, 82, 90–*91*, 91, 106, 108, 110, 130, 135, 140, 141, 142, 143, 148, 151, 155
Public transcripts 53
- and public discourse 52
- Definition *50–51*
- in the Roman Empire *68–91*

Reformation 116
Research 1–2, 3, 6, *21–22*, 35, 39, 66
Resistance *See* Hidden transcripts, *See* Criticism
Resonance 148, 157
Resurrection 37, 112, 116, 117, 119, 120, 147
rex See King(ship)
Roma 73
Roman religion 126, *See* Pagan gods
Roman Republic 74, 85, 111
Romanisation 90, 108
Rome 74, 75, 76, 84, 88, 93, 111, 120
Rumors 54

Satan 113, 119, 120, 122, 123
Satire 40, 83, 84
Satisfaction 142, *See* Echoes
Saviour 82, 103, 112, 116, 119, 122, 143, 144, 154, *See* Greek terms and phrases: σωτήρ
securitas See Greek terms and phrases: εἰρήνη καὶ ἀσφάλεια
Sejanus 88
Senate 76, 87, 88
Sin 113, 118, 119, 120, 122
Slaves 59
- of Artemis 151
- of Christ 151, 155
- US South 53
Smyrna 73
Society *See* Elite

Index of Subjects 199

- Alternative 60
- and pagan gods 68, *126*–27

Son of David 144, 149
Son of god 75, 82, 104, 111, 120, 143, 144, 149, 151, 154
Songs 54
Spain 111
Spirit 119, 122, 144
Subtext
- and heterogeneity of congregations 130–31
- and Roman identity 129
- Effectiveness (for persuasion) 136–38
- Modification *138*
- Narrative 136
- Proposals *21–24*, *See* Persecution, *See* Danger

Suffering *See* Persecution
Syria 111
Syrian Antioch 95

Tacitus
- *Barbarenrede* 72

Tarsus 94
Temple
- Imperial *See* Imperial cults
- in Jerusalem 151, 152
- — and Qumran 153
- of God 151, 152
- Pagan *See* Pagan gods

termini technici 157
Tertullian 77
Textbooks 92
Theatre 37, 39, 54, 87, 105
Thematic Coherence 38, 110, 112, 145, *See* Echoes
Theophanes 155
Thessalonica 59, 63, 94, 96
Thessaly 96
Treason 86, 87
Triumphal procession 108, 158, 159

Volume 39, 114, 142, 147, *See* Echoes
Voluntary associations *See collegia*

Worldview
- and perception 99–104
- and the place of the Empire 3, 29, *110–25*
- Apocalyptic 30, 55, 113–14, 114–16
- Critique 137
- Monotheism *See* Jews
- Narrative 136
- Perception 137
- Plight and solution 116–25

Xerxes 9

Zeus 99, 101

www.ingramcontent.com/pod-product-compliance
Lightning Source LLC
Chambersburg PA
CBHW071158070526
44584CB00019B/2843